# Across the Spectrum of Women and Crime

# Across the Spectrum of Women and Crime

## Theories, Offending and the Criminal Justice System

Edited by

**Susan F. Sharp**
**Susan Marcus-Mendoza**
**Kathleen A. Cameron**
**Elycia S. Daniel-Roberson**

CAROLINA ACADEMIC PRESS

Durham, North Carolina

Library of Congress Cataloging-in-Publication Data

Names: Sharp, Susan F., 1951- editor.
Title: Across the spectrum of women and crime : theories, offending, and the criminal justice system / edited by Susan F. Sharp, Susan Marcus-Mendoza, Kathleen A. Cameron, and Elycia S. Daniel-Roberson.
Description: Durham : Carolina Academic Press, 2016. | Includes bibliographical references and index.
Identifiers: LCCN 2015041594 | ISBN 9781594600319 (alk. paper)
Subjects: LCSH: Female offenders. | Women--Crimes against. | Women--Drug use. | Prostitution. | Women criminal justice personnel.
Classification: LCC HV6046 .A197 2016 | DDC 364.3/74--dc23
LC record available at http://lccn.loc.gov/2015041594

CAROLINA ACADEMIC PRESS, LLC
700 Kent Street
Durham, North Carolina 27701
Telephone (919) 489-7486
Fax (919) 493-5668
www.cap-press.com

Printed in the United States of America.

# Contents

# Introduction

*Susan F. Sharp, Ph.D.*

An edited volume is a labor of love that frequently takes on a life of its own, and this volume is no exception. We envision this book as a resource for those wanting to better understand the relationship between women and offending, using original chapters written for this text. The book provides important insights into female offending because so much of the research is qualitative, allowing the voices of the women themselves to reveal and help interpret the themes addressed by the authors.

The book covers three fundamental—but not necessarily mutually exclusive—areas related to women and offending. Broadly defined, the three areas are theoretical applications, varieties of female offenders (especially those less commonly studied such as female drug traffickers and female terrorists), and the system's response to women. Thus, it offers a view of women and crime across the spectrum—from explanations of women's offending to specific types of offending. Most importantly, we then turn to how the system—and society—respond to the woman offender.

The book is divided into three parts, reflecting the three major themes. Each reading is followed by discussion questions designed to provoke thought. In the first four chapters, original research helps inform important theoretical approaches. In Chapter 1, Van Gundy-Yoder explores the cases of two women, Andrea Yates and Lisa Montgomery, to illustrate how a gendered approach to Agnew's General Strain Theory can help explain their crimes. Using Broidy and Agnew's gender-specific approach to identifying strains and their impact on behavior, she provides support for a gendered approach to General Strain Theory and how to apply the characteristics common to women in the analyses.

Smith and Klepfer, in Chapter 2, explore the relationship between intimate partner victimization and offending among women with a focus on how failures in the system contribute to the problems of female offenders. This chapter illuminates the barriers faced by women who offend. To illustrate how this plays out, they utilize Maslow's "hierarchy of needs" as a framework to help us better understand the behaviors of the women. Simply put, the women's behaviors are efforts to meet needs. Using in-depth interviews, their analyses add to our knowledge of the role between intimate partner violence and female offending.

Chapter 3, by Sharp, uses a case study to illustrate how being marginalized in multiple ways can contribute to excessive punishment. Wanda Jean Allen was the first African American female executed in the United States since the 1950s as well as the first woman executed in the state of Oklahoma. Jean, as she liked to be called, was disadvantaged in several interacting dimensions, leading to a death sentence for a crime that probably should have resulted in a far less severe penalty. A young, black female lesbian, she was portrayed by the prosecution as a vicious and hardened criminal who "played the role of the man in her lesbian relationship." Poor, uneducated and brain-damaged, she was unable to obtain an even minimally functional defense. Thus, race, gender, class, sexual orientation, and mental handicaps worked against her in a synergistic manner. Using firsthand observations, observations of legal proceedings and communications with her legal team, Sharp develops Wanda Jean Allen's story as a case study of how multiple forms of marginalization result in more than the sum of the individual disadvantages.

The theme of intersectionality in continued in Chapter 4. Using national data (NIBRS), Durfee examines the patterns of arrest of teens for dating violence and how the intersection of race and gender plays an important role. She focuses on the role of mandatory and pro-arrest laws in the likelihood of arrest, specifically in dating relationships. She then further explores the role of race, finding that African American girls are the most likely to be arrested, controlling for legal factors.

The next four chapters focus on several types of female offending. Topics include studies of women who kill their children, women who participate in stripping and the sex industry, women in the methamphetamine trade, and women as suicide bombers.

Dragon, Oberman and Meyer use both qualitative and quantitative data in Chapter 5 to examine the role of their relationships with men in explaining women who kill their children. They illustrate that domestic violence and learned helplessness often play a role in women killing their children. Additionally, in some cases, the male partner plays a significant role, and at times the woman did not even participate in the homicide but was instead blamed for her failure to protect her child. The authors then turn to the differential response of the criminal justice system to women who kill their children, illustrating how societal expectations of mothers lead to harsh punishments.

In Chapter 6, Caputo takes the reader into the world of legal sex work among women who use drugs. She ties together the relationship between sex work and drug use with histories of abuse and impoverishment in both childhood and adulthood. She further adds to our knowledge by examining the relationship between legal sex work (such as dancing) and illegal sex work (prostitution).

Chapter 7 focuses on the experiences of women in the methamphetamine trade. Jenkot explores the motivations of women who sell or trade illegal drugs, using a gendered pathways framework that focuses on relationships, economics, gender norms and abuse. Using in-depth interviews, he explores several themes, including the women's identification (or lack thereof) as drug dealers, their perception of themselves as being involved more in trading than selling, the norm of sharing or reciprocity, and the risk of being coerced to trade sex for drugs.

In the final chapter in Part II (Chapter 8), Markovic examines women as suicide bombers, tracing the history of female suicide bombers as well as the motivations. She explores both personal and organizational motivations among women who engage in this practice. The chapter examines the recent emergence of female suicide bombers in Nigeria and which countries use female suicide bombers the most often and with the most deadly impact.

The final five chapters examine various aspects of women and the criminal justice system. Topics include wrongful convictions, imprisonment, access to treatment within the criminal justice system, desistance from offending, and reintegration into society.

In Chapter 9, Fox asks three important questions about women who are unjustly convicted of murder: how, who, and why? Looking at five cases in the U.S. and Japan, he explores the misogynistic approach of a system that places unrealistic expectations on women and then punishes them for their failure to meet those expectations. He hypothesizes that women who are seen as "bad" may be given long sentences as a form of eugenics, keeping them in prison so that they cannot have children.

The focus of Chapter 10 is to give voice to women who are or have been incarcerated. Using qualitative data, Lawston illustrates to the reader how women's experiences of prison often mirror their traumatic pre-prison lives. The intrusive and coercive nature of supervision, often by men, leads to sexual and other traumas while in prison. This is further compounded by failure to provide appropriate medical and mental health care. The result is a chapter that paints a disturbing picture of the lives of women prisoners. However, she points out that, despite the restrictive and coercive nature of the prison, women still finds ways to resist.

The theme of medical neglect is carried on by McGee et al. in Chapter 11. Noting that women who are arrested, especially for drug offenses, often have chronic health issues, McGee et al. juxtapose the need for substance abuse, mental health and physical health treatment with the limited availability of programs and resources. They then go on to demonstrate the unequal treatment availability for minorities. Supplementing analyses from a quantitative survey with interviews, they allow the voices of the women to tell the stories.

Chapter 12 focuses on women who get a second chance to live prosocial lives through their roles as grandparents. Kerrison and Bachman take an innovative approach to understanding women offenders' desistance from crime and drugs. They propose that identity change may result when the woman is able to redefine her role on the basis of being a grandmother. They explore the importance of this prosocial role through in-depth interviews with more than one hundred participants.

The final chapter (Chapter 13) by Sharp and Ortiz examines the experiences of women who returned to prison versus women who not only did not recidivate but successfully reintegrated. They found that not only were the women who returned less able to access resources and lacking outside support, but they also often lacked the belief that they could thrive in a post-prison world.

Marcus-Mendoza then recapitulates the chapters in the book, finding that they illustrate total system failure. In other words, prior to, during and after incarceration, women who offend are often as much victims of a society that neither cares nor understands as they are offenders.

We hope that the readers of this volume enjoy the contributions as much as we have enjoyed working with these authors. We believe that this book offers a refreshing look at women caught up in the criminal justice sytem.

# Part I

# Theorizing about Crime and Women

# Chapter 1

# Exploring the Relationship between Gender and Strain: Two Case Studies

*Alana Van Gundy-Yoder, Ph.D.*

Feminist criminologists have long called for the examination of the ability of criminological theory to understand, predict, and respond to female criminality. This chapter will attempt to qualitatively address their inquiry by focusing on the relationship between strain theory and female offending. Components of Agnew's general strain theory will be presented along with Broidy and Agnew's extension of strain theory's theoretical concepts. The chapter will then explore the case studies of Andrea Yates and Lisa Montgomery in an attempt to better investigate how gender may condition the relationship between strain and female offending.

## Agnew's General Strain Theory

Stemming from Robert Merton's concepts of structurally induced strain and modes of adaptation, Robert Agnew proposed that the root of crime can be traced to different forms of strain (Agnew, 1992, Merton, 1938). He argued that strain can occur through a) the actual, anticipated, or perceived *loss* of positive stimuli and/or b) the actual, anticipated, or perceived *presentation* of negative stimuli. When presented with either positive or negative stimuli, individuals can cope in many ways, both criminal and non-criminal.

Agnew proposed a conditional relationship between strain and criminal behavior and focused on numerous components of strain. One component of Agnew's theory of strain was the general relationship between the individual and strain. In other words, the more that strain presents itself, the more likely the individual is to become engaged in deviant behavior. He also proposed that while strain may aid in understanding individual actions, theorists must also examine the reasoning behind why some individuals do not engage in deviant behavior despite having high levels of strain. Lastly, Agnew also included the component of emotions, in particular anger, when examining how an individual responds to strain (Agnew, 1992).

## Broidy and Agnew's Extension of Strain Theory

Broidy and Agnew's 1997 article was divided into two sections. The first section identified, discussed, and explored four explanations as to why males commit more crime than females. Those explanations included:

1.  Males are subject to more strains or stressors than females;
2.  Males are subject to different strains then females, with the strains that males experience being more conducive to criminal behavior;
3.  In comparison to females, males have an emotional reaction to strains that are more likely to result in criminal behavior; and
4.  Males are more likely to respond to strain with crime (Broidy & Agnew, 1997).

The second section of their article focused on how strain theory may be able to explain female crime. They argue that strain theory can explain both male and female behavior, but when examining the relationship between gender and strain, researchers must focus on how gender conditions the response to strain. For example, when measuring one of strain's major components, the failure to achieve positively valued goals, special attention should be paid to the concern that females place on close, interpersonal, and/or intimate relationships with others and the increasing concern of females for financial security (Broidy & Agnew, 1997).

As identified by Broidy and Agnew, the following variables related to strain's major components may also induce or inhibit unique and gendered reactions to strain with regards to females: high rates of divorce and abuse (family, emotional, physical, and/or sexual abuse), single parent responsibilities, the desire to be treated in a just and equitable manner, levels of responsibility at home (often times coupled with unique responsibilities at work), employment in service sector or lower skill jobs, lower levels of compensation, gendered reactions to loss (friendships, intimate relationships, death etc.), barriers to social participation and gender valued behaviors, negative stimuli that are associated with gender-related roles (being female itself, housewife etc.), and being presented with unique forms of harassment, such as sexual harassment.

In 2001, Agnew again extended strain theory by differentiating between different types of strain. He discussed four factors which affect the relationship between strain and crime (but did not have a primary focus on gender) by identifying conditions under which the adaptation will likely be deviant behavior:

1. If the strain is seen as unjust;
2. If the strain is high in magnitude;
3. If the strain is caused by or associated with low social control; and
4. If the strain creates some pressure or incentive to engage in criminal coping (Agnew, 2001).

## *Gender and Strain Theory*

What is important about these extensions is the implication for theoretical testing. While the components of strain theory may explain female engagement in delinquent or criminal behavior, the key is that these components might need to be *measured* differently. They also must consider gender role, identification with gender role, whether or not the role itself is considered positive or negative, and what other conditioning factors exist indirectly through being female. Subsequent studies of Broidy and Agnew's work has shown that key aspects do differ when measuring strain, the reaction to it, and it's implication for females (Piquero & Sealock, 2004; Jennings et al., 2009, and Piquero, et al. 2010). Two case studies are presented below in order to qualitatively explore the relationship between gender and strain.

### Andrea Yates

Andrea Yates was a bachelor-degree-educated woman who worked as a registered nurse at a Cancer Treatment Center. By most accounts, she was a quiet and introverted woman that was very focused on her religious beliefs. Andrea met and married Rusty Yates, became a housewife, concentrated on having children, and was the sole individual responsible for the children, even to the point of home-schooling them. Despite Andrea's husband's job at NASA, she was forced to live in a small trailer (reportedly 38 feet long) with her children because her husband wanted to live frugally.

Throughout the marriage, Yates attempted suicide twice, was hospitalized numerous times for psychosis and major depressive disorder, reported having hallucinations and began self-mutilating. At the urging of Andrea's family, Rusty agreed to eliminate some of the difficulty of her living conditions by purchasing a home in a small neighborhood. Once Andrea was in the home and her living conditions improved, some of her hallucinations and delusions were disappearing and she began leaving the house more to resume normal activities.

Yates later approached her husband and let him know that she was concerned, because she had been planning to kill her children, but she didn't want to act on her plan. After going on and off numerous medicines, two different doctors notified her and her husband that if she chose to get pregnant again, her struggles with mental illness would re-surface. Yates notified her husband that she did not want to have sex with him because she didn't want to get pregnant again and possibly hurt her children. Her husband told her that she was a good mother, she could handle it, and it was her religious responsibility to be a dutiful wife and mother.

At her husband and pastor's urging, Andrea went off of her medicines and became pregnant with her fifth child. Months after delivering her final child, Andrea was again returned to the hospital. Her doctor notified Rusty Yates and her family that she should be monitored at all times and never be left alone with her children, but for health insurance reasons, her doctor released her from the hospital. On June 20th, 2001, Andrea Yates methodically drowned all five of her children in the bathtub. She then calmly called her husband and the police, told them what she had done, and was arrested.

Agnew's original concepts of strain (loss of positive stimuli and presentation of negative stimuli) are applicable to the case of Andrea Yates. Actual or perceived loss of positive stimuli could have included Andrea's loss of friendships, connections, and jobs by staying home. It could also have included the loss of her independence to a domineering husband, the loss of personal time with the addition of so many children and the loss of her freedom to her relationships and religion.

Presentation of a mental illness would also be a primary negative stimulus for Andrea. To live in cramped quarters, to have the physical difficulties of stopping and starting different medicines and their side effects, and to have hallucinations and delusions would cause numerous negative situations, beliefs, and feelings (fear, anger, terror, etc.). Depending on her internal reaction to the lifestyle changes mentioned above, those changes in and of themselves could be viewed as negative stimuli (quitting her job, the addition of more children may have been a negative stimulus for her, and the rules imposed on her from her religion).

While the two main concepts of strain are present (loss of positive stimuli, presentation of negative/noxious stimuli), strain theory and its power becomes clearer when Broidy and Agnew's concepts of gender specific conditions are included. Broidy and Agnew argued that divorce and abuse are important factors when considering the effect that strain has on female involvement in criminal behavior. Interestingly, in this situation, divorce may have been a positive or negative situation for Andrea. To others, her husband would appear to be a major source of strain; by placing a lot of pressure on her and by emotionally persuading her with religious arguments to have sex with him (let alone be impregnated again) he emotionally and sexually abused her. As evidence of his callousness to her fragility, at her trial he was reportedly discussing his fantasies of having more children with her. Her religion would have condemned divorce, so that might have brought upon additional strains for her, but maybe by turning to family (her mother in particular) she may have been able to better cope with her strains/stressors.

Broidy and Agnew also focused on the impact of single parent responsibility and the level of responsibility at home (and work). While Andrea was technically a married woman, she stayed at home all of the time with her children. She did not have daycare help, she was responsible for feeding and educating her children, and was told by her husband and her religion that her duty was to her children. She essentially was the sole parent to these children and the magnitude of those responsibilities coupled with the isolation that she experienced by not working, not having friends, giving up exercising, etc., would appear to be a tremendous strain. Her structural position in the home and society would have placed her as "employed" (without pay—another strain) in the service/home sector and left with no level of monetary compensation, two strains both identified by Broidy and Agnew.

The last forms of strain identified by Broidy and Agnew can also be applied to Yates, but not necessarily in the manner generally expected (according to the authors these could either induce or inhibit criminal behavior). They discuss examining the conditioned gender response when a person is not treated in a just and equitable manner, gendered reactions to loss, barriers to social participation and gender-valued behaviors and negative stimuli associated with gender-related roles. The religion Andrea strove to follow places women in a subordinate position as a rule, touts motherhood as the highest honor, promotes staying away from sinful behavior and endorses what others would view as negative stimuli, but what she would/may consider positive stimuli. Thus, where theorists may have considered her lifestyle as conducive to strain, Andrea herself, may not have. She may not have had the desire to be treated as just and equitable, may have felt that her losses were necessary to be sent to Heaven, may have become reclusive because that was what she felt was important to attain the level of motherhood she wanted, and she may have seen subordinate, care-taking, and mothering behavior as her personal and internally gender-valued behavior. The key component here is her gendered and conditioned response to her religion, the position it places women in, as well as the mandated rules that come with that position/religion. Without knowing Andrea's internal response, we don't know how or if these strains affected her but it is clear that being female would be an important determinant in her reaction.

The last concept discussed by Broidy and Agnew is being presented with harassment. Many on the outside of her relationship would consider almost all of her close, interpersonal, and intimate relationships harassment. Her husband pushed her to have children after she begged him not to be forced to have any more and he used the Bible to force and reiterate his beliefs on her. Little is said in research about her personal relationships, but one significant relationship did appear prominent. Her relationship with her pastor would also appear from the outside to be a negative relationship. Her pastor and his wife were said to have sent her letters condemning some of her behavior, focusing on her lack of parenting, and sending notes of personal judgment and derision. To others, this would seem as if she were being dominated and harassed, but again, to Andrea, with her strict belief in her religion, it did not seem to make her angry at her harasser, but at herself.

Agnew's 2001 extension of strain theory leaves question about the ability of strain theory to fully predict Andrea's behavior. While an external evaluator can "score" or "measure" Andrea Yates high on strain because: her relationships and position in life appear unjust, her strains are viewed as being high in magnitude, and that these strains may create pressure or incentives to engage in criminal behavior, it is unclear whether Andrea considered the aforementioned issues as strain or stress. Conversely, she did not push or seem to desire to be treated as just, but was compliant because that is what her religion deemed a woman should be. She did not appear to outwardly get upset at her husband or pastor, but followed (and requested) their bidding. Her life was rigidly planned and evidenced a high level of social control instead of evidencing a low level of social control as suggested by Broidy and Agnew. Lastly, her belief system and religion would have condemned her killing as a failure and a sin as a mother. Andrea's experienced strain and the magnitude, impact, and gendered reaction to it is unclear. From available research, it can be deducted that her gender has both a direct and indirect relationship to her reaction to strain.

One of the central issues here is where exactly Andrea Yates felt strain. Society assumes that women rebel against being subordinate, against identifying with a primary role such as motherhood instead of being self-focused, and that classifying themselves within a gender role is a negative thing. In this case, Andrea Yates's largest strain may have come from not attaining what she felt was the highest honor and most important gender role, being a good mother (which is directly related to her religion and society's view on the roles of females).

Both her husband and her pastor preyed on this vulnerability/strain. She was told despite her one documented request (that she not have more children out of fear she might hurt them) that she must continue producing children. She was given one job and one job only: to be a worthy mother. As she was increasingly unable to do this due to her living conditions, her isolated lifestyle, and her mental illness, her personal and emotional condition worsened. So in this case, the gender role that she identified with was a high honor to her and worthy of attaining, and when she was unable to meet the demands of it, not attaining the gender role may have been more of a strain to her than the responsibilities of the gender role itself.

In this case, strain appears to be related to the crime Andrea committed and is conditioned by her gender indirectly via religion. The original components (positive and negative stimuli) of strain appear strongly related to Andrea's reaction to her life, her roles, her responsibilities, and her rigid attempts and expectations of meeting them. It would be easy to predict that Andrea Yates had a high amount of strain in what theorists consider traditional areas of strain, but strain is in the eye of the beholder and is conditioned by the structural, emotional, and physical position one occupies in society. Without measuring how Andrea's emphasis on religion may have magnified or diluted her strain when the religion deems subordination, motherhood, and obeying to be the highest honors, a full picture of Andrea's reaction to her strain cannot be provided.

## Lisa Montgomery

Lisa Montgomery was also an individual who was convicted of murder, but the background, circumstances, and victim are in stark contrast to the previous case study. Lisa was an outgoing woman who enjoyed talking about herself and being the center of attention. Her original marriage did not work out and her ex-husband publicly spoke out about her continuous and creative ability to lie. He reported she viewed pregnancy as a way to be the center of attention and described her as a "selfish, chronic liar, with low self-esteem, and critical of others" but stated that throughout their marriage she did not show signs of violence (Sable, n.d.). During their marriage she had four children in less than four years, cheated on her husband, and claimed to be pregnant twice when she was not.

After her divorce, Montgomery took her children and moved in with another man. Together they had seven children, all teenagers. Montgomery again claimed (twice) that she was pregnant when she was not and she went as far as wearing maternity clothes and cutting back on her work hours as she was supposedly getting closer to her due date. Unfortunately, her husband believed her lies and genuinely believed that she was pregnant and due to deliver.

In 2004, Montgomery began working on her plan to steal someone's baby. She was unable to have any more children because she previously had her tubes tied, but continued her lies of being pregnant. She posed as a pregnant woman in online chat rooms, ordered a birthing kit, and studied online how Caesarean sections were performed. Through a chat room, Montgomery met a pregnant dog breeder named Bobbi Jo Stinnett and pretended that she was interested in purchasing a dog from her. Bobbi Jo provided directions to her home and made an appointment with Montgomery.

The day before her meeting with Bobbi Jo, Montgomery made the drive to her house and back to time how long it would take. The next day she drove to Bobbi Jo's house and strangled her. When she cut her open with a kitchen knife to steal Bobbi Jo's baby, Bobbi Jo woke up and struggled and Montgomery strangled her again. The Coroner report stated that Bobbi Jo had "eight jagged cuts across her abdomen and defensive wounds on her hands, face, and elbows" (Montaldo 2007) that came from attempting to protect her child and fight for her own life.

Montgomery took the baby, drove back to her town, called her husband, and told him she had delivered the baby while she was out of town. Montgomery and her husband went around town showing the baby to friends, family, and her pastor and his wife. Bobbi Jo was found in a pool of blood by her mother and an Amber Alert was issued. A participant in the chat room reported Montgomery's meeting with Bobbi Jo and she became a person of interest. She was charged with 'kidnapping resulting in death' at the federal level because she crossed state lines with one of her victims (in this case, the child). Montgomery initially blamed her brother for the murder but later claimed insanity.

Tenets of Agnew and Agnew and Broidy's theoretical concepts are also apparent while examining the case of Lisa Montgomery. Montgomery's largest loss of positive stimuli appears to be related to the role of motherhood. She had a few miscarriages and was eventually the recipient of a tubal ligation (both would qualify as the presentation of negative stimuli). The loss of feeling, acting, and being pregnant affected her so greatly that she created multiple pregnancies when she was physically unable to become pregnant. The attention that came from being pregnant was also a positive stimulus for her, and when she was not pregnant that stimuli was missing from her life. As a result, she pretended to be pregnant, wear maternity clothes, and discuss her pregnancy experiences as if she truly believed she was pregnant. The strain from losing positive stimuli and being presented with negative stimuli was so great that her adaptation was to alleviate that strain by living in a world created by her lies.

Agnew's 2001 extension focused on the causes, magnitude, justness, and incentive of strain. The main cause of her strain was the inability to continue to reproduce and the attention that came with being pregnant. This strain multiplied as her lies continued regarding her fictitious pregnancies and her due date neared. Montgomery's husband, children, and community expected her to deliver but internally, she knew she would not. She might have felt that it was unjust that she was unable to deliver while around her community and chat rooms, she was continuously hearing about the pregnancy of others. The environments that she chose to be in focused on the importance of pregnancy and motherhood and thus, heightened her strain, anxiety, and possibly feelings of injustice. Incentives to engage in criminal behavior may have included; following through on her pregnancy by "delivering," gaining attention by passing around a newborn baby and claiming that it was hers, and attaining what she felt was so important, attention via motherhood.

Broidy and Agnew's gender-specific conditions also appear to play a role in Montgomery's crime. While she was previously divorced (again, this could be a positive or negative stimuli, but Broidy and Agnew clearly identify it as a gender-specific condition), research did not disclose Montgomery as a victim of family, emotional, physical, and sexual abuse. However, it is possible to deduce it was in her life and possibly not in the direction expected (statistically speaking). Specifically, Montgomery could actually be considered as someone who precipitated abuse of others. Lying to her first and second husband about miscarriages and pregnancies could be considered emotional abuse towards them and family abuse could be viewed in the manner she treated her current children; neighbors reported her home was filthy, that she laid around all day with "morning sickness," and that the seven children were always running around dirty and neglected.

Similar to Yates, strain could have been a factor for Montgomery through her parental responsibilities for seven children, her non-employment, and thus low levels of compensation, and her perceived levels of responsibility at home. What differed between the two however, was the priority that the two women placed on the children themselves. Yates's role as a mother placed priority on the children while Montgomery seemed to place priority on the act of being pregnant, delivering a child, and gaining the resultant attention. So while the role of motherhood was an important source of strain for both women, different aspects of the role were valued by each, and as a result, the strain differs in magnitude, timing, and duration.

In the Montgomery case, a few key components emerge. Montgomery's gendered reactions to loss, barriers to gender-valued behaviors, and stimuli associated with gender-related roles greatly differ from that of Yates. Montgomery was unable to physically have children anymore and whether that loss revolved around the experience of pregnancy or it revolved around the inability to have another actual child isn't important, but the significance here is that this loss was traumatic for her. This also acted as a barrier to her attaining what she viewed as gender-valued behavior, the ability to deliver a child. Lastly, both women were stay-at-home housewives (Montgomery quit her job as she was approaching her fictitious due date) and Broidy and Agnew argue that the negative stimuli associated with this role causes strain. However, Montgomery seemed to appear to savor this role. Unlike Yates, who was under the thumb of a domineering husband, Montgomery seemed to maintain control of her environment and enjoy being pregnant, being a housewife, and being female.

In contrast to Yates, Montgomery also differed on her level of self-control. Yates was non-emotional, did not like to be the center of attention, and appeared to have a high level of self-control, even to the point of trying to control a mental illness without medication. She was dominated and controlled by others (both personally and religiously) and strove to please those around her. Montgomery appeared to love to be the center of attention, was gregarious, and evidenced low levels of self-control. She seemed to want to please herself and showed little regard for those around her as evidenced by her painful lies to those closest to her and the neglect of the children and home she already had. Broidy and Agnew suggest that low levels of self-control are critical when examining gendered responses to strain, but it may be possible that, as deduced by control theory, an excess of control would also be important to consider.

# Summary

Feminist criminologists repeatedly call attention to the numerous and unique conditions that distinctly face women and that arguably should be included in theoretical testing. These conditions include: co-occurring disorders, partner abuse, domestic violence, negative emotionality, financial strain, structural position, mental illness, and alcohol and substance abuse. While males may experience some of these conditions, the magnitude and reaction differ in comparison to females. Through the examination of the two preceding case studies, it calls to question that gender conditions the response to strain and its resultant criminal behavior. For Andrea Yates, motherhood was inescapable, but for Lisa Montgomery, motherhood was unattainable. This affected their behavior, their victims, those that were involved, and the final outcome of their respective trials.

At a minimum, this chapter should reiterate the complexity of women's lives and call to light the role that gender and gender roles play while examining the relationship between strain and criminality. Andrea Yates' mental illness and devotion to her religion may have conditioned a gendered response to her strain in both a positive and negative manner. Lisa Montgomery's need for attention and inability to physically attain the gender role she deemed most important resulted in a gendered reaction to strain as well. The crucial point here is that both of their reactions and behaviors were controlled by *how they personally viewed their gender and their gender role.* The strain they experienced was conditioned by their gender, their gender-valued roles, and their ability or inability to attain those roles.

# References

Agnew, R. (1992). Foundation for a general strain theory of crime and delinquency. *Criminology, 30(1),* 47–87.

______. (2001). Building on the foundation of General Strain Theory: Specifying the types of strain most likely to lead to crime and delinquency. *Journal of Research in Crime and Delinquency, 38,:* 319–361.

Broidy, L. & Agnew, R. (1997). Gender and crime: A General Strain Theory perspective. *Journal of Research in Crime and Delinquency, 34(3),* 275–306.

Jennings, W. G., Piquero, N. L., Gover, A. R., & Pérez, D. M. (2009). Gender and general strain theory: A replication and exploration of Broidy and Agnew's gender/strain hypothesis among a sample of southwestern Mexican American adolescents. *Journal of Criminal Justice, 37(4),* 404–417.

Merton, R. (1938). Social structure and anomie. *American Sociological Review, 3,* 672–82.

Montaldo, C. (2007). The murder of Bobbie Jo Stinnett. Retrieved may 27, 2015, from http://crime.about.com/od/current/a/stinnett.htm.

Piquero, N. L., Fox, K., Piquero, A. R., Capowich, G., & Mazerolle, P. (2010). Gender, general strain theory, negative emotions, and disordered eating. *Journal of youth and adolescence, 39(4),* 380–392.

Piquero, N.L. & Sealock, M.D. (2000). Generalizing General Strain Theory: An examination of an offending population. *Justice Quarterly, 17,* 449–84.

Sable, Kari. (n.D. True crime and justice. Retrieved May 27, 2015, from http://karisable.com.

# Chapter 2

# Female Offenders as Victims of Intimate Partner Violence (IPV): Exploring Maslovian Cracks in the System

*Alisa Smith, J.D., Ph.D., and G. Jeffrey Klepfer, Ph.D.*

Social and criminal justice resources are available to battered women. Hundreds of agencies and programs provide services, including shelter, mental health counseling, legal and employment services. The law supports battered women with pro- or mandatory arrest law,[1] no-drop prosecution policies[2] and loosened restrictions on restraining-order[3] criteria now being employed by most states (Belknap, 1995; Hilton, 1993). Despite the availability of these widespread resources, one and a half million women a year are battered and few actually access them (Tjaden & Thoennes, 2000; Grotpeter, Menard & Gianola, 2009). Why? And what do the women who are rejecting legal and social support think will help them?

Most of the research targeting victims of IPV has examined perceptions, decisions, and behavior of women who initiate formal help seeking from shelters or police. Female offenders, however, face barriers to formal help seeking some personal and cultural, others systemic and societal and unique to their situation, including structural barriers to housing, good-paying jobs, and so-

---

1. Mandatory and pro-arrest policies require police to arrest for domestic violence misdemeanor violence without a warrant.

2. No-drop prosecution policies prohibit prosecutors from dismissing charges even if victims desire dismissal.

3. These are civil-court orders issued to prevent direct or indirect contact between abusers and victims. Although the initial orders are imposed during civil court proceedings, violating restraining orders is typically a criminal offense.

cial or governmental assistance (Moe, 2004, 2007; Hirsch, 2001). In this chapter, we review the literature regarding change in the response to battered women and barriers that remain in seeking help. In addition, we include initial research findings from a qualitative study in which one author, Alisa Smith, conducted hour-and-a-half interviews with four battered women who were also offenders, court-ordered into a residential program, asking them whether their interactions with the police, courts, shelters and medical professionals were beneficial, and what suggestions they propose to help women like them. In concluding, Maslow's hierarchy of needs is applied to understand battered offenders and alternatives to meet their needs.

# History of Change

In the 1970s and 1980s, Straus (1978) and Gelles and Straus (1988) interviewed families about wife beating, and were surprised to find that it was far more common than expected. One in every six wives, in 1975, reported being hit by her husband (Gelles & Straus, 1988). That criminal justice ignored this frequent and pervasive social problem raised serious concern among advocates, who urged that wife-beating be treated like other crimes (Buzawa & Buzawa, 2003). By the late 1970s and early 1980s, shelters provided safe havens for battered women, sporadic legislation allowed protective orders against family members and funding was provided for battered women services (Dobash & Dobash, 1977); feminists fought for even more far-sweeping changes.

In the mid-1980s, lawsuits resulting in big damage awards against police departments for not protecting victims and the research findings of Sherman and Berk (1984) that arrest may not deter recidivism were the catalysts for mandatory and pro-arrest laws (Sherman & Berk, 1984; *Thurman v. City of Torrington*). By the late 1980s, forty-seven states eased access to restraining orders, permitted warrantless arrests for misdemeanor domestic violence, and recognized Battered Woman Syndrome as a defense to the killing of batterers (Fagan, 1996).

In the early 1990s, special prosecution units and no-drop policies were adopted to reduce case dismissal rates (Fagan, 1996). Legislation that required medical professionals, including doctors, to report suspected battering to police passed in forty-two states (Smith, 2000, Smith, 2001). Specialized and coordinated domestic violence courts, with trained courtroom personnel, were created (Tsai, 2000, Keilitz, 2002).

# Barriers to Help-Seeking

## *Policing*

Despite the changes and increased resources, few victims of IPV seek help from shelters, social services, or police (Grotpeter, Menard, & Gianola, 2009). Most rely on family, friends and clergy (Grotpeter et al., 2009). Using a longitudinal, multigenerational, national probability sample, Grotpeter et al. (2009) found victims of partner violence rarely called the police: "[A]mong female IPV [intimate partner violence] victims of any type, 7% contacted the police and 93% did not" (Grotpeter et al. (2009, p. 56). Barriers which impaired access to the police included: (1) batterers physically preventing victims from calling the police, (2) batterers threatening retaliation, and (3) negative experiences with the police curtailed reporting (Fleury, Sullivan, & Bybee, 1998; Zweig, Schlichter, & Burt, 2002). Battered women don't call the police because (1) they don't believe the abuse is important enough, (2) they fear reprisal, or (3) they believe the abuse is a private matter and the police can't help them (Fleury et al., 1998; Grotpeter et al., 2009). Some women love their abusers, hope they will change or fear loss of financial stability.

Women of color, immigrant women, non-English-speaking women, older women, and women living in rural areas confront additional hurdles to accessing police assistance (Abraham, 2000; Straka & Montminy, 2006; Willis, 1998; West, Kantor & Jasinski, 1998). Some women face multiple barriers, suffering from substance abuse, mental health issues, and learning disabilities. (Zweig et al., 2002). Others are incarcerated or engage in prostitution (Zweig et al., 2002). These barriers prevent victims from calling the police because they fear being deported, arrested, retaliated against, humiliated, or simply not believed (Zweig et al., 2002). Being under the influence of drugs or injuring their abusers thwarts police involvement (Kingsnorth & MacIntosh, 2004). Because so many victims won't call police, their barriers become tools for batterers who threaten, exploit and further victimize these women (Zweig et al., 2002).

Women who have been seriously physically or psychologically injured, those who struggled with mothering, and women with substantial support from friends and family are more likely to contact the police (Wright & Johnson, 2009; Lee, Park, & Lightfoot, 2010). The police response for these battered women, however, is mixed and complex (Kingsnorth & MacIntosh, 2004; Grotpeter et al., 2009). When police demonstrated a lack of sympathy for victims or arrested batterers against victim preference, victims were less likely to follow through with prosecutions (Erez & Belknap, 1998). Battered women reported being most satisfied when police honored their preference to arrest or not (Buzawa & Austin, 1993; Miller, 2003). Pro-arrest policies used to justify arresting victims chilled future calls for police help (Miller, 1989, 2001; Nichols & Felty, 2003; Rajah, Frye & Haviland, 2006). Arresting victims means the police do not view the women as victims, reducing them from 'self-confident,' 'strong,' and 'independent' women to 'worthless,' 'powerless,' and 'frightened' women (Rajah et al., 2006, p. 909).

## *Prosecution and Courts*

Prosecutors dismiss most domestic violence cases (Rebovich, 1996). An early study found that prosecutors filed charges in only 10% of cases (Fagan, 1989). No drop policies were intended to shrink dismissal rates, even when victims sought dismissal, (Lerman, 1981; Smith 2001, Corsilles, 1994) and by 1996, two-thirds of prosecution offices adopted no-drop policies (Rebovich, 1996). Victims who wanted prosecutions are happy, but victims who asked to drop charges are ignored and left dissatisfied (Ford, 1991; Ford & Regoli, 1992). Battered women ask to drop charges because initially they viewed the threat of prosecution as a tool to ameliorate violence, reasserting power and control. Once achieved, actual incarceration of abusers appeared to them unnecessary (Fischer & Rose, 1995; Ford, 1991; Ford & Regoli, 1992, 1993; Richman, 2001). "Uncooperative" victims have been held in contempt, arrested, and incarcerated to force their participation in prosecutions (Ford, 2003; Chesney-Lind, 2002). Battered women who dropped charges, dismissed restraining orders or challenged threatened or imposed punishment for refusing to prosecute faced more hostility from prosecutors and judges when they later returned to court for help (Fischer & Rose, 1995). Essentially, the battered women were punished for not prosecuting abusers or following-through with restraining orders.

Systemic barriers impede battered women's participation in prosecuting abusers (Bennett, Goodman, & Dutton, 1999). Battered women give up on prosecuting because the system is confusing and frustrating (Bennett et al., 1999). Battered women, unfamiliar with the courts, confused criminal prosecution and civil restraining order proceedings (Bennett et al., 1999). Since judges do not impose jail time during restraining order proceedings, battered women became disgusted by the leniency and refused to appear at other court proceedings, including criminal prosecutions (Bennett et al., 1999). Disappointed by non-arrest or immediate release from jail pending prosecution, battered women became frustrated with increased fear of reprisal or confronting abusers in court (Bennett et al., 1999). Financial dependence, lengthy incarceration periods, and conflicts about separating fathers from their children diminished victim support for prosecution or restraining orders (Bennett et al., 1999; Kingsnorth & MacIntosh, 2004).

For women who continued to pursue prosecutions or requests for restraining orders, in spite of cultural, systemic and personal barriers, courts erected other barriers (Ptacek, 1999). Battered women confronted court personnel who were insensitive, incapable of communicating information, or biased (Miller, 2003; Taylor, Magnussen & Amundson, 2001). When restraining orders have been refused, their credibility attacked or lenient sentences imposed, victims felt further victimized by the system (Eigenberg, 2001; Erez & Belknap, 1998). They confronted judges who held gendered stereotypes, unwilling to separate batterers from their children:

> Many times, judges are skeptical of victims' claims or unwilling to "break up the family" or deprive victims and their children of a breadwinner by sending the abusers to jail. They might also think treatment of some sort is better than incarceration (Ames & Dunham, 2002, p. 7).

Women experienced the courts as hostile with their credibility and behavior particularly scrutinized and challenged (Hartley, 2003; Jordan, Nietzel, Walker & Logan, 2004; Wan, 2000). If convicted, few abusers were incarcerated (Ames & Dunham, 2002) and frequently victim safety was overlooked (Pence, 2001). Denying restraining orders created barriers for women, who then end up staying with abusers and refusing to return to the legal system for help (Fischer & Rose, 1995; Gist, McFarlane, Malecha, Fredland, Schultz, & Willson, 2001; Holt, 2006; Keopsell, Kernic, & Yearwood, 2005). When granted, battered women don't get full relief. Rarely have judges ordered temporary custody of children to victims, treatment for batterers, or confiscated batterers' firearms in compliance with federal law (Yearwood, 2005). Enforcing restraining orders was difficult (Chaudhuri & Daly, 1992; Efkerman, 1997; Kane, 2000; Keilitz, Hannaford & Keilitz, 1994; Rigakos, 1997; Wan, 2000). Arrest was likely only with evidence of forced entry or physical injury, testimony from other witnesses, or if batterers were caught in the act by police (Chaudhuri & Daly, 1992; Efkerman, 1997; Kane, 2000; Keilitz, et al., 1994; Rigakos, 1997; Wan, 2000).

African-American women have been reluctant to employ a criminal justice system that they perceived as racist, and they experience pangs of guilt when they do (Kingsnorth & MacIntosh, 2005; Weisz, 2005). Asian women rarely call the police and prosecute abusers because doing so was perceived as "bringing shame" to their families (Bhuyan, Mell, Senturia, Sullivan, & Shiu-Thornton, 2005; Bui, 2005). Rural women believed politics and gender stereotypes held by rural judges created barriers to seeking safety (Shannon, Logan, Coe & Medley, 2006; Websdale, 1995). For battered women, the criminal justice system has been the weakest link in the societal response to victims, peppering their attempts at help with a series of obstacles, hurdles and barriers (Zweig, Schlichter & Burt, 2002).

Prior research focusing on marginalized battered women located those participants in programs or shelters, as such identifying women who sought some type of help (e.g., Burgess-Proctor, 2008). No research has focused on marginalized women who were also offenders, and who did not seek help from the criminal justice system, but were punished by the system. This research was intended to explore this gap by examining help seeking by women who have been punished by the criminal justice system. Each was court-ordered to attend a residential program as part of their criminal punishment. These women volunteered to be interviewed because they thought it was important for their voices and perspectives to be heard. As discussed below, battered female *offenders* confront nearly insurmountable barriers accessing help, and the legal system is largely unavailable to them.

# Research Methods

Originally, this research project was focused on battered offenders' perceptions of and experiences with criminal justice agents (e.g., police, prosecutors and judges), family court (e.g., divorce lawyers) and dependency court. During preliminary meetings with the battered offenders, it became apparent that few had sought formal assistance from criminal justice, family or dependency systems or social services. The structure of the hour-and-a-half interviews focused on the women's life histories, their perceptions and experiences of seeking help or why they didn't, and ways they thought the system could improve for women like them. This study is *exploratory*, interviewing only four women by conducting semi-structured questions, and allowing the women to guide the focus of the conversations about their stories, experiences and recommendations.[4]

Following the interviews, the women's responses were transcribed, and their answers categorized and coded, looking for general themes in their responses (Berg & Lune 2011). Using a grounded theory approach, the content of the interviews were reviewed allowing themes to emerge from the data (Glaser & Strauss, 1967; Strauss, 1987). The women provided detailed answers, and the research took on a more case study approach.

---

4. Ten women were interviewed, but a technology problem resulted in the loss of six interviews.

## The Women

At the time of the interviews—Spring 2008—the women were living in transitional housing under court supervision. Each was convicted of at least one felony and self-reported domestic violence victimization. Each participant volunteered for the study. Names of the victims and abusers are changed to protect the women's identities.

The four battered offenders are different from each other, but all four found themselves on the receiving end of criminal punishment, and each reported a reluctance to seek help for abuse from that very same system. The women faced significant barriers to formal help-seeking, and over time, each confronted barriers to getting help from friends and family members. One of the interviewed women was African-American, and the other three were Caucasian. All had at least one child. One woman was in her 20s (Barb), one in her 30s (Vivian), one in her 40s (Francis), and one in her 50s (Janet). The two older women remained married to their abusers; the younger two were not. Vivian reported abuse by several partners, including the father of her child. Francis had been married to her husband for more than 20 years, and she remained married, but not living with him, at the time of the interview. Janet was married for five years before she killed her husband by stabbing him with a knife. The two older women, at one time, held professional jobs and had some college education; the younger two dropped out of school. Three of the four grew up in homes with violence, witnessing fathers or father figures abusing their mothers. Three of the four admitted to drug or alcohol abuse problems. The same three had previous convictions for a variety of crimes. Janet had only a prior DUI charge that predated her violent relationship by 20 years.

Janet has an adult son. Francis, Vivian and Barb have younger children, but none had custody. Francis has four children, two are now adults and two young children are in elementary school. Vivian has one child. Barb has three children, but had lost her parental rights to the youngest child. A priority for the women was to regain custody of their children. Francis's and Barb's children are parented by their abusers, and Vivian's child is parented by her abuser's mother.

# Perceptions, Decision-Making and Help-Seeking

Each woman was shown the power and control wheel developed by the Domestic Abuse Intervention Programs in Duluth, Minnesota.[5] We discussed whether they perceived themselves as "survivors" of abuse, or helpless to stop it. Each had periods where they felt trapped, but they saw themselves as survivors, and each expressed their preference for that label as more empowering. Their relationships were emotionally, financially, and physically abusive. Barb was raped several times by her abuser. The women reported that they returned to their boyfriends and husbands many times. Janet went back because she was lonely. Vivian returned because she wanted her child to have a father. Barb returned because she needed her children's father's financial support. Francis reunited with her husband because she loved him.

## *Police*

Barb, Francis and Vivian were raised in families that experienced domestic violence, and these early contacts with the police dissuaded them from calling the police to address their own domestic violence. Barb became involved with her boyfriend at 15 years of age. She was reared in an abusive home, where she regularly witnessed her step-father—an alcoholic and drug addict—physically abuse her mother:

> [S]ee, I was brought up in an abusive relationship; I seen my dad beat my mom for 16 years. He shot her in the mouth; he did everything. And, he put my mom through a lot. I've seen every beatin' since I was five. And, cops were called all the time. When cops came to the house, they'd be like eight, nine cops showed up just to pick up my dad because my dad always fought the cops. But he'd get out of jail two days later, and this is every single time he beat my mom. Cops would be called, somebody would always call the cops, my dad got arrested, but he was always released a day later, two days later.

---

5. The power and control wheel was developed based on the reports of domestic violence survivors in Duluth, MN, and it describes the most common behaviors or tactics used by abusers to control and victimize women, including financial, physical, sexual and psychological abuse. Domestic Abuse Intervention Project, 202 E. Superior Street, Duluth, MN 55802.

Barb did try to get help from the police early in her relationship, but that experience reinforced her observation that the police either wouldn't or couldn't help her:

> With me, it's about my kids' father. When I first got with him, I was like 15 years old, and things were great in the first year or two, and after the second year, I guess, he realized he had me and he started hitting me, and I tried to get away. [At 16] I went to the police and they didn't do nothin' about it. I ran from the house, and went to the police department, and they didn't do nothin' about it. They basically made, this is what they said, they said it was my fault for staying with him, if he continued to hit me. And I told 'em that it was hard 'cause he's all I had, ya know. I didn't know where else to go. I didn't know what else to do. And, so basically, they didn't do anything. So, I just left … and I went back to him.

Vivian's mother had several boyfriends who physically abused her. As a teenager, she remembers calling the police for help:

> [S]he was like in love with this one. I mean he, like he bought everything for us the first, I'd say the first three years. He gave us whatever we wanted. And then slowly, but surely, things start to like … Mom would stay closed up in her room; she'd never come out. I'd hear noises, but never could make that out, and she'd come out and her face would be all swollen up and she'd be like, "Go call the police." He was in there sleeping, and I'd do that. I think that was the only time he got arrested. But he fought his way out: he still … I don't think he even got arrested. They caught him at his momma house. So, he ran from the police.

Vivian had several abusive relationships, the first when she was 17. She was with him for 18 months, but he became jealous when he saw her sitting in another man's car, and he pulled her out by her hair. He hit her in front of a number of people, and when the people left, it got worse. But she never called the police: "I mean they didn't do too much for my momma, so what would they do for me?" She also explained that in her community, people didn't call the police. Self-help was the preferred way of extricating oneself from an abusive relationship:

> No, 'cause this is in the projects. That is like a rule, you don't call the police. When you have relationships, that's something I just picked up from the street, when you have relationships, you don't call the police, you try to handle your situation yourself. Because, if you in-

volve the police, then that means that you really don't want that person. So, I really wanted him, so I didn't call the police. And I didn't.

Francis grew up in a violent home. She lived in a small town, and her abusive father was a captain with a local police department. The police came to her home on several occasions, and never arrested him:

> I was raised by a policeman. My mom and he had six children. My dad was very abusive; … he beat my mom severely. And I used to run down the stairs to get him to stop, and he would come after me. And I would run up the stairs in the bedroom and lock the door. I don't think he really tried, except the one time. I used to shimmy down the two-story window to get help, and the police didn't do anything because he was a captain in the police department. Sometimes, after the police were there, he'd leave and I was able to get help for my mom.

Francis, like Vivian, called the police to report the abuse against her mother. She reported calling 15 times, but they never intervened, even when her mother was hospitalized:

> My mom was in the hospital because he busted everyone of her ribs. But, she didn't do anything or say anything. I was four the first time it happened; the last was when I was about 16. My dad got a girlfriend and it stopped.

The first seventeen years of Francis's marriage were not abusive, and then, she did not call the police when her husband, while drunk, shoved her up against the kitchen cupboards. But she did take matters into her own hands:

> My husband hit me one time because he got drunk. He didn't even hit me; he grabbed a hold of me and lifted me up and slammed my back into the kitchen cupboards. I waited until the next day, until he was straight, and the next night he wasn't drinking. I sat on him with a butcher knife to his throat and said, "If you ever touch me again, I'll kill you." And he said it'll never happen again. And it didn't happen again until my drug issues. But I was violent, I became just as violent as he was.

When she called the police, he was not arrested. But Francis almost was:

> No, because every time I've dealt with the police, I've almost went to jail because I was the one that was mad. I've had to leave my house once. They gave me a choice to leave or go to jail because I was hysterical, and he wasn't. They didn't believe me. They were laughing with my husband; he knows how to talk to people. He knows how to play the games. He plays really

good games … I called the police six times. He was never arrested and never threatened with arrest, but I was almost arrested three times.

Francis put it simply:

I don't think it's fair what the law does. I was harassed by the police, my husband got the police working for him to harass me…. Anyone can scream anything, and you get arrested.

Janet had no issues with police growing up. She did not grow up in a violent home. In fact, her first marriage, resulting in the birth of her child, was not abusive. She met her abuser in her mid-50s. Within a few months of her marriage, her husband hit her and forced her to quit her job. The first time he hit her, she didn't call the police:

Because I didn't think it was that big a deal. Every time he hit me, he was drunk. And I didn't think it was that big a deal. It was a long time before I called the police…. They didn't want to arrest him: "Can you work this out?" "No, I'm scared." I was hysterical, and that's not me. I am a calm person, and I was hysterical. I was all black and blue.

When Janet called the police, they did not arrest him. And, during her last call for help, the police indicated that if they were called to her home again, they would arrest both her and her husband:

They said if I come back here one more time, your both going to get arrested. And that scared me because I was afraid of being arrested. And he was the one hitting on me. I had no defense against the guy.

After the police left, her husband reminded her that she would get arrested if she called again. She felt like the police couldn't be bothered with helping her, even though she was obviously injured and bruised:

They ignored it, like, "Oh God, I'll have to do paperwork. Is there any place you could go, so I don't have to do paperwork?" I wasn't happy with the police. I shouldn't even have called them because they made me feel, I don't know, not good. I wanted help, but I didn't feel like I was getting help. And I knew that my husband would come back, and he'd be really angry. Then I'd really get it, and that is exactly what happened.

Unsurprisingly, without arrests for the abuse, none of the women pursued prosecutorial or criminal court resources.

## *Restraining Orders*

None of the women obtained restraining orders, nor had they ever requested information about restraining orders. Janet and Barb concluded that restraining orders would not help them. Barb: "Honestly, that would not have stopped him. See, I was brought up in an abusive [home]." Francis thought about a restraining order only after she was arrested: "I thought about a restraining order, after I got out of jail and got custody of my kids, but it never got that far. I've not gotten the kids back." Vivian said that she didn't know if a restraining order would help her.

## *Shelters*

Francis never thought about going to a shelter, she had friends to live with. Barb also didn't consider going to a shelter, but because she was scared:

> No, I was too scared to do all that. Because I was always hearing stories that if you go there, your kids would get taken away from you, and I just didn't want to lose my kids.

Vivian was afraid of the shelter, but for a different reason. She thought most people in her community knew where it was and it wasn't a safe place:

> I know too many people who know about that. You don't have to bring it up, and some people bring it up and in conversations, and I just heard somebody say, "Oh yeah, well I know where that's at, that over by such and such." And, I was like, man, it ain't a secret place. There's a lot of people who know about it. 'Cause a lot of women done been there and then you got women sittin' around and you got men sittin' around there and that's just how it is.

Janet was the only one of the four who went to a shelter, and she had a good experience. She escaped her abuser, and a helpful police officer directed her to a shelter:

> I took domestic violence classes. This shelter was domestic violence shelter for women and children. I liked it there; I felt safe. They helped me. I got my stuff back, and I got a job. And I walked to work. And then I hurt my foot and hobbled to work, but that was okay. I got an apartment. I got a voucher for furniture, pots, pans, and things. Rent was based on my income. They helped me. I got all set up, went to work. I did my routine every day.

Janet stayed away from her abusive husband, living in her apartment, and walking to her job for several months. But she got lonely, and called her husband. She went back to him and the abuse resumed. She felt trapped, and on the day she killed her husband, he was drinking and abusive, and he attacked her while she was cooking dinner, holding a knife. She stabbed him once. He died, and she was prosecuted. She entered a plea to manslaughter, but served several years in jail before the plea. She is serving a ten-year probation, and the transitional placement is part of her probation.

## Hospital

Barb, Janet and Vivian went to hospitals because of injuries, sometimes more than once. Most often, they lied about how they got hurt, and the doctors and nurses didn't call the police or provide any information about domestic violence or community resources. Barb was hospitalized twice, once while she was pregnant:

> No, they just asked me what happened, and I told them that my boyfriend got upset and he hit me. They didn't call the police. After that, I left the hospital and I started thinking I can't do this on my own. When I found out I was pregnant, I am just gonna go back to him, I love him, and maybe he just, was just doing it. He got upset. He was drinking, or whatever.

> Nobody, the doctors and nurses came in and checked the baby. The doctor came in one time to let me know the baby was fine, that the heart rate was a little low, but after that they just let me go. Nobody came and talked to me about anything. The nurses didn't ask me what happened. The doctors didn't ask me what happened. I mean, no cop came to visit me at the hospital.

Vivian went to the hospital. She reported that she was brought by her abuser because he didn't want the paramedics asking questions. She had been choked by her boyfriend, and the nurses asked if she wanted to call the police: "They asked, do you want to [call the police] and I said no."

Janet went to the hospital three times, including one time with a broken arm and another for brain surgery because of the abuse by her husband. She made up excuses: "I made up an excuse. I didn't tell them the truth." While at the hospital with her brain injury, she told the doctor that she fell off a ladder. The doctor replied that that wasn't possible, but no social worker or police officer came to the hospital to speak to her. She received no information about domestic violence.

## *Information*

The women were asked what would help them, what changes might help women like themselves. Barb thought help and information needed to be more easily accessible.

> They could've helped me a lot more by maybe explaining things to me, giving me places to go to, places that would help me. Getting my own place, help me raise my kids on my own without being in an abusive relationship. Without having to deal with that. They say there's places out there, but where do you go to find these places. They say look in a phone book. I looked in a phone book and the places that you call, they say, "Oh, this is not the number; you have to call somebody else." But they don't help you. I don't even know how to explain, or I don't even know how to tell you what I want because I don't know how to get it. I just think they need to help people more than what they do.

Janet believed that jails and prisons are missing opportunities to educate battered women:

> I think they should have, when I was sitting in jail, and if they would have had resources like AA, but for abused women, and they go to meetings like AA or to get help, to learn how to deal with it, or to get away from it or something. I would have gone. I would have found a way to go to a meeting to help me. To help me, to either get away or deal…. In jail they always talk about drugs; 75% I think of the girls in jail are related to drugs…. Only one program dealt with domestic violence….

Vivian suggested alternatives to shelters, renaming battered women's classes, and providing programs in jails and prisons:

> I think they should have like, they have a lot of battered women classes. But maybe if they changed up the name, so it doesn't sound like battered woman, like "survivor." Something they can come to so that they don't feel embarrassed. Put them in the projects, but the women won't go because they don't want people to know that is what is going on inside in their house…. But I think more programs like this [the program in the transitional housing], because the majority of the one's I know are incarcerated, the classes should be in jails and prisons. It should be pounded in their heads.

## *Practical Help*

Barb felt frustrated by the lack of practical help, and that her criminal and drug history impeded her ability to get support in leaving her abusive relationship:

> And stop looking at the people, like for example my background, yeah I have drug charges, now I have violent charges, and it's gonna be really hard for me to get my life together because of my violent charges. So what am I supposed to do about that? Where am I supposed to go? And, here [the transitional housing program], they send you out a month before you leave to go find a place to live. I honestly know right now from girls coming back, I'm not, it's gonna be hard for me to get a place to live. A place for me to afford because I'm working for $7 an hour job, and I have to take a bus back and forth to work, and I want to fight for my kids.

Barb also felt the system was working against her. She indicated that she didn't know how she was going to turn her life around. She stated that more needs to be done with education, training, work and housing:

> But, how am I gonna do that, how am I gonna make these people realize that I deserve a chance to get a place to live, and I wanna go back to school? I wanna learn. I wanna get a better job because I quit in 5th grade. I have no education. I just, how about help with going to get my GED. I actually have to study, I need somebody to help me one on one to teach me things. Not just to throw a book at me and say, here, study this, because I wouldn't know how to do it. Ya know what I'm sayin'? I think they have to help people more with resources and to help them more with through the state. Instead of just givin' certain people, people out there working, who are trying. I think they should help those people.

# Applying Maslow's Hierarchy of Needs

Basically, these women are not having basic needs met, and in some instances that drove them back to their abusers, or in others, struggling to get their lives back on track. They suggest the system improve by providing information, resources, and fulfilling basic needs. Fulfilling fundamental needs is the foundation of Maslow's (1954) theory of human motivation and personality. Knowing how and where to get help to achieve independence, safety, connectedness, and confidence are essential to escaping and surviving domestic violence.

Maslow's (1954) theory posits a hierarchy of seven basic needs: (1) physiological homeostasis,[6] (2) safety, (3) belonging and love, (4) esteem, (5) self-actualization, (6) knowledge and understanding and (7) aesthetics (Maslow, 1954). Any assessment of human tragedy, loss or injury, may apply Maslow's paradigm in an attempt to determine the nature of the psychological threat experienced by the individual.

Applying Maslow's hierarchy to address the issues surrounding IPV victimization is present, if not prominent, in the literature. Kaslow (2008) identified family violence and the phenomenon of battered women as a "megatrend" depriving the family, on an international scale, of the fulfillment of its members' basic needs. Abrahams (2007) applied Maslow's theory to an understanding of the toll that domestic IPV takes on battered women, in terms of their loss of a sense of safety and security, community belonging and self-esteem. Joseph, Govender and Bhagwanjee (2006) reported on the threat to the satisfaction of their safety needs that children experience when confronted with their mothers' IPV victimization. Baumeister and Leary (1995) documented the power of the need for love and belonging, even in the face of violent relationships, as demonstrated when battered women return to their abusive partners.

Maslow held that satisfaction of the seven basic human needs is contingent upon various situational or environmental preconditions, such as "freedom to speak, freedom to do what one wishes so long as no harm is done to others, freedom to express oneself, freedom to investigate and seek for information, freedom to defend oneself, justice, fairness, honesty, orderliness in the group...." (Maslow, 1954, p. 92). When these preconditions are restricted or negated, the person experiences threat, because they are so closely aligned with the person's basic needs that their inhibition is certain to follow.

Maslow proposed that a person might become motivationally threatened when basic needs are deprived. Maslow assumed that threat to the personality might be experienced as "catastrophic" when the basic human needs are so completely thwarted that no alternatives for their satisfaction remain. He explained that severe illness or accident would result in catastrophic threat when the person perceives that "he is not the master of his own fate and that death is ever at his door" (Maslow, 1954, p. 161).

The more continuous the catastrophic threat, the weaker and less effective one's personal system of defenses becomes in protecting oneself from the psy-

---

6. Examples are hunger, sex, and sleep.

chological assault. Then, according to Maslow, one's behavior degenerates into a purposeless and disorganized expression of hopelessness: "Such people may come to the point where they simply give up trying, mostly because they seem to see no use in it. If one hopes for nothing, one fights for nothing" (Maslow, 1954, p. 192).

Certainly, IPV strikes at the heart of the victim's need for safety. Safety, for Maslow, was not only a matter of physical, but also of psychological, security—the need for "a predictable, orderly world" (Maslow, 1954, p. 86). Maslow suggested that people most rely on the need for safety to mobilize their resources when they are in emergency situations. He believed that, when one's safety is catastrophically threatened, then one might likely become a "safety-seeking mechanism." The prototype of this obsession with safety, according to Maslow, is the child in abusive family circumstances: "Also parental outbursts of rage or threats of punishment directed to the child, calling him names, speaking to him harshly, handling him roughly, or actual physical punishment sometimes elicit such total panic and terror that we must assume more is involved than the physical pain alone" (Maslow, 1954, p. 86).

Maslow recognized that a person's experience of physical and/or psychological threat is often registered on more than one need level at a time. Under even the best of circumstances, none of the needs are ever fully satisfied and, therefore to different degrees, a person is living to fulfill multiple need levels simultaneously. For victims of IPV, the next two higher needs seem to be equally, if not as basically, engaged. Belongingness and love needs are most intensely stimulated when significant others are persistently absent or attempts to fit in with a community is somehow prevented or affection and trust is violated.

Esteem needs consist of the human urge both for self-respect and for the respect of others. For Maslow, it takes two forms, that of personal mastery and competence, and that of reputation and status. As the most direct precursor of self-actualization, esteem is essential for the development of "self-confidence, worth, strength, capability, and adequacy, of being useful and necessary in the world. But thwarting of these needs produces feelings of inferiority, of weakness, and of helplessness" (Maslow, 1954, p. 91).

Battered women experience IPV as a threat to their psychological well-being, their basic needs for safety, belongingness and love and esteem. When law enforcement and judicial systems fail these women, the intensity of the threat is compounded. But, as the literature and the interviews cited in this chapter suggest, when in addition they don the offender status, that threat becomes catastrophic. Police, prosecutors, courts, along with health, social service and penal institutions, it seems, tend to focus on the woman-as-offender to the neglect of woman-as-victim.

The battered female offenders here identified many of the same barriers to help-seeking that non-offender victims of IPV identify. The difference was that their offender status made access to practical help and relevant information even more difficult to access because their interactions with the police, prosecutors and judges, in shelters, hospitals and jails depleted their alternatives for satisfying the most basic needs for safety, belonging and esteem. Their normal defenses have broken down and their efforts to help themselves have become erratic and, even in some cases, hopeless.

# Conclusion

For battered offenders, the system is not working. They are not accessing legal or social resources, information, resources or practical help. Programs should be created in jails and prisons to educate women about domestic violence and the means to escape abusive relationships. Social programs should include information about domestic violence without the "battered woman" label, which some women find off-putting. Safety and security are essential, so women must be provided with economic, child-care, educational, and employment assistance. As important, however, women need connections to other people, intimate, but not necessarily romantic, relationships with others to fill that void. Connecting with others, achieving goals and developing social circles will help women satisfy some of the foundational needs of Maslow's hierarchy, so they may improve their self-esteem, and perhaps escape the violence.

# References

Abrahams, H. (2007). *Supporting women after domestic violence: Loss, trauma and recovery.* London: Jessica Kingsley Publishers.

Abraham, M. (2000). *Speaking the unspeakable: Marital violence among South*

Ames, L. J., & Dunham, K.T. (2002). Asymptotic Justice: Probation as a criminal justice response to intimate partner violence. *Violence Against Women,* *8*(1), 6–34.

Asian immigrants in the United States. New Brunswick, NJ: Rutgers University Press.

Baumeister, R. F. & Leary, M. R. (1995). The need to belong: Desire for interpersonal attachments as a fundamental human motivation. *Psychological Bulletin, 117* (3), 497–529.

Belknap, J. (1995). Law enforcement officers' attitudes about the appropriate response to woman battering. *International Review of Victimology 4*, 47–62.

Bennett, L., Goodman L., & Dutton, M.A. (1999). System obstacles to the criminal prosecution of a battering partner: A victim perspective. *Journal of Interpersonal Violence 14*(7), 761–772.

Berg, Bruce L. & Lune, H. (2011). *Qualitative Research Methods for the Social Sciences* (8th Edition). Boston MA: Pearson.

Bhuyan, R., Mell, M., Senturia, K., Sullivan, M., Shiu-Thornton, S. (2005). Women must endure according to their karma: Cambodian immigrant women talk about domestic violence. *Journal of Interpersonal Violence 20*(8), 902–921.

Bowman, C.G. (2003). Domestic violence: Does the African context demand a different approach? *International Journal of Law and Psychiatry 26*(5), 473–491.

Bui, H. (2005). Perceptions of intimate partner violence and attitudes toward interventions: The role of acculturation. *Journal of Ethnicity and Criminal Justice 3*(4): 1–27.

Burgess-Proctor, A. (2008). *Understanding the help-seeking decisions of marginalized battered women*. Dissertation, UMI Number: 3312668.

Buzawa, E. & Austin, T. (1993). Determining police response to domestic violence victims: The role of victim preference. *American Behavioral Scientist 36*(5): 610–623.

Buzawa, E. S., & Buzawa, C.G. (2003). *Domestic violence: The criminal justice response*. Thousand Oaks, CA: Sage.

Chaudhuri, M. & Daly, K. (1992). Do restraining orders help? Battered women's experience with male violence and legal process. In Buzawa, E.S. & Buzawa C.G. (Eds.) *Domestic violence: The changing criminal justice response*, Greenwood Press, Westport CT, pp. 227–252.

Chesney-Lind, M. (2002). Criminalizing victimization: The unintended consequences of pro-arrest for girls and women. *Criminology and Public Policy 2*(1), 81–90.

Corsilles, A. (1994). No-drop policies in the prosecution of domestic violence cases: guarantee to action or dangerous solution? *Fordham Law Review 63*(3): 853–881.

Dobash, R.E. & Dobash, R. P. (1977). Wives: The "appropriate" victim of marital violence. *Victimology, 2*, 426–242.

Eigenberg, H. M. (2001). *Woman battering in the United States: Till death do us part*. Prospect Heights, IL: Waveland Press.

El-Khoury, M., Dutton, M.A., Goodman, L.A., Engel, L., Belamaric, R.J. & Murphy, M. (2004). Ethnic Differences in Battered Women's Formal Help-

Seeking Strategies: A Focus on Health, Mental Health, and Spirituality. *Cultural Diversity and Ethnic Minority Psychology* 10(4): 383–393.

Erez, E. & Belknap, J. (1998). In their own words: Battered women's assessment of the criminal justice response. *Violence & Victims* 13(3): 3–20.

Fagan, J. (1989). Cessation of family violence: Deterrence and dissuasion. *Family Violence* (pp. 377–425). Chicago, IL: University of Chicago Press.

Fagan, J. (1996). *The criminalization of domestic violence: Promises and limits.* Wash. DC: National Institute of Justice.

Fischer, K. & Rose, M. (1995). When "Enough is Enough": Battered women's decision making around court orders of protection. *Crime and Delinquency* 41(4): 414–429.

Fleury, R., Sullivan, C., & Bybee, D.I. (1998). Why don't they just call the cops?: Reasons for differential contact among women with abusive partners. *Violence and Victims* 13(4): 333–346.

Ford, D. (1991). Prosecution as a victim power resource: A note on empowering women in violent conjugal relationships. *Law and Society Review 25,* 313–334.

Ford, D. (2003). Coercing victim participation in domestic violence prosecutions. *Journal of Interpersonal Violence* 18(6), 669–684.

Ford, D. & Regoli, J. (1992). The preventive impact of policies for prosecuting wife batterers. In Buzawa, E. & Buzawa, C. (Eds.), *Domestic violence: The changing criminal justice response* (pp. 181–207). Westport, CT: Greenwood.

Ford, D. & Regoli, J. (1993). The criminal prosecution of wife assaulters: Process, problems, and effects. In Hilton, N.Z. (Ed.) *Legal responses to wife assault: Current trends and evaluation* (pp. 127–164). Newbury Park, CA: Sage.

Gelles, R., & Straus, M. (1988). *Intimate violence.* NY: Simon & Schuster.

Gist, J.H., McFarlane, J., Malecha, A., Fredland, N., Schultz, P. & Willson, P. (2001). Women in danger: Intimate partner violence experienced by women who qualify and who do not qualify for a protective order. *Behavioral Sciences and the Law* 19(5/6), 637–47.

Glaser, B.G. & Strauss, A.L. (1967). *The Discovery of Grounded Theory: Strategies for Qualitative Research.* Piscataway, New Jersey: Transaction Publishers. Grotpeter, J., Menard, S., & Gianola, D. (2009). *Intimate partner violence: Justice system response and public health service utilization in a national sample.* Washington, DC: National Institute of Justice.

Hartley, C.C. (2003). A therapeutic jurisprudence approach to the trial process in domestic violence felony trials. *Violence Against Women* 9(4): 410–437.

Hilton, Z. (Ed.) (1993). *Legal responses to wife assault: Current trends and evaluation.* Newbury Park, CA: Sage.

Hirsch, A.E. (2001). The world was never a safe place for them: Abuse, welfare reform, and women with drug convictions. *Violence Against Women, 7,* 159–175.

Jordan, C.E., Nietzel, M. Walker, R. & Logan T.K. (2004) *Intimate partner violence: A clinical training guide for mental health professionals.* New York: Springer.

Joseph, S., Govender, K., & Bhagwanjee, A. (2006). "I can't see him hit her again, I just want to run away … hide and block my ears": A phenomenological analysis of a sample of children's coping responses to exposure to domestic violence. *Journal of Emotional Abuse, 6* (4), 23–45.

Kane, R. J. (2000). Police responses to restraining orders in domestic violence incidents: Identifying the custody-threshold thesis. *Criminal Justice and Behavior 27*(5), 561–580.

Kaslow, F. W. (2008). Sameness and diversity in families across five continents. *Journal of Family Psychotherapy, 19* (2), 107–142.

Keilitz, S. (1994). Civil protection orders: A viable justice system tool for deterring domestic violence. *Violence and Victims 9*(1): 79–84.

Keilitz, S. (2002). Improving judicial system response to domestic violence: The promises and risks of integrated case management and technology solutions. In Albert Roberts (Ed.) *Handbook of Domestic Violence Intervention Strategies: Policies, Programs and Legal Remedies.* Oxford: Oxford University press (pps. 147–172).

Keilitz, S., Hannaford, P. & Efkeman, H.S. (1997). *Civil Protection Orders: the Benefits* and limitation for victims of domestic violence. Williamsburg, VA: National Center for State Courts.

Keopsell, J., Kernic, M. & Holt, V.L. (2006). Factors that influence battered women to leave their abusive relationships. *Violence and Victims 21*(2), 131–147.

Kingsnorth, R. F. & MacIntosh, R.C. (2004). Domestic violence: Predictors of victim support for official action. *Justice Quarterly 21*(2), 301–328.

Lee, H.Y., Park, E., & Lightfoot, E. (2010). When does a battered woman seek help from the Police? The Role of Battered Women's Functionality. *J. Fam. Viol. 25*: 195–204.

Lerman, L. G. (1981). *Prosecution of spouse abuse: Innovations in criminal justice response.* Wash DC: Center for Women Policy Studies.

Maslow, A. H. (1954). *Motivation and personality.* New York: Harper & Brothers.

Miller, J. (2003). An arresting experiment: Domestic violence victims' experiences and perceptions. *Journal of Interpersonal Violence 18*(7), 695–716.

Miller, S. L. (1989). Unintended side effects of pro-arrest policies and their race and class implications for battered women: a cautionary note. *Criminal Justice Policy Review 3*(3), 299–317.

Miller, S. L. (2001). The paradox of women arrested for domestic violence: Criminal justice professionals and service providers. *Violence against Women 7*(12), 1339–1376.

Moe, A. M. (2004). Blurring the boundaries: Women's criminality in the context of abuse. *Women's Studies Quarterly, 32,* 116–138.

Moe, A. M. (2007). Silenced voices and structural survival: Battered women's help seeking. *Violence Against Women, 13,* 676–699.

Nichols, L. & Felty, K. (2003). The woman is not always the bad guy": Dominant discourse and resistance in the lives of battered women. *Violence Against Women 9*(7): 784–806.

Pence, E. (2001). Safety for battered women in a textually mediated legal system. *Studies in Cultures, Organizations and Society 7,* 199–229.

Ptacek. J. (1999). *Battered women in the courtroom: The power of judicial responses.* Boston: Northeastern University Press.

Rajah, V., Frye, V. & Haviland, M. (2006). "Aren't I a victim?": Notes on identity challenges relating to police action in a mandatory arrest jurisdiction. *Violence Against Women 12*(10), 897–916.

Rebovich, D.J. (1996). Prosecution response to domestic violence: Results of a survey of large jurisdictions. In Buzawa, E. & Buzawa, C. (Eds)., *Do arrests and restraining orders work?* (pp. 176–191). Thousand Oaks, CA: Sage.

Rigakos, G.S. (1997). Situational determinants of police response to civil and criminal injunctions for battered women. *Violence Against Women 3*(2): 204–16.

Shannon, L., Logan, T.K., Cole, J. & Medley, K. (2006). Help-seeking and coping strategies for intimate partner violence in rural and urban women. *Violence and Victims 21*(2), 167–181.

Straka, S. & Montminy, L. (2006). Responding to the needs of older women experiencing domestic violence. *Violence Against Women 12*(3), 251–267.

Straus, M. (1978). Wife-beating: How common and why. *Victimology, 2,* 443–458.

Strauss, A. L. (1987). *Qualitative Data Analysis for Social Scientists.* New York: Cambridge University Press.

Sherman, L.W. & Berk, R.A. (1984). The specific deterrent effects of arrest for domestic assault. *American Sociological Review 49,* 261–272.

Smith, A. (2000). It's my decision, isn't it?: A research note on battered women's perceptions of mandatory intervention laws. *Violence Against Women: An International and Interdisciplinary Journal 6*, 1384–1402.

Smith, A. (2001). Domestic violence laws: The voices of battered women. *Violence and Victims 16*(1), 91–111.

Straka, S. & Montminy, L. (2006). Responding to the needs of older women experiencing domestic violence. *Violence Against Women 12*(3), 251–267.

Taylor, W. K., Magnussen, L. & Amundson, M.J. (2001). The lived experience of battered women. *Violence Against Women 7*(5): 563–585.

*Thurman v. City of Torrington*, 595 F. Supp. 1521 (D. Conn. 1984).

Tjaden, P., & Thoennes, N. (2000). *Extent, nature, and consequences of intimate partner violence: Findings from the National Violence Against Women Survey* (NCJ 181867). Washington DC: National Institute of Justice.

Tsai, B. (2000). The trend toward specialized domestic violence courts: Improvements on an effective innovation. *Fordham Law Review 68*, 1285–1327.

Wan, A. M. (2000). Battered women in restraining order process: Observations on a court advocacy program. *Violence Against Women 6*(6), 606–632.

Websdale, N. (1995). Rural woman abuse: The voices of Kentucky women. *Violence Against Women 1*, 309–388.

Weisz, A. N. (2005). Reaching African American battered women: Increasing the effectiveness of advocacy. *Journal of Family Violence 20*(2), 91–99.

West, C.M., Kantor, G. K., & Jasinski, J. (1998). Sociodemographic Predictors and Cultural Barriers to Help-Seeking Behavior by Latina and Anglo American Battered Women. *Violence and Victims, 13*(4), 361–375.

Willis, S. M. (1998). Recovering from my own little war: Women and domestic violence in rural Appalachia. *Journal of Appalachian Studies 4*(2), 255–70.

Wright, C.V. & Johnson, D.M. (2009). Correlates for Legal Help-Seeking: Contextual Factors for Battered Women in Shelter. *Violence and Victims 24*(6): 771–785.

Yearwood, D. L. (2005). Judicial dispositions of ex-parte and domestic violence protection order hearings: A comparative analysis of victim requests and court authorized relief. *Journal of Family Violence 20*(3), 161–170.

Zweig, J. M., Schlichter, K.A. & Burt, M.R. (2002). Assisting women victims of violence who experience multiple barriers to service. *Violence Against Women 8*(2), 162–180.

# Chapter 3

# Wanda Jean Allen: A Case of Multiple Marginality

*Susan F. Sharp, Ph.D.*

On January 11, 2001, Wanda Jean Allen became the first African American female to be executed in the United States since reinstatement of capital punishment in 1976. Moreover, she was the first African American woman executed in the United States since 1954, and the first woman executed in the state of Oklahoma since statehood in 1907. Thus, her execution garnered considerable publicity both nationally and globally. There was substantial controversy surrounding her execution due to the many disadvantages faced by Allen, which are the subject matter of this chapter.[1]

Not only was Wanda Jean Allen an African American female, but she was also a lesbian and borderline mentally retarded. Additionally, she was from a very low socioeconomic group. Across virtually every dimension, she was marginalized. Those factors all worked against her in her trial for the murder of her lover, Gloria Leathers.

Understanding Wanda Jean Allen's execution requires comprehension of how different forms of social inequality may intersect. Her story illustrates how her multiple layers of disadvantage worked against her, and consequently it serves as a good case study of multiple marginalities. As Daly (1997) suggests, story-telling is perhaps one of the best ways to reveal the interconnected impact of multiple forms of disadvantage.

---

1. I attended her clemency hearing and was privy to a number of conversations with key figures in her appeals process, thus some of the observations in this chapter may differ from published reports.

# Multiple Marginalities

The perspective of the intersection of multiple marginalities argues that one cannot examine simply how gender (or race, class) disadvantage the individual. Instead, the individual experiences life from a unique position resulting from many different social statuses or relationships. From a feminist perspective, this means that we cannot explain inequities simply on the basis of gender, assuming the experiences of all women are the same. Instead, the feminist researcher must take into account the relative lack of power of the subjects, which varies by race, class and sexual orientation (Daly & Chesney-Lind, 1988; Daly, 1997; Burgess-Proctor, 2006). Avoiding the trap of essentialism, the intersectionality or multiple marginalities approach acknowledges that all women do not have the same experiences (Flavin, 2001). A brief examination of how gender, race, education, disability (mental health and mental deficiency), SES and sexual orientation may marginalize offenders may help illuminate the disadvantages faced by Wanda Jean Allen.

## *Gender*

Violence is often viewed as the domain of males. In contrast, women who engage in violent crimes, especially in homicides, may be seen as acting in a gender-inappropriate manner. Thus, they are doubly-deviant: deviant for committing the crime and deviant for violating gender roles (Schur, 1983). Historically, women who kill have been viewed as "devious, cunning, and deceitful" (Mann, 1996, p.1). Because women kill far less often than men, their actions often become sensationalized, and this may have serious repercussions in the criminal justice system. Contrary to popular media representations, female violence has not increased significantly (Steffensmeier et al.; 2006; Lauritsen et al., 2009a, 2009b; Schwartz et al., 2009). Women continue to account for only a fraction of all murders. In 2007, the most recent year for which data are available, women were the known offenders in only 7.1% of the murders known to law enforcement (U.S. Department of Justice, 2008).

Family members and sexual intimates are the most common victims of women who kill (Belknap, 2007; Mann, 1996; Peterson, 1999). Furthermore, we know that when women commit homicides, there is frequently little if any planning involved (Peterson, 1999). Instead, women seem more likely to kill in response to an immediate threat, whether to personal safety or of loss of a relationship. Additionally, victim precipitation appears to play a significant role in homicides committed by women. In fact, in one study of women who killed, the majority of the offenders appear to have been provoked by their victims (Mann, 1996).

Prior research suggests that the societal response is harsher towards women who kill their lovers or spouses compared to the response toward men who kill their lovers or partners (Mann, 1996). Despite the lack of malice aforethought and the likelihood that the victim played a major role, the response to homicide by women tends to be harsh.

## *Race*

Prior research suggests that race remains a significant factor in sentencing, even when controlling for legal factors (Chiricos & Crawford, 1995). Legal representation may also be affected by race, with African Americans being more likely to be represented by a public defender (Bureau of Justice Statistics, 2000). However, the lack of private representation is only somewhat disadvantageous, as having a private attorney is only beneficial to whites (Spohn & DeLone, 2000).

The impact of Allen's status as an African American woman cannot be ignored. As Britton (2000) points out, the media representation of the new breed of bad, dangerous women focuses primarily on women of color. Furthermore, African American women and other women of color tend to be the target of highly discriminatory prosecution and treatment by the system (Burgess-Proctor, 2006; Potter, 2006; Potter, 2008). Although they are not inherently more violent, some evidence suggests that African American women may be more likely than other women to respond to abuse they receive with violence (Miller, 2005).

In one of the most vivid and compelling descriptions of how African American women are viewed by both society and the criminal justice system, Young (1986) eloquently portrays how these women are portrayed. The self-sufficiency attributed to African American women means they do not need chivalry or protection. Furthermore, the woman engaging in violence may be characterized as a "sinister sapphire," someone "inherently violent" and "treacherous" (Young, 19 86, p. 323). It is clear that this is how Allen was portrayed in her trial.

On a more global level, there is a belief that African American communities are inherently more violent. However, research suggests that African American women who kill are not more violent, that there is not an underlying subculture that promotes more violence (Mann, 1996). Nonetheless, this belief has serious implications, impacting the treatment of African American women by the criminal justice system.

## *Education/Mental Illness/Mental Retardation*

Deinstitutionalization of the mentally ill in the mid-twentieth century has resulted in more individuals with mental illnesses and operating with limited abilities being in our communities. As a result, their behaviors have frequently come under the purview of the criminal justice system. Indeed, they are far more likely to be arrested than those without mental health and functionality problems (Teplin, 2000). Law enforcement officers find themselves often acting as *de facto* social workers for these people due to societal failure to adequately provide for them (Blevins & Arrigo, 2009; Dodge & Schreiber, 2009).

Mental retardation and low educational achievement can also marginalize individuals. Low educational achievement can be linked to harsher sentencing (Belknap, 2007) as well as increased likelihood of incarceration (Casey & Keilitz, 1990). Furthermore, those who are mentally retarded or deficient may be less likely to be able to help in their own defense, and their testimony is often viewed as less credible. They often make little effort to conceal their crimes and may willing admit their culpability to law enforcement in a misguided effort to please (Petersilia, 1997; RAND, 1997). In the case of Wanda Jean Allen, this is apparent. First, she shot Leathers in the parking lot of the police station with Allen's mother witnessing the act. Second, she admitted her culpability to police. Finally, some of her testimony, particularly her inflating of her educational achievements, worked against her. She lacked the capacity to understand that by portraying herself as someone capable of attending college, she increased her perceived culpability.

## *SES*

Socioeconomic status plays a major role in the prosecution and disposition of homicides. It may also frame how law enforcement personnel respond to domestic violence calls. Officers may label both victims and offenders in lower-class neighborhoods negatively and see the violence as just another aspect of what they perceive as a lifestyle among the poor (Miller, 2005, p. 70). Not only are the poor likely to be negatively stereotyped, but they also lack the resources to obtain adequate and fair representation. Again, we see this in Allen's situation. Her representation at trial was noteworthy for its defects. A poorly paid and ill-prepared defense attorney did little research into mitigating evidence and thus provided her with a totally inadequate defense.

## Sexual Orientation

Research by Renzetti (1992) on battering in lesbian relationships has indicated that substance abuse and emotional abuse are important factors in violent lesbian relationships. Moreover, it appears that abuse is more likely to be bi-directional in homosexual relationships than in heterosexual relationships (Renzetti, 1992). On the other hand, some research has suggested that battering in gay and lesbian relationship, as in heterosexual relationships, is still a function of unequal power (Miller, 2005). It is important, however, to acknowledge that little is actually known about the dynamics of these relationships and the abuse that occurs. Because lesbians are a hidden population, most research on lesbian couple violence is based on clinical samples. To document the dynamics of these relationships requires self-disclosure of sexuality, thus many may remain hidden (Miller, 2005). What we do know suggests that prior histories of violent offending are common in lesbians who engage in intimate partner violence (Renzetti, 1992). In the case of Allen and Leathers, both women had documented histories of violence, as will be described in more detail below.

Within the criminal justice system, there is evidence that lesbian women receive harsher sanctions than heterosexual women. They are overrepresented in the criminal justice system and may experience harassment due to their sexual orientation (Belknap, 2007; Belknap & Holsinger, 2006).

Wanda Jean Allen's social placement placed her in the position to be likely to receive harsh punishment. As Belknap (2007: 154) concludes, the criminal justice system does not treat all women equally, stating, "As a rule, women of color, poor women, younger women, women immigrants, and lesbians are afforded less leniency or are processed more prejudicially than other females." It is imperative to remember that the impact of these statuses is not simply additive but instead constitutes a complex and interwoven pattern. Meeting all the above criteria except being an immigrant, it is not surprising that Allen was sentenced to death for what was most likely a crime of passion. As a young, poor, African American lesbian with limited education and low intellectual functioning, both her actions and her death sentence were highly predictable. This is especially true in Oklahoma, where her crime was committed. Oklahoma has the highest female incarceration rate in the nation as well as the highest per capita execution rate. So, in addition to being marginalized in a variety of ways, Allen was in a locale where punitive responses were the norm.

# Wanda Jean's Story

The path to the execution of Wanda Jean Allen, who preferred to be known to her friends and supporters as Jean, began in childhood. Born into a very disadvantaged family, she was the oldest daughter in a family of eight children. At an early age, she took responsibility for her younger siblings, helping to raise several after her father abandoned the family. The family lived on welfare, in public housing (Potter, forthcoming).

There is some evidence that her mother drank during her pregnancy with Jean (ACLU, 2004; Cohen, 2001). Additionally, Jean suffered documented developmental disabilities and brain-damage, at least partly related to two injuries received in childhood. First, she was hit by a truck at age 12. Second, she was stabbed in the temple at age 14. While there is no decisive link between those injuries and her impulsive and sometimes violent behavior, there is documented evidence from childhood that she was mentally impaired. By her mid-teens, Jean was placed first in foster care and then in a youth detention program. While there, psychological testing indicated borderline mental retardation as well as serious cognitive impairment related to her injuries. A psychologist recommended that Allen receive further testing, training and protective control to deal with her problems. However, Jean never received these or any other interventions (Rust-Tierney, 2001). In 1995, a comprehensive psychological evaluation of Allen was conducted. Again, evidence of limited functioning was reported. Although the psychologist reported her IQ then tested at 80, he also reported that she evidenced significant dysfunction in the left hemisphere of her brain that could impair her ability to effectively understand cause and effect. Furthermore, he reported that her impairment placed her at high risk of becoming overwhelmed by everyday stressors, with the likely result of losing control under stress (Amnesty International, 2000). In the words of clinical psychologist Martin Krimsky:

> Wanda achieved a Verbal IQ of 62 (mental deficiency), a Performance IQ of 78 (border-line) and a Full Scale IQ of 69 which is just within the upper limit of the classification of mental retardation. The combined mental age equivalent is nine years seven months…. [Wanda Jean] does very poorly on Similarities which requires abstract and conceptual thinking. The Verbal subtests are severely lowered and all fall within the range of retardation. Certain methods she utilizes in solving perceptual and cognitive tasks resemble those methods which are frequently used by individuals with cerebral damage…. In view of these findings, a neurological assessment would be most appro-

priate … In view of the intellectual deficit and the marked inability to cope with a variety of complex situations *I would recommend some form of protective control with emphasis on socialized and vocational training* (Presson, n.d.).

Like many from impoverished backgrounds, Jean was often in trouble with the legal system. During adolescence, she was responsible for helping to provide for her younger siblings, and she often engaged in petty theft to supply needed food and clothing. These thefts resulted in her detention as a juvenile. Eventually, her actions culminated in her first incarceration in 1981 for manslaughter in the death of her long-time friend, Dedra "Sweet Pea" Pettus. There is some disagreement about the circumstances surrounding the shooting. Some sources claim that Allen cold-bloodedly shot Pettus with a concealed gun during an argument in a parking lot (Clark Country Prosecutor, n.d.). Others claim that it was self-defense, with Jean defending herself from gunfire from Pettus' boyfriend (Cohen, 2001). Regardless, Jean pled guilty to manslaughter and was sentenced to four years in prison.

It was during this incarceration that she met Gloria Jean Leathers. Allen was released from prison in 1984, and Leathers' release followed. The two began living together in what has been characterized as a turbulent and often violent relationship. There were frequent calls to the police made by both women for domestic disputes that turned violent. Indeed, Jean was not the only one with a past history of engaging in violence. Gloria Leathers also had a history of violent behavior. She had been accused of the shooting death of another woman, Sheila Barker, in 1979, although she was never prosecuted. There is evidence, as well, that she had also been violent towards Allen (ACLU, 2004). On at least one occasion, Allen had filed a battery complaint against Leathers (Presson, n.d.).

In fact, on the day she was shot, evidence suggests that both women had been violent towards each other. Earlier in the day of December 1, 1988, the two had engaged in an argument at home and then at a store that resulted in police being called to the scene. There is also the suggestion that Leathers had attacked Allen earlier in the day with a hand rake, including a wound on Allen's face still visible five days later when she was booked for first-degree murder (Amnesty International, 2000). After the police left, Leathers and her mother headed to the Village police station, where Leathers planned to file charges against Allen. Jean confronted Gloria and her mother in the parking lot of the police station. Here, the story becomes somewhat muddled. Allen claimed that she thought Leathers was going to attack her again and shot her in self-defense. In fact, the hand rake was purportedly with Gloria's belongings in the vehicle, and Jean claimed that Gloria again came after her with it, so she fired a single shot at her. The rake was never found, and it was not until the clemency hearing that her attorneys heard what might have become of it. One of Gloria's family members said it was given to a relative in Tulsa to dispose of following the shooting (Presson, n.d.)

In contrast, the prosecutors claimed that Allen stalked Leathers to the police station with the intent of killing her. What is indisputable, however, is that Allen shot Leathers in the stomach. Several days later, Gloria Leathers died, and first-degree murder charges were filed against Allen (Clark County Prosecutor, n.d.; CCADP, 2001). The state argued that Allen had pre-meditated the murder, acting "with malice aforethought." However, given that the shooting occurred at the police station, it is difficult to view this as a calculated, pre-meditated act.

# The Trial

Jean's economic disadvantage did not end with her childhood. Indeed, the effects of her low socioeconomic status became more pronounced during her trial. Like many poor, black families, Jean and her family did not trust the court-appointed attorney system. Thus, they hired a private attorney, Bob Carpenter, to represent Allen in what was expected to be a manslaughter or second-degree murder case. Nor am I the only one to believe that this is how the case should have been filed. During her federal appeal, the Honorable Wade Brorby, judge on the U.S. Tenth Circuit Court of Appeals asked the prosecution, "How in the world did this case become a death penalty case? In my experience as a judge and prosecutor, this would not have been anything more than second degree murder, and probably manslaughter at the most" (Presson, n.d.).

Carpenter took the case for a $5,000 fee, although all he ever received was an initial $800 down payment on his fee. When the state filed first-degree murder charges and announced its intent to seek the death penalty, Carpenter approached the court, asking to be released, but his request was denied. He then offered to act as co-counsel for free, requesting that a public defender be appointed. This was opposed by the prosecution, and he was forced to remain as counsel of record. He was also denied a court-appointed investigator to assist him in preparing for trial. Allen therefore received the best defense that $800 could buy. This meant that little if any research into mitigating factors was accomplished, and no evidence of her limited functioning and brain-damage were introduced at the trial (ACLU, 2004; Amnesty International, 2000; personal conversations with appellate attorney; clemency hearing). The jury was given the impression that Allen had a happy and normal childhood, rather than a borderline mentally retarded woman brought up in a highly dysfunctional family living in "abject poverty" (Presson, n.d.).

Her sexuality also became a major focus during the trial. She was portrayed to the jury and court as a lesbian, acting as the dominant "male" partner in the relationship (Cohen, 2001). Prosecutors even argued that she was a "hunter," hunting down Leathers like an animal (Presson, n.d.). The defense was barred from introducing evidence of Gloria's prior violent behavior or testimony from those who knew the couple. The prosecutor even used Jean's choice to be called by her middle-name as evidence of her "masculinity," implying that she wanted to be known as "Gene," a man's name (Cohen, 2001). The jury was left with the impression that Wanda Jean Allen was a masculine, aggressive woman who had deliberately committed an intentional murder. Gloria Leathers, in contrast, was portrayed as a woman often victimized by her violent partner. The jury had little difficulty reaching a unanimous decision to sentence Allen to death.

# The Clemency Hearing

At her clemency hearing on December 15, 2000, United Church of Christ minister Robin Meyers was the major witness for Allen. He reiterated her disadvantaged background, her mental impairment, and her inadequate defense at the trial. Trial attorney Bob Carpenter testified that he had not been aware of the early IQ testing indicating borderline retardation. He additionally admitted his failure to adequately research the case, as well as the fact that he received only $800 total for her defense, had no experience with capital cases, and was not allowed to step down. During the clemency hearing, board member Currie Ballard became incensed at the implication that Jean's low IQ might have contributed to the crime. Ballard, who himself had a brother with Downs' Syndrome, stated that he was offended by the suggestion that mental retardation could be linked to violence or that Oklahoma would execute a mentally retarded person. In a vitriolic diatribe, he lambasted Meyers and the appellate attorney for introducing that argument, possibly affecting the votes of other board members.

Nor was Ballard's reaction the only bizarre occurrence. Sandy Howard represented the Oklahoma Attorney General at the hearing and sought to dispel any idea that Allen was mentally retarded by using a statement made by Allen during her trial. Allen thought that it might look better for her if she lied about her level of education, and she had testified that she had completed high school and attended Rose State College, obtaining an associate's degree. The reality was that she had dropped out of high school and attended only one day of certified nursing assistant training at Rose State, unable to comprehend the readings. However, she was ashamed of her lack of education and lacked the capacity to understand how her falsehood might eventually be used against her. Assistant Attorney General Howard had been provided with the complete appellate file documenting Allen's educational achievements (or lack thereof), the IQ score of 69, and the psychologist's recommendations. However, she instead focused on Allen's earlier statement and argued effectively to the Pardon and Parole Board that the diminished capacity argument was merely a smokescreen.

In the state of Oklahoma, clemency is a two-pronged process. First, the Pardon and Parole Board must vote by a majority to recommend clemency. Then, the governor has thirty days to consider that recommendation before making his or her final decision. However, without the Board's recommendation, the governor cannot grant clemency. As one of almost two hundred people attending Wanda Jean Allen's clemency proceeding, I found the entire process surreal. I have attended a number of clemency hearings in the state, but no hearings before or since have borne even slight resemblance to that one. First, due to the high profile nature of the case, hundreds of people from around the country arrived at the prison. Several hundred remained outside, led in an organized protest. To even get into the prison, one had to drive through the gauntlet of protestors and some supporters of the execution.

The room in which the clemency hearing took place was packed with attendees, including a number of members of Leathers' family who were to testify against clemency. Jean's family was spread throughout the courtroom. One brother, who sat directly in front of me, almost got into a physical altercation with one of Leathers' brothers, who somewhat ambivalently argued against clemency. Another of Allen's brothers, who suffered from Tourette's Syndrome, stood at the side of the room. Successful initially in suppressing the involuntary movements, as the hearing continued, his ability to contain the tics decreased, resulting in highly visible jerky movements that at one point caused the prison guards surrounding the room to move towards him. Allen herself was so intimidated that she was difficult to hear, with her voice frequently breaking. Additionally, the Oklahoma process requires a board vote with no deliberation. Two board members spoke after the two sides presented their cases. First, Board chair, Susan Bussey, asked if there was anyone who could testify from a sociological perspective. The appellate attorney ran down the aisle to me. After a quick consultation, we decided that we were unsure what she wanted and that I did not have data with me to adequately address the issues. Then, Ballard gave his explosive condemnation of the discussion regarding mental retardation. The Board then had to vote, with no time to discuss the issues. Ballard voted first with a vivid "thumbs down." Only Bussey voted in favor of clemency. Allen was then told that her request was denied and led from the room by guards. One of her younger sisters jumped up and ran to the door, beating on it and sobbing that she had to get out. After determining she was no threat, guards lead her to the appropriate door so that she could leave. Most clemency hearings are not fraught with this type of drama, and attendees left the room virtually silently.

## The Execution

Race became a major focus in the days leading up to the execution. The Reverend Jesse Jackson, Jr., came to Oklahoma City to protest her execution. He met with the governor to plead Allen's cause and garnered national headlines for his arrest for trespass onto the prison grounds. The latter was a planned nonviolent protest, designed to garner media coverage. Jackson also met with Allen as one of her spiritual advisors, again garnering headline coverage.

Allen was transferred to McAlester State Penitentiary for the execution. Last-minute efforts to stop the execution failed. She spent her last evening reassuring the investigator on her case and his brother, one of her appellate attorneys. Lying on the gurney, she playfully stuck her tongue out at the investigator, and then she quoted the scriptures before being put to death.

In one final note about the case, the day following the execution, I was approached by one of the students in my senior capstone class. We cover capital punishment, particularly in terms of race, and we had discussed the case at length. Ryan asked to speak to me in private. In a halting voice and with tears in his eyes, he told me that Jean had been his babysitter at the time of her arrest. The family found out about it on television. He said she had been the best babysitter that he had ever had, loving and playful. It was clear that he had been devastated by her execution.

## Multiple Marginalities and Wanda Jean

Wanda Jean Allen was as much a victim of her social placement as of her own actions. The prosecution and execution of Wanda Jean Allen was clearly affected by her various forms of disadvantage. She was disadvantaged as a female who had committed a crime antithetical to traditional conceptions of femininity. As an African American, she was viewed as a more dangerous and violent type of person. As a lesbian, she was portrayed as mannish and aggressive, the dominant and violent partner in the relationship. As a mentally-challenged woman, she tried to make herself look more intelligent, which ultimately was used against her. During her trial and in subsequent proceedings, the State crafted a portrait of an almost demonic woman, ruthless and cunning, the ultimate villainess.

Because of her poverty and distrust of the justice system, Allen ended up with what can be viewed as an almost criminally inadequate defense. The private attorney hired by her family did not anticipate trying a capital case. The facts of the case suggested that Leathers' death would be prosecuted as second-degree murder or perhaps even manslaughter. Thus, he thought that the $5,000 fee he was charging would be adequate for plea-bargaining her case. He did not anticipate not receiving more than the initial down payment, much less having to try a capital case for only $800. His efforts to be removed from the case or to obtain assistance from a public defender were denied. Thus, the defense Wanda Jean Allen received was woefully inadequate. It is, of course, a moot point now as to whether a more rigorous defense that addressed her documented brain damage and low level of functioning would have resulted in a different outcome. The point is, she was presented to the jury as the worst type of individual, "social junk" (Spitzer, 1980) to be discarded by society and viewed as having no redeeming qualities. Not any single status can fully explain this. Instead, it is the complex interwoven nature of her sex, her sexual orientation, her race, her poverty and her disabilities that contributed to the portrayal of Wanda Jean Allen as a vicious and predatory offender, deserving of death. She was an easy target for an ambitious prosecutor. Because of societal perceptions about African American women and of lesbian relationships, it took little effort to paint a picture of a cunning and violent woman who did not deserve to live. Furthermore, her marginalized position made it easier for a jury to essentially "write her off." Allen was portrayed as the stuff of nightmares—cunning, domineering and violent. Lacking a defense team that could highlight her disadvantages and the role of Leathers in the relationship, she was powerless to deflect the negative labels and ultimately powerless to prevent her own execution.

Far more vicious crimes often result in far less harsh sentencing. In Jean's case, we have a volatile relationship between two women that was characterized by mutual abuse. Additionally, both women had histories of violence. But, in the conservative state of Oklahoma, prejudices against minorities, homosexuals, and women who violated gender-role explanations all worked against Allen. The complex interactions of her various social placements ultimately assured that she would receive no compassion—from the prosecutor, the jury, or the Pardons and Parole Board. Although her cause was championed by those fighting for the rights of both minorities and homosexuals, neither status can be fully blamed for the outcome of her case. Instead, the case of Wanda Jean Allen is best understood by using a multiple marginality framework to highlight the inequities in the system.

# References


American Civil Liberties Union & American Friends Service Committee. (2004). *A forgotten population: A look at death row in the United States through the experiences of women.* Retrieved May 28, 2009, from http://www.deathpenalty.org/downloads/womenondeathrow.Dec.2004.pdf.

Amnesty International. (2000). Amnesty International Execution Alert 17 November 2000. Retrieved February 1, 2009, from http://www.clarkprosecutor.org/html/death/US/allen687.htm.

Belknap, J. (2007). *The invisible woman: Gender, crime and justice (3rd ed.).* Belmont, CA: Wadsworth.

Belknap, J. & Holsinger, K. (2006). The gendered nature of risk factors for delinquency. *Feminist Criminology, 1,* 48–71.

Blevins, K. R. & Arrigo, B. A. (2009). Ethics, female offenders and psychiatric illness: How the justice and mental health systems fail and abandon women. In R. L. Gido and L. Dalley (eds.), *Women's mental health issues across the criminal justice system* (pp. 244–260). Upper Saddle River, NJ: Prentice-Hall.

Britton, D. (2000). Feminism in criminology: Engendering the outlaw. *Annals of the American Academy of Political and Social Science, 57,* 57–76.

Bureau of Justice Statistics. (2000). *Defense counsel in criminal cases.* Washington, DC: U.S. Department of Justice.

Burgess-Proctor, A. (2006). Intersections of Race, class, gender and crime: Future directions for feminist criminology. *Feminist Criminology, 1,* 27–47.

Canadian Coalition to Abolish the Death Penalty (CCADP). (2001) Wanda Jean Allen. Retrieved February 1, 2009, from http://www.ccadp.org/wandajeanallen-news.htm.

Casey, P. & Keilitz, I. (1990). Estimating the prevalence of learning disabled and mentally retarded juvenile offenders: A meta-analysis. In P. E. Leone (Ed.), *Understanding troubled and troubling youth* (pp.80–101) Newbury Park, CA: Sage.

Chiricos, T. G. & Crawford, C. (1995). Race and imprisonment: A contextual assessment of the evidence. In D. Hawkins (ed.), *Ethnicity, race and crime* (pp. 281–309). Albany, NY: SUNY Press.

Clark County Prosecutor. (n.d.). Wanda Jean Allen. Retrieved May 29, 2009, from http://www.clarkprosecutor.org/html/death/US/allen687.htm.

Cohen, A. B. (2001). Who was Wanda Jean?—Black woman executed in the United States. *The Advocate*. Retrieved May 15, 2009 from http://www.thefreelibrary.com/Who+was+Wanda+Jean%3F-a071763690.

Daly, K. (1997). Different ways of conceptualizing sex/gender in feminist theory and their implications for criminology. *Theoretical Criminology, 1*, 25–51.

Daly, K. & Chesney-Lind, M. (1988). Feminism and criminology. *Justice Quarterly, 5*, 497–538.

Dodge, M. & Schreiber, T. (2009) The challenges of policing the mentally ill: An exploration of gendered and ungendered perspectives. In R. Gido & L. Dalley (eds.), *Women's mental health issues across the criminal justice system* (pp. 71–83). Upper Saddle River, NJ: Prentice-Hall.

Flavin, J. (2001). Feminism for the mainstream criminologist: An invitation. *Journal of Criminal Justice, 29*, 271–285.

Lauritsen, J., Heimer, K., & Lynch, J. P. (2009a). Trends in the gender gap in violent offending: New evidence from the National Crime Victimization Survey. *Criminology, 47*, 361–399.

______. (2009b). The National Crime Victimization Survey and the gender gap in offending: Redux. *Criminology, 47*, 427–438.

Mann, C.R. (1996). *When women kill*. Albany, NY: SUNY Press.

Miller, S. L. (2005). *Victims as offenders: The paradox of women's violence in relationships*. New Brunswick, NJ: Rutgers University Press.

Meyers, R. (2001). Killing Wanda Jean. Retrieved May 1, 2009, from http://www.ucc.org/ucnews/feb01/killing.htm.

Petersilia, J. (1997). Justice for all? Offenders with mental retardation and the California corrections system. *The Prison Journal, 77*, 358–380.

Peterson, E.S.L. (1999). Murder as self-help: Women and intimate partner homicide. *Homicide Studies, 3*, 30–46.

Potter, H. (2010). Wanda Jean Allen. In V. Jensen & K. Baird-Olson (Eds.), *Women and crime: An encyclopedia of issues and cases*. Westport, CT: Greenwood Press.

______. (2008). *Battle cries: Black women and intimate partner abuse*. New York: New York University Press.

______. (2006). Black feminist criminology. *Feminist Criminology, 1*, 106–24.

Presson, S. (n.d.). The case of Wanda Jean Allen: First woman executed in Oklahoma history. Retrieved June 14, 2009, from http://www.stevepresson.com/Allen_Case.html.

RAND. (1997). Criminal justice policies toward the mentally retarded are unjust and waste money. Retrieved June 4, 2009, from http://www.people1.org/articles/article_criminal_justice_unjust.htm.

Renzetti, C. (1992). *Violent betrayal: Partner abuse in lesbian relationships.* Newbury Park, CA: Sage.

Rust-Tierney, D. (2001). Wanda Jean Allen clemency letter, January 3, 2001. Retrieved May 29, 2009 from http://www.aclu.org/capital/clemency/10356lgl20010103.html.

Schur, E. M. (1983). *Labeling women deviant: Gender, stigma and social control.* Philadelphia: Temple University.

Schwartz, J., Steffensmeier, D., Zhong, H. & Ackerman, J. (2009). Trends in the gender gap in violence: Reevaluating NCVS and other evidence. *Criminology, 47,* 401–425.

Spitzer, S. (1975). Toward a Marxian theory of deviance. *Social Problems, 22,* 638–651.

Spohn, C. & DeLone, M. (2000). When does race matter? An examination of the conditions under which race affects sentence severity. *Sociology of Crime, Law & Deviance, 2,* 3–37.

Steffensmeier, D., Zhong, H., Ackerman, J., Schwartz, J. & Agha S. (2006). Gender gap trends for violent crimes, 1980–2003. *Feminist Criminology, 1,* 72–98.

Teplin, L. A. (2000). Keeping the peace: Police discretion and mentally ill persons. *National Institute of Justice Journal, July,* 8–15.

U.S. Department of Justice. (2008). Crime in the United States, 2007. Washington, DC: U.S. Government Printing Office.

Young, V. (1986). Gender expectations and their impact on black female offenders and their victims. *Justice Quarterly, 3,* 305–327.

# Chapter 4

# Arresting Girls for Dating Violence: The Importance of Considering Intersectionality

*Alesha Durfee, Ph.D.*

## Introduction

There seems to be an increased willingness on the part of all authorities to both police and punish youth violence, particularly if those exhibiting the behavior are females and especially if they are African American. It may be that the systems of social control have shifted from policing girls' sexuality, as was the case for most of the last century, to instead policing girls' violence … and *most particularly the violence of young African American girls* (Stevens, Morash, & Chesney-Lind, 2011, p. 740; emphasis added).

This chapter analyzes law enforcement data in order to better understand the potential impacts of the extension of domestic violence (DV) mandatory and pro-arrest laws on reported cases of adolescent intimate partner violence (IPV). Nearly 36% of American women and 29% of American men report that they have experienced some form of IPV; more than one in five of those women and one in seven of those men were first victimized before the age of 18 (Breiding, Chen, & Black, 2014). Despite increasing awareness about DV, current rates of IPV among teenagers are also "disturbingly common" (Hamby, Finkelhor, & Turner, 2012, p. 122). Slightly more than six percent of youth surveyed for the National Survey of Children's Exposure to Violence stated that they had experienced physical IPV (Hamby, Finkelhor, & Turner, 2012); other studies with high-risk populations have found rates between 43% and 57% (Molidar, Tolman, & Kober, 2000; Watson et al., 2001).

In an effort to combat high rates of DV and IPV among adults, all jurisdictions in the United States have adopted some form of a warrantless arrest policy for DV. The criminalization of DV, the implementation of mandatory and pro-arrest policies, and the creation of no-drop prosecution policies were seen as ways to hold perpetrators "accountable for their violence" (Zosky, 2010, p. 362). The intention of such policies was to deter abusers from committing acts of DV and IPV through the threat of criminal sanctions, decrease rates of recidivism for DV offenders, and ensure that victims could use the criminal justice system as a resource to achieve safety and obtain justice. After the widespread adoption of these types of legal interventions for DV, the prevalence of IPV decreased, reporting rates increased, and the arrest rates for reported cases of IPV increased (Cho & Wilke, 2005; Dugan, 2003; Eitle 2005; Hirschel et al. 2007; Jones & Belknap 1999; Mignon & Holmes 1995; Pattavina et al. 2007).

Given the apparent success of mandatory arrest policies in cases of adult IPV, some have argued that mandatory and pro-arrest laws should be applied in cases of IPV with adolescent victims and perpetrators (Moak, 1995; Sousa, 1999; Zosky, 2010). From a policy perspective, this makes sense—if mandatory arrest laws are having the desired effect on adult IPV, then they should be effective at combating adolescent IPV as well. Several states already include dating relationships in their mandatory arrest statutes, so extending it further to juvenile dating relationships is, at face value, a relatively simple policy solution. Finally, the idea of mandating arrests and the rhetoric of "accountability" for adolescent offenders is aligned with the slow shift of the juvenile justice system from rehabilitative to punitive.

However, missing from those conversations is a comprehensive evaluation of the problems associated with mandating arrest in cases of adult IPV reported to law enforcement. First, there is not a clear and consistent effect of arrest on IPV recidivism (Maxwell, Garner, & Fagan 2001; Sherman, Schmidt, Rogan, & Smith, 1992) and in some cases arrest may increase and/or escalate the violence. Second, mandatory arrest policies have also led to an increase in the number of dual arrests (where both the victim and perpetrator are arrested) (Durfee, 2012; Eitle 2005; Hirschel et al. 2007). Crager, Cousin, and Hardy (2003) documented the arrest and prosecution of victims who were misidentified by police as the offenders, and, in her book *Victims as Offenders*, Susan Miller (2009) describes how batterers often control victims by manipulating police officers, prosecutors, and judges into arresting, prosecuting, and convicting victims of IPV.

This research, however, has focused almost exclusively on adult IPV, even though juveniles can and have been arrested for DV. The absence of research on the effects of mandatory arrest laws on juveniles is particularly troubling given that, by definition, officers must make an arrest if an act of DV has occurred, regardless of why or how it occurred. Self-report data from the Youth Risk Behavior Survey (CDC, 2011) shows relatively equal rates of IPV perpetration by girls and boys, even though the context, motivation, and consequences of the violence are markedly different (for example, girls often use defensive violence and girls are more likely to describe themselves as fearful of their dating partner). Because of the illusion of gender symmetry in IPV, mandatory arrest laws may prove to be even more problematic for teenage girls than for adult women.

This chapter builds on extant research on mandatory arrest laws by examining the impacts of these laws on arrests for adolescents who have perpetrated acts of IPV. The analysis is structured around three core research questions.

1.  Do mandatory arrest and pro-arrest laws increase the likelihood that a juvenile offender will be arrested for IPV (as in cases of adult IPV)?
2.  Is the gender and/or race of a juvenile offender a significant factor in the arrest decision for cases of IPV after controlling for legally relevant characteristics of the incident (as in cases of adult IPV)?
3.  Does the use of an intersectional framework significantly change any patterns of effects of gender, race, and/or mandatory arrest policies on arrests for juvenile perpetrators of IPV?

To answer these three questions, I conduct two sets of analyses. The first examines the impact of the type of arrest policy, as well as the gender and race of the offender, on the probability of arrest after controlling for the age of the offender and legally relevant incident characteristics. The second set uses an intersectional framework and includes an interaction term indicating whether the offender is an African-American teenage girl. This helps address the following questions: Does the pattern of results change with the addition of this interaction term, with a greater likelihood of arrest for African-American teen girls accused of committing IPV? If so, what are the implications of this for research on legal interventions for DV?

# Understanding Teenage IPV

Teenage IPV is a pattern of abusive actions perpetrated by an adolescent under the age of 18 towards a current or former dating partner in order to gain coercive control over that person (National Resource Center on Domestic Violence, 2004). While an advocacy-based definition of IPV includes a wide range of actions, including emotional, verbal, sexual, and physical violence that is threatened, attempted, or completed, the legal definition of teenage IPV is far more restrictive and varies widely from state to state. While women are more likely to be the victims and men are more likely to be the offenders in cases of adult IPV, estimates of the prevalence of IPV among teenagers showed a marked gender symmetry in victimization and offending. According to the Youth Risk Behavior Survey, the IPV victimization rates for boys (9.5%) and girls (9.3%) are nearly identical (CDC, 2012); the difference in boys' (8.6%) and girls' (6.3%) IPV victimization rates[1] for teenagers as reported by Hamby & Turner (2013) is not statistically significant. Furthermore, the prevalence of IPV among teenagers varies by race and ethnicity; Black teens are more likely to be victimized by a dating partner (12%) than Hispanic (11%) or White (8%) teens (CDC, 2013). Black and Hispanic boys are slightly more likely to be victimized than Black and Hispanic girls, and White girls are slightly more likely to be victimized than White boys, but the differences are insubstantial.

IPV victimizations have serious impacts on teens, including an increased likelihood for drug use, alcohol use, eating disorders, sexual activity, pregnancy, suicidal ideation, and partner victimization in adulthood (Ackard & Neumark-Sztainer, 2002; Foshee et al, 2013; Holt, Buckley, & Whelan, 2008; Silverman et al., 2001). They also have differential impacts based on the gender of the victim and offender as the type, motivation, and the consequences of violence perpetrated by girls is dramatically different than that perpetrated by boys. In a study by Molidar & Tolman (1998), boys most frequently reported being slapped (26%) and pinched (20%) by their girlfriends; over half said that they laughed at their girlfriend when this happened and a third said they ignored her. In comparison, girls reported more serious forms of victimization such as punching (17%) and forced sexual activity (18%) that resulted in significant injury, fear, and caused the girls to subsequently "obey" their boyfriends (p. 187). This may be due in part to the motivation for the violence—while over one-third of girls said that they fought back when physically assaulted, only 12% of boys fought back, suggesting that a significant proportion of IPV "perpetrated" by girls may actually be self-defensive actions.

---

1. Hamby & Turner (2013) provide prevalence estimates of TDV using seven different definitions. I use here the combined measure of physical and sexual force, which I argue is a more accurate assessment of TDV than measures which privilege physical over sexual abuse, especially given the severe effects that sexual violence has on victims.

# Domestic Violence Mandatory Arrest Laws and Teenage IPV

The gender symmetry in IPV prevalence estimates for teenagers, combined with the gender asymmetry in the actual experiences and consequences of the abuse pose a significant obstacle in combating IPV through mandatory arrest policies, which focus exclusively on whether an act that meets the legal definition of DV in that state has occurred. There is a minimum threshold in effect that impacts the arrest decision in states with mandatory arrest laws—determinations about the context of the broader relationship, motivation for the action, level of severity, and consequences of the action shape what the offender is arrested for, whether the prosecutor determines to proceed with the case, and what the offender is prosecuted for, but not (if the minimum threshold is reached) whether the offender is arrested or not.

In the 1980s, DV mandatory arrest laws were widely adopted by police departments across the United States as the initial results from the Minneapolis Domestic Violence Experiment (Sherman & Berk, 1984) indicated that arrest reduced the likelihood that an offender would commit additional acts of DV. All 50 states and the District of Columbia now have one of three types of warrantless arrest policies for DV—discretionary arrest, pro-arrest, and mandatory arrest. *Discretionary arrest* policies are the least restrictive arrest policy, and simply state that an officer may make an arrest for DV without a warrant if they believe that either an assault occurred or the victim is in imminent danger of an assault. A *pro-arrest* policy states that arrest is the "preferred" option, but do not require officers to make an arrest in cases of DV. *Mandatory arrest* policies are the most restrictive; under a mandatory arrest policy, if an officer determines that a qualifying act of DV has occurred, they must arrest the offender. The threshold for a qualifying act varies considerably from state to state. In some states the act must be a felony and/or have occurred within the past 12 hours, while in other states officers must make an arrest if any domestic assault occurred. Some states specifically exclude certain relationships from mandatory arrest statutes (dating relationships, same-sex relationships, etc.) while others include these relationships. The wide variation in mandatory and pro-arrest policies from state to state (and within states, by jurisdiction) may be one of the reasons why the enforcement of mandatory and pro-arrest policies has not been uniform. Even in mandatory arrest states, estimates of arrest rates for reported IPV vary from 33–50%—but prior to the passage of mandatory arrest laws, arrest rates were incredibly low and ranged from 7–15% (Durfee, 2012; Mignon & Holmes, 1995; Jordan, 2004; Eitle 2005; Hirschel et al., 2007; Pattavina et al., 2007).

At the same time that mandatory arrest policies were widely adopted and arrest rates for DV and IPV were increasing, the gender gap in arrests for juveniles was dramatically decreasing. According to the Federal Bureau of Investigation, the proportion of juvenile arrests that were of girls increased from 22% in 1986 to 29% in 2013 (US Department of Justice, 1996; US Department of Justice, 2014). The major reason for this increase was due to a sharp increase in the arrest of girls for "simple" assault; between 1986 and 1995, the number of girls arrested for simple assault skyrocketed from 15,948 to 40,515— an increase of 154%—even though the overall number of arrests of girls decreased (US Department of Justice, 1996). Chesney-Lind & Irwin (2008) argue that parents started using the juvenile justice system more frequently during this time period by calling the police to control the behavior of their teenage daughters. Although mandatory arrest was initially intended to be used in cases of intimate partner violence (IPV), violence in other "domestic" relationships— including parents and their teenage girls—also fell under the scope of the new mandatory and pro-arrest laws. In states with mandatory arrest laws, "assaults" of parents, caregivers, and other family members were classified as DV and thus fell under the scope of the new arrest laws that suggested or required arrest, even in situations where previously officers may have issued a warning to the teen. Race was an important factor in the arrest decision for these types of assaults, as the percentage of Black girls arrested was and is disproportionate to the U.S. population.

## Gender and Discourse about Teenage IPV

Many of the arguments made to support the extension of mandatory arrest laws to cases of teenage IPV employ gendered language when describing the situations where such laws could be used to "enforce accountability with perpetrators" (Zosky, 2010: 365), even though violence perpetrated by both boys and girls would fall under the scope of the law. For example, the law article by Moak (1995) includes a section on "the boys who perpetrate violence" (there is no similar section for girls) and "the relationship" where "the male acts dominant while the female plays the 'submissive woman'" (43). Again, no other types of teen relationships are described. These arguments also do not include issues of race, ethnicity, class, sexuality, or other dimensions of marginalization and identity, even though it is clear that a White, economically advantaged, heterosexual perspective has been incorporated. For example, Murray

(2001) makes a number of suggestions as to how parents can keep their "girls" from becoming victims or help their daughters leave abusive boyfriends. She argues that one of the key reasons why girls "choose abusive relationships" is because they have not had "time to attend to … developing a sense of her own identity" because they face "unnatural" pressure to take AP classes, study for the SAT, and engage in community service to be more competitive on their college applications (78–79). While girls of every demographic groups take AP classes, study for the SAT, and engage in community service, some of the immediate realities of girls struggling with DV and childhood victimization, racism, parental or familial incarceration, parental absence, homelessness, residential instability, poverty, and/or are who are juggling school and working to support their families are not reflected here, even though the author is writing to (all) "parents" about (all) "girls." As Donnelly, Cook, Van Ausdale, and Foley (2005) note, "White is seen as neutral and normal—the standard to which all other groups are compared" (p. 7). This omission is especially notable as many of these scholars are either implicitly or explicitly arguing for the use of the juvenile justice (and perhaps the adult criminal justice) system as a resource to protect "victims" (girls) of IPV from "perpetrators" (boys), yet both have a legacy of disparate treatment of individuals of color.

The problem is that "victims" and "perpetrators" are not simply girls and boys—they are a complex combination of social identities that include gender, race, ethnicity, class, immigration status, sexuality, ability, etc.—and thus one cannot discuss responding to IPV by only relying on a gendered framework. The idea that "multiple grounds of identity" operate to shape the experiences and resources of individuals is the core premise of intersectionality (Crenshaw, 1991). Intersectionality has become increasingly employed in both the social sciences and humanities because it is a useful framework that can be used to study the effects of gender, race, class, sexuality, documentation status, etc. simultaneously rather than in isolation. Structural intersectionality focuses on how "seemingly neutral" institutional practices have differential impacts on individuals based on their social location (their gender, race, class, sexuality, documentation status, etc.). This reproduction of broader social inequalities need not be intentional—in fact, it is because they are often unintentional that they appear to be neutral. When individuals interact with institutions, they do not do so as "women" or "men," "Blacks" or "Whites." Institutions and individuals within institutions react to, process, sanction, and provide services to people based on the sum of their complex social identities, and thus any differential impacts cannot be identified, analyzed, and considered separately.

Most of the existing research on legal responses (arrests, prosecutions, sentences) to adolescent dating violence where the victims are "girls" and the perpetrators are "boys" rely on the assumption that only two dimensions of identity are significant—age and gender. Other markers of identity, such as the race and ethnicity, economic status, immigration status, etc. of the victim and perpetrator, are often included in quantitative analyses as separate independent variables. The results are then used to illustrate the impact (or lack of impact) of these characteristics on legal responses. For example, the authors may talk about the impact of being Black or Hispanic on the likelihood of a perpetrator being arrested for DV.

The fundamental flaw with this assumption is that structuring the analysis and discussion of results around individual dimensions of identity ignores the complexity of the social world highlighted by intersectionality. If, in theory, the conception of "teen girls" is a miscategorization of a group of individuals that ignores other dimensions of inequality, then empirical analyses of legal responses to DV where the independent variables fail to account for the intersecting nature of multiple forms of identity may be fundamentally flawed. This analysis first addresses the question as to whether mandatory and pro-arrest laws have any impact at all on arrests for IPV. Then I explore whether incorporating an intersectional perspective, as opposed to analyzing gender and race separately, makes a difference when analyzing the impacts of mandatory arrest laws on arrests in cases of teenage IPV.

# Data and Methods

The data for this chapter comes from the 2010 National Incident Based Reporting System (NIBRS) Victim File. The NIBRS contains information on all incidents of crime reported to the police in participating jurisdictions in 35 states in 2010. There are several reasons why the NIBRS is preferable than the Uniform Crime Report (UCR) to analyze the arrest decision in cases of IPV.

First, unlike the UCR (which contains aggregate data), the structure of the NIBRS allows researchers to use the individual incident as the unit of analysis. With aggregate data, one cannot link demographic information (such as the race or gender of the victim and offender) for a specific case and a specific case outcome. The NIBRS contains incident-level information on victim and offender demographics, characteristics of the incident (as recorded by the responding officer), the type of offense, and, perhaps most importantly, the relationship between the victim and offender. By using the information on the victim–offender relationship, it is possible to identify and analyze cases of IPV. It is not possible to separate cases of IPV from other cases of physical and sexual assaults in the UCR.

Second, the NIBRS is preferable to the UCR because the NIBRS contains information on a maximum of ten different offenses for each incident. In contrast, only one offense per incident is recorded in the UCR. To determine which offense is recorded, the jurisdiction uses a standardized data "hierarchy" in which only the most severe offense (as defined by the FBI, not the victim) is recorded. Thus, if an individual is both sexually and physically assaulted and the physical assault reaches the level of an "aggravated assault," only the aggravated assault is reported. This leads to an undercount of offenses that have been defined as "less serious."

Finally, the NIBRS includes information about 46 different crimes, while the UCR only has information on eight "index" crimes (murder and nonnegligent manslaughter, forcible rape, robbery, aggravated assault, burglary, larceny-theft, motor vehicle theft, and arson (United States Department of Justice, 2008)). Cases of intimidation, forcible sodomy, sexual assault with an object, forcible fondling, simple assault, and/or intimidation would not appear in the UCR but are included in the NIBRS. Given that most incidents of DV are not "index" crimes, the NIBRS allows for a more comprehensive (and realistic) assessment of officer decision-making in regards to arrests for DV.

The sample for this analysis consists of 1,933 cases of teen dating violence. The sample was selected using six criteria. First, in order to be classified as an incident of teen dating violence, both the victim and offender had to be between 13 and 17 years of age. Second, to focus on dating violence the sample was restricted to those cases where the victim and offender were identified as "boyfriend-girlfriend." Third, the sample was limited to heterosexual couples because previous research indicates that officer decision-making is different in cases of same sex IPV; many states also explicitly exclude same sex IPV from their DV statutes (Durfee, 2013; Pattavina et al., 2007).

Fourth, in order to meet the legal definition of IPV, at least one of the recorded offenses had to be coded as intimidation, a sexual assault, or a physical assault. Sexual assault was defined as "forcible rape," "forcible sodomy," "sexual assault with an object," and/or "forcible fondling," while physical assault included both "aggravated assault" and "simple assault." Fifth, as some incidents of violence include multiple victims and multiple offenders, only cases with one victim and one offender were included in these analyses. Finally, as the race of the offender is a critical variable for these analyses, only those cases where the offender's race was known were included in these analyses.

# Measures and Characteristics of the Sample

Of the 1,933 cases included in this analysis, 34% ended in the arrest of the juvenile offender (659 cases). Thirty-five percent of the cases where the offender was a girl ended in an arrest; 34% of the cases where the offender was a boy ended in an arrest. This apparent gender symmetry in arrest rates is similar to the studies discussed earlier in the chapter.

The key independent variables for this analysis include the state arrest policy and the gender and race of the offender. In the second model, an interaction term for Black and female is included to capture the additional impacts of being a Black teenage girl on the arrest decision.

Table 4.2 provides information about the types of arrest policies for DV by state for the 35 states participating in the NIBRS in 2010. Twelve states had discretionary arrest policies, five had pro-arrest policies, 13 had mandatory arrest policies that did not include dating relationships, and five had mandatory arrest laws that included dating relationships (American Bar Association, 2007).

While individual jurisdictions within a state may adopt a more restrictive arrest policy, no jurisdiction may adopt a less restrictive policy, so the arrest policy variable actually reflects the least restrictive policy that would apply to the incident. Data on the arrest policies of each individual jurisdiction is not available. As shown in Table 4.1, 36% of the incidents included in the sample occurred in states with discretionary arrest policies, 20% in states with pro-arrest policies, 39% in states with mandatory arrest policies that did not include dating relationships, and five percent in states with mandatory arrest policies that included dating relationships.

The other primary variables of interest were the gender and race of the offenders. The majority of the sample were boys (89%) and were White (70%); 11% were girls and 30% were Black. Three percent of the offenders were Black teenage girls, 8% were White teenage girls, 27% were Black teenage boys, and 62% were White teenage boys. As the most of the relationships were intra-racial rather than inter-racial, and all of the relationships were heterosexual, only the race and gender of the offender were included in this analysis.

Other independent variables include the type of offense committed, the state DV arrest policy, whether the officer noted that the offender used alcohol or drugs during the incident, whether the officer noted any injuries to the victim, and the age of the offender. Most incidents were classified as physical assaults—58% percent were physical assaults, 29% were sexual assaults, and 13% were cases of intimidation. For the purposes of this analysis, physical assault includes both "aggravated assault" and "simple assault." Incidents of sexual assault include "forcible rape," "forcible sodomy," "sexual assault with an

## Table 4.1. Descriptive Statistics (N=1,933)

| Variable | Mean | Percent |
|---|---|---|
| **Arrested** (Dependent Variable) | | 34% |
| **Offense Type** | | |
| Sexual Assault[1] | | 29% |
| Intimidation | | 13% |
| Physical Assault | | 59% |
| **State Arrest Policy** | | |
| Discretionary Arrest Provisions[1] | | 36% |
| Pro/Preferred Arrest Provisions | | 20% |
| Mandatory—All Relationships | | 39% |
| Mandatory—Except Dating Relationships | | 5% |
| **Substance Use by Offender** | | 2% |
| **Injury to Victim** | | |
| No Injury[1] | | 66% |
| Minor Injury | | 32% |
| Major Injury | | 3% |
| **Offender Demographics** | | |
| Age | 16.21 (.98) | |
| White[1] | | 70% |
| Black | | 30% |
| Female | | 11% |
| Male[1] | | 89% |
| White Female | | 8% |
| White Male | | 62% |
| Black Female[2] | | 3% |
| Black Male | | 27% |

[1] Reference category for logistic regression analyses. [2] Interaction term for Model 2.

object," and/or "forcible fondling." The FBI defines intimidation as placing "another person in reasonable fear of bodily harm through the use of threatening words and/or other conduct but without displaying a weapon or subjecting

Table 4.2. Type of Arrest Provisions for
Domestic Violence by State (35 States)

| Discretionary (n=12) | Pro/Preferred (n=5) | Mandatory (n=13) | Mandatory (n=5) |
|---|---|---|---|
| Alabama | Arkansas | Arizona | Maine |
| Delaware | Massachusetts | Colorado | Oregon |
| Georgia | Montana | Connecticut | Rhode Island |
| New Hampshire | North Dakota | Iowa | Washington |
| Idaho | Tennessee | Kansas | Washington D.C. |
| Illinois | | Louisiana | |
| Kentucky | | Missouri | |
| Michigan | | Ohio | |
| Nebraska | | South Carolina | |
| Texas | | South Dakota | |
| Vermont | | Utah | |
| West Virginia | | Virginia | |
| | | Wisconsin | |

the victim to an actual physical attack"—thus stalking is included under "intimidation" (FBI, 2000, p. 23).

Officers suspected substance use by the offender (either alcohol or drugs) in only three percent of the cases. Officers noted "apparent minor" injuries to the victim in 32% of these cases and major injuries (broken bones, internal injuries, loss of teeth, severe laceration, unconsciousness, and "other major" injuries) to the victim in only two percent of these cases. Officers did not note an injury to the victim in 65% of the cases. In most incidents, the offender was slightly older than the victim (16.21 versus 15.53 years of age). Most of the offenders were the same age as the victim so only the offender's age is included in the analysis.

# Analytic Technique

To analyze the relationship between offender gender, race, and the arrest decision in cases of teenage IPV, I conducted two logistic regressions. When an officer responds to a call and determines that a crime has occurred, if the offender is at the scene the officer has two options—to arrest the offender or not. When statistically analyzing the choices made between two options, researchers often use logistic regression. The first model includes the type of offense committed, the state arrest policy, whether the officer suspected the offender of using alcohol or drugs, whether any injuries to the victim were noted by the officer, and the age, gender, and race of the offender. The key element in the first model is that the effects of gender and race are considered *separately*. However, in the second model I add an interaction term which allows me to see if there is an additional effect of being both Black and female on the probability of being arrested beyond what would be predicted by adding together the effects of being Black and the effects of being female.

To measure the magnitude of the effects of the independent variables on arrest outcomes, I calculate the odds ratio for each independent variable. The easiest way to interpret odds ratios is that if the odds ratio is less than one, that variable decreases the odds of being arrested for IPV. If the odds ratio is more than one, the variable increases the odds of being arrested for IPV.

# Results

Table 4.3 contains the results of the two logistic regression analyses. For Model 1, which only examines the effects of gender and race separately, there are two key results that are important in relation to research question #1. First, mandatory arrest and pro-arrest policies are significantly associated with a higher probability of arrest. After controlling for incident and demographic characteristics, reported incidents of IPV perpetrated by teenagers in states with mandatory arrest policies that include dating violence are 1.34 times more likely to result in an arrest than in states with discretionary arrest policies. Thus they appear to be having the desired effect of increasing the arrest rate for juvenile perpetrators of IPV.

Interestingly, incidents in mandatory arrest states that exclude dating relationships are no more likely to result in arrest than incidents in discretionary arrest, suggesting that there is no "spillover" effect of mandatory arrest on cases that do not meet the legal relationship requirement. Pro-arrest laws are also significantly and positive associated with arrest—incidents in states with pro-

### Table 4.3. Multinomial Logistic Regression Results (n=1,933)

| | Model 1 | | | Model 2 | | |
|---|---|---|---|---|---|---|
| Variable | B | SE B | OR | B | SE B | OR |
| **Offense Type** | | | | | | |
| Intimidation | -1.29** | .19 | .28 | -1.30** | .19 | .27 |
| Sexual Assault | -1.54** | .15 | .22 | -1.55** | .15 | .21 |
| **State Arrest Policy** | | | | | | |
| Pro Arrest | .30* | .14 | 1.34 | .28* | .14 | 1.33 |
| Mandatory— No Dating | .22 | .12 | 1.25 | .22 | .12 | 1.24 |
| Mandatory—All | .86** | .23 | 2.36 | .85** | .23 | 2.34 |
| **Substance Use by Offender** | .10 | .33 | 1.11 | .08 | .33 | 1.08 |
| **Injury to Victim** | | | | | | |
| Minor Injury | .35** | .12 | 1.42 | .36** | .12 | 1.43 |
| Major Injury | 1.19** | .33 | 3.28 | 1.13** | .34 | 3.10 |
| **Offender Demographics** | | | | | | |
| Age | -.01 | .05 | .99 | -.00 | .05 | 1.00 |
| Female | -.26 | .16 | .77 | -.47* | .19 | .63 |
| Black | -.18 | .12 | .83 | -.27* | .12 | .77 |
| Black Female | — | — | — | .70* | .35 | 2.02 |
| **Constant** | -.31 | | | -.33 | | |
| *= p ≤ .05 | | **= p ≤ .01 | | | ***= p ≤ .001 | |

arrest laws are 1.34 times more likely to result in an arrest than in states with discretionary arrest laws.

Second, after controlling for the other independent variables, neither offender gender nor offender race is associated with arrest—girls are no more likely to be arrested than boys, and Blacks are no more likely to be arrested than Whites. Additionally, the age of the offender does not appear to impact the likelihood of arrest, but that may be due to the fact that the range of ages in the sample is quite small by definition. This analysis indicates that there is no evidence that officers are considering either the gender or the race of an offender when determining whether or not to make an arrest—that the criminal enforcement of laws prohibiting IPV are gender- and race-neutral.

In addition to the arrest policy, both the type of violence committed and the degree of injury suffered by the victim are significantly related to the probability of arrest. Cases of sexual violence and cases of intimidation are less likely to result in an arrest than are cases of physical violence. This is consistent with patterns of arrest for DV offenses committed by adults (Durfee, forthcoming), but a full discussion of this result is beyond the scope of this limited chapter.

Model 2 incorporates an intersectional perspective through the addition of an interaction term indicating whether the teenage offender is a Black girl. As is shown in Table 4.3, the pattern of the results for Model 2 is identical to those for Model 1, with one notable exception — both gender and race, as well as the interaction between gender and race — are statistically significant at the .05 level. Teenage girls and Blacks are significantly less likely to be arrested for reported IPV than are teenage boys and Whites. However, Black girls are far more likely to be arrested for IPV as compared to all of the other teenage offenders in the sample. This suggests that neither gender nor race were statistically significant predictors of arrest in Model 1 because the increased likelihood that Black girls would be arrested was offset by the decreased likelihood that girls (and here, White girls) will be arrested for IPV. Similarly, the decreased likelihood of Black teenage boys to be arrested was masked by the increased likelihood that Black girls would be arrested. The conclusion that the criminal enforcement of laws against acts of IPV committed by juveniles has been gender and race neutral is not supported by Model 2; in fact, when the effects of gender and race are considered together, the data suggests that criminal sanctions for IPV are disproportionately imposed on Black teenage girls.

# Discussion

The analyses presented here address three key research questions. First, are mandatory and pro-arrest laws increasing the likelihood of arrest in cases of teenage IPV reported to the police? The results of both Models 1 and 2 indicate that they are — but mandatory arrest laws only increase the likelihood that a juvenile perpetrator of IPV will be arrested when they explicitly incorporate dating relationships. When violence in dating relationships is not included in the scope of the mandatory arrest policy, the mandatory arrest law does not appear to have any kind of "spillover" effect by increasing arrests for cases not included in the statute. In addition, pro-arrest laws are also having the desired effect of increasing arrests of juveniles for IPV. The impacts of these policies on arrest remain even after controlling for incident and offender characteristics. This finding is consistent with studies focusing on arrest laws and arrests for cases of adult IPV (Durfee, 2012; Eitle, 2005; Hirschel et al, 2007); given the small number of cases in the NIBRS that are IPV, this analysis is an important extension of this previous work. If the goal of implementing mandatory arrest policies is to increase arrests for teenage perpetrators of IPV, then it appears from this study that pro-arrest laws and mandatory arrest laws that explicitly include dating relationships are effective in achieving that goal.

An important part of any criminal justice policy evaluation is considering whether the policy is applied equally, or whether extra-legal characteristics influence whether and how any criminal sanctions are applied. Hence the second research question is whether the gender or race of the offender (both extra-legal characteristics) are associated with the probability of arrest for IPV—that is, whether girls are more likely to be arrested than boys, and teenage Blacks more likely to be arrested than teenage Whites, in reported cases of IPV. According to Model 1, neither gender nor race influence an officer's decision to make an arrest—only incident characteristics such as the type of violence, the arrest policy, and the level of injury are significantly associated with the arrest of the offender.

However, when an intersectional framework is used, the gender and the race of the offender are important factors in predicting arrest . While teenage girls and African-Americans are less likely to be arrested for IPV than are teenage boys and Whites, African-American teenage girls are significantly more likely to be arrested than any other offenders in the sample, even after controlling for the type of violence committed, the degree of injury to the victim as a result of that violence, the arrest policy of the state, whether the officer noted that the offender had used alcohol or drugs, and the age of the offender.

This finding is consistent with research on the overrepresentation of girls and women of color in the juvenile justice and criminal justice system, as well as their differential experiences in them as compared to White girls and women. Black girls are more likely to be arrested and receive harsher dispositions than do White girls, even after controlling for other factors (Moore & Padavic, 2010; Stevens, Morash, & Chesney-Lind, 2011). Although law enforcement officers and other legal actors who interact with girls of color may recognize that race and gender are important factors that shape these girls' pathways into and through the juvenile justice system, they may still make "inappropriate assessments" based on racial and cultural stereotypes that lead to differential outcomes for girls of color (Gaarder, Rodriguez, and Zatz, 2004). Gaarder et al. (2004) suggest that culturally specific training, services, and resources are needed in order for girls of color to be adequately served by the juvenile justice system. While their study focused on probation officers, police officers responding to IPV incidents involving girls of color may make assessments about IPV using the same racial and cultural stereotypes—which can lead to the increased probability of arrest for Black girls reported here.

One example of an anti-violence policy targeting teens that has had severe unintended consequences for girls of color are zero-tolerance policies in schools. While zero-tolerance policies are intended to protect students and decrease the likelihood of victimization, in practice zero-tolerance policies often result in an increased vulnerability of girls of color to sexual and physical violence. In her book *Getting Played* (2008), Jody Miller documents astoundingly severe and frequent acts of sexual violence against urban Black girls in schools, neighborhoods, and dating relationships. She documents the problems faced by these girls, one of which is that under zero-tolerance policies, girls could either (1) fight back when boys attempted to sexually harass, coerce, or assault them, at which point they could be suspended or expelled; or (2) ignore or minimize the victimization, which usually led the girls to become the targets of more frequent and severe violence as the boys knew that there would be no consequences for their actions.[2] For these urban Black girls, zero-tolerance policies that did not allow for defensive violence were more harmful than protective.

Like zero-tolerance policies in schools, mandatory arrest laws may result in an increased vulnerability to IPV, especially when the victim fights back. Girls of color disproportionately use defensive violence, and when adult women fight back, they are more likely to be arrested under mandatory arrest laws. Durfee (2012) examined the arrest decision in cases of "situational ambiguity"; cases where police cannot clearly identify the victim and offender. In these cases, mandatory arrest laws are associated with higher rates of dual arrest and female-only arrests. Survey data suggests that incidents of IPV may be situationally ambiguous due to the gender symmetry in prevalence estimates (CDC, 2012; Hamby & Turner, 2013) and that one-third of girls who experience IPV fight back (Molidar & Tolman, 1998). As one Latina teen told Lopez, Chesney-Lind, and Foley (2012):

> We'll start fighting and stuff, and like, we'll stop and then be happy again, and then we go somewhere, he is looking at this girl, and I tell him, okay? And he is like, oh so this and that, and we go back to where

---

2. Teachers who witnessed victimization of girls in schools often ignored them or minimized the significance and consequences of those victimizations; few teachers intervened in these cases.

> we are supposed to be, and then he'll be after me [again], and then talk-
> ing stuff, so then I just get mad, and yell back at him, and then he
> hits me, then I hit him back. (p. 686)

As both dating partners committed a physical assault, officers in states with mandatory arrest laws would be required to arrest both people, even if the girl's violence is only defensive or did not harm her boyfriend or induce fear. The level of severity and the motivation for the violence influence charging and prosecutorial decision-making, not the arrest decision. Once the arrest has been made, a series of institutional responses are set into motion, the consequences of which can be even more severe if the girl is already on probation or under supervision. The results of previous qualitative studies, in conjunction with the analyses presented here, indicate that extending mandatory arrest laws to cases of IPV with juvenile offenders may pose more problems than it resolves.

It is important to note the limitations with this analysis. First, the sample size is relatively small. The sample size would be increased if all jurisdictions participated in the NIBRS; at the time that this data was collected (2010), only 35 states participated in the NIBRS. With a larger sample the analysis could be expanded to examine patterns of arrests for Asian/Pacific Islander and American Indian/Alaska Native offenders (the NIBRS only contains information on ethnicity for arrestees, not for offenders who are not arrested, so ethnicity cannot be incorporated no matter what the sample size). It is difficult to comprehensively discuss the impacts of gender and race on arrest when analyzing only Black and White offenders.

Despite these limitations, this analysis should serve as a cautionary tale about the potential problems of extended legal interventions for DV to cases of teenage IPV. A careful assessment of the impacts that mandatory arrest laws have on juvenile victims and perpetrators of IPV is clearly needed. Although these policies are facially neutral, in practice they have differential impacts on Black girls. Whether these policies have similar impacts on other teenage girls of color would be a fruitful avenue for future research. Other directions for future research include collecting qualitative data to explore further the quantitative findings presented here as mixed-methods approaches are often the best way to integrate an intersectional framework into research on gender and crime (Burgess-Proctor, 2006). Finally, tracking girls as they are swept into the juvenile justice system via their arrest for IPV is critically important to understanding whether mandatory arrest laws are appropriate or effective or instead exacerbate existing inequalities and become avenues for social control.

# References

Ackard, D. M. & Neumark-Sztainer, D. (2002). Date violence and date rape among adolescents: Associations with disordered eating behaviors and psychological health. *Child Abuse and Neglect*, 26, 455–473.

American Bar Association Commission on Domestic Violence (2007). *Domestic Violence Arrest Policies by State*. Downloaded on January 15, 2014 from http://www.americanbar.org/content/dam/aba/migrated/domviol/docs/Domestic_Violence_Arrest_Policies_by_State_11_07.authcheck-dam.pdf.

Arriaga, X.B. & Foshee, V.A. (2004). Adolescent dating violence: Do adolescents follow in their friends', or their parents', footsteps? *Journal of Interpersonal Violence*, 19(2), 162–184.

Buel, S.M. (2003). Addressing family violence within juvenile courts: Promising practices to improve intervention outcomes. *Journal of Aggression, Maltreatment, and Trauma*, 8(3), 273–307.

Burgess-Proctor, A. (2006) Pathways of victimization and resistance: Toward a feminist theory of battered women's help seeking. *Justice Quarterly*, 29(3), 309–338.

Centers for Disease Control and Prevention (2011). Youth risk behavior surveillance—United States, 2011. *Morbidity and Mortality Weekly Report*, 61(4). Downloaded on November 8, 2014 from http://www.cdc.gov/mmwr/pdf/ss/ss6104.pdf.

Chesney-Lind, M. & Irwin, K. (2008). *Beyond Bad Girls: Gender, Violence and Hype*. New York: Routledge.

Cho, H. & Wilke, D. (2005). How has the violence against women act affected the response of the criminal justice system to domestic violence? *Journal of Sociology and Social Work*, 32(4), 125–139.

Crager M., Cousin M., & Hardy T. (2003). Victim-defendants: An emerging challenge in responding to domestic violence in Seattle and the King County region. Retrieved from http://www.mincava.umn.edu/documents/victimdefendant/victimdefendant.pdf.

Crenshaw, K. (1991). Mapping the margins: Intersectionality, identity politics, and violence against women of color. *Stanford Law Review*, 43, 1241–1299.

Dugan, L. (2003). Domestic violence legislation: exploring its impact on the likelihood of domestic violence, policy involvement, and arrest. *Criminology & Public Policy*, 2(2), 283–312.

Durfee, A. (2012). Situational ambiguity and gendered patterns of arrest for intimate partner violence. *Violence Against Women*, 18(1), 64–84.

Eitle, D. (2005). The influence of mandatory arrest policies, police organizational characteristics, and situational variables on the probability of arrest in domestic violence cases. *Crime and Delinquency*, 51(4), 573–597.

Federal Bureau of Investigation. (2000). National Incident-Based Reporting System Volume 1: Data collection guidelines. Retrieved from http://www.fbi.gov.ezproxy1.lib.asu.edu/ucr/nibrs/manuals/v1all.pdf.

Finkelhor, D., Ormrod, R.K., & Turner, H.A. (2007). Poly-victimization: A neglected component in child victimization. *Child Abuse & Neglect*, 31, 7–26.

Foshee, V.A., McNaughton Reyes H.L., Gottfredson, N.C., Chang, L.Y., & Ennett, S.T. (2013). A longitudinal examination of psychological, behavioral, academic, and relationship consequences of dating abuse victimization among a primarily rural sample of adolescents. *Journal of Adolescent Health*, 53(6), 723–729.

Gaarder, E., Rodriguez, N., & Zatz, M. (2004). Criers, liars, and manipulators: Probation officers' views of girls. *Justice Quarterly*, 21(3), 547–578.

Hamby, S., Finkelhor, D., & Turner, H.A. (2012). Teen dating violence: Co-occurrence with Other Victimizations in the National Survey of Children's Exposure to Violence (NatSCEV). *Psychology of Violence*, 2(2), 111–124.

Hamby, S. & Turner, H.A. (2012). Measuring teen dating violence in males and females: Insights from the National Survey of Children's Exposure to Violence. *Psychology of Violence*, 3(4), 323–339.

Hirschel, D., Buzawa, E., Pattavina, A., & Faggiani, D. (2007). Domestic violence and mandatory arrest laws: to what extent do they influence police arrest decisions. *The Journal of Criminal Law and Criminology*, 98(1), 255–298.

Holt, S., Buckley, H., & Whelan, S. (2008). The impact of exposure to domestic violence on children and young people: A review of the literature. *Child Abuse & Neglect*, 32, 797–810.

Lopez, V., Chesney-Lind, M., & Foley, J. (2012) Relationship power, control, and dating violence among Latina girls. *Violence Against Women*, 18(6), 681–690.

Maxwell, C., Garner, J., & Fagan, J. (2001). The preventive effects of arrest on intimate partner violence: Research, policy, and theory. *Criminology and Public Policy*, 2(1), 51–95.

Mignon, S. & Holmes, W. (1995). Police response to mandatory arrest laws. *Crime and Delinquency*, 41(4), 430–442.

Moak, D.P. (1996). Teenage dating violence: A problem without a legal solution. *Adelphia Law Journal*, 11, 39–60.

Molidar, C. Tolman, R.M., & Kober, J. (2000). Gender and contextual factors in adolescent dating violence. *Prevention Research*, 7(1), 1–4.

Moore, L. & Padavic, I. (2010) Racial and ethnic disparities in girls' sentencing in the juvenile justice system. *Feminist Criminology*, 5(3), 263–285.

Pattavina, A., Hirschel, D. & Buzawa, E. (2007). A comparison of the police response to heterosexual versus same-sex intimate partner violence. *Violence Against Women*, 13(4), 374.

Silverman, J., Raj, A., Mucci, L., & Hathaway, J. (2001). Dating violence against adolescent girls and associated substance abuse, unhealthy weight control, sexual risk behavior, pregnancy, and suicidality. *Journal of the American Medical Association*, 286(5), 572–279.

Sherman, L., Smith, D., Schmidt, J., & Rogan, D. (1992). Crime, punishment, and stake in conformity: Legal and informal control of domestic violence. *American Sociological Review*, 57(5), 680–690.

Sherman, L. & Berk, R. (1984). The specific deterrent effects of arrest for domestic assault. *American Sociological Review*, 49, 261–272.

Sousa, C. (1999). Teen dating violence: the hidden epidemic. *Family and Conciliation Courts Review*, 37(3), 356–374.

Stevens, T., Morash, M., & Chesney-Lind, M. (2011). Are girls getting tougher, or are we tougher on girls? Probability of arrest and juvenile court oversight in 1980 and 2000. *Justice Quarterly*, 28(5), 719–744.

United States Department of Justice, Office on Violence Against Women, National Advisory Committee on Violence Against Women, Subcommittee on Teen Dating Violence (2010). *Teen Dating Violence: Next Steps in Our National Response* (executive summary). Retrieved November 3, 2014 from http://www.justice.gov/archive/ovw/docs/execsum-tdv.pdf.

United States Department of Justice, Federal Bureau of Investigation (1996). Crime in the United States, 2013. Retrieved November 3, 2014 from http://www.fbi.gov/about-us/cjis/ucr/crime-in-the-u.s/1995.

United States Department of Justice, Federal Bureau of Investigation. (2008). Crime in the United States, 2007. Retrieved from http://www.fbi.gov.ezproxy1.lib.asu.edu/ucr/07cius.htm.

United States Department of Justice, Federal Bureau of Investigation (2014). Crime in the United States, 2013. Retrieved November 3, 2014 from (http://www.fbi.gov/about-us/cjis/ucr/crime-in-the-u.s/2013/crime-in-the-u.s.-2013.

Watson, J.M., Cascardi, M., Avery-Leaf, S., & O'Leary, K. D. (2001). High school students' responses to dating aggression. *Violence and Victims*, 16(3), 339–348.

Zosky, D.L. (2010). Accountability in teenage dating violence: A comparative examination of adult domestic violence and juvenile justice systems policies. *Social Work*, 55(4), 359–368.

# Part II

# Varieties of Female Offenses

# Chapter 5

# Gender, Romance, and Filicide

*Wendy R. Dragon, Ph.D., Michelle Oberman, J.D., and Cheryl L. Meyer, J.D., Ph.D.*

In the United States, scarcely a week passes without a news story about a mother killing one or more of her children. Usually, these stories focus on the mothers and their children; they seldom discuss the children's fathers, stepfathers, or the men in their mother's lives. Often, the biological fathers were no longer involved in their children's lives. Certainly, most were not there when their children died. Even when fathers or father figures were present in these children's lives, typically they remained a mystery to the public. The same is not true of cases involving fathers who kill their children. In those cases, we tend to hear a lot about the mothers; indeed, many mothers have been prosecuted and convicted for having failed to protect their children from the fathers.

In this chapter, we build on earlier research on mothers who kill their children (Meyer & Oberman, 2001; Oberman & Meyer, 2008) by exploring the part men played in the women's lives, particularly at the time of their crimes. We also examine societal factors that may play a role in the tragic deaths of these children. We look at the extent to which the criminal justice system responds differently to these mothers and their crimes than it does to similar crimes when committed by fathers. Finally, we explore possible ways of preventing similar tragedies in the future.

Our research is drawn from quantitative and qualitative data sources. The quantitative data source was described in detail in the book *Mothers Who Kill Their Children* (Meyer & Oberman, 2001). In that book, the second and third authors recounted their search of LexisNexis, a news database which provides full-text articles and publications from newsmagazines, regional and national newspapers, newsletters, trade magazines and abstracts, and legal documents such as appeals, for cases of filicide from January 1990 through December 1999. These cases were reviewed and assigned to one of five categories. The categories were filicide related to an ignored pregnancy, purposeful filicide when the mother acted alone, filicide due to neglect, abuse-related filicide, and assisted or coerced filicide. Mothers who committed filicide related to an ignored pregnancy committed neonaticide (killing a child within 24 hours of birth) after either denying or concealing their pregnancies (Resnick, 1970). Mothers who decided to kill their child or children fit into the purposeful filicide category. Mothers who killed their children by omission (e.g., leaving a child in the bathtub unattended) or commission (e.g., placing a bag over the child's head to stop the child from crying) were placed into the neglectful filicide category. When mothers killed a child out of abuse, it was classified it as accidental, as most of these victims died in discipline-related incidents rather than in premeditated murders.

Mothers in the first four categories acted alone and, in fact, were rarely involved in a romantic relationship at the time of their children's death. In contrast, male partners played an integral role in the crimes for which women in the assisted-coerced category were convicted. These represented a small percentage of our overall data set (5%). In some of these cases, it was the woman's partner who killed the child, and the woman only became implicated after the fact, either for failing to protect the child, or for assisting her partner in concealing the child's death. In general, the men involved in the "assisted-coerced" set of cases were romantically involved with the mothers but were not the child's biological father.

If the woman *was* directly involved in the incident leading to her child's death, it was classified as active participation. Women who became implicated either due to a failure to protect or by concealing the crime after it occurred were placed into the passive category.

The qualitative source of data for this chapter is drawn from the second and third authors' book, *When Mothers Kill: Interviews from Prison* (Oberman & Meyer, 2008). That book is based on 40 interviews conducted with mothers who were incarcerated for killing their children. During the interviews, we asked the women about their lives, including their experiences in romantic relationships. Five years later, nine of the women were re-interviewed to gain greater depth and understanding of their experiences.

From those interviews, one interesting theme arose regarding the relationship (or lack thereof) that the fathers had with the children at the time of their deaths. In most neonaticides, the biological father of the child was either unaware of the pregnancy or distanced himself from the mother prior to the birth. Often, these cases involved teenagers in short-term romances. In neglect and abuse cases, the biological fathers were either completely absent or sporadically involved with child care. In the purposeful category, mothers often were separated or in the midst of a divorce. In short, these fathers were involved in the crime by virtue of their absence. Had any of these fathers been consistently present, their support may have lessened the burdens on the mother and/or prevented the crime. In this way, they were indirectly involved in the child's death.

The assisted-coerced category stands in marked contrast to the other four groupings: these are the only cases in which men were consistently and actively involved with the women at the time of the crime. They are not simply present as the mothers' romantic partners. Instead, in this category of cases, the men are involved in bringing about the child's death.

Across all categories, many of the women that were interviewed, particularly those in the neglect, abuse-related, and assisted-coerced categories, experienced interpersonal violence long before they became involved with the men who fathered their children. Later in this chapter, we will be focusing on the role of violence in the lives, and specifically in the relationships, of women in the assisted-coerced category.

Taken as a whole, the stories and data constitute a Venn diagram of sorts. They describe the tragic cases arising at the intersection of motherhood and violent intimate relationships. In the following pages, the stories related to us by mothers incarcerated for the crime of filicide help us to demonstrate both the pervasive nature of violence in their intimate relationships, as well as the ways in which violence shaped their relationships with their children. To begin to orient you to these women, we will review some basic information on intimate partner violence (IPV), tying it to our sample.

## An Overview of Intimate Partner Violence

Many of the women we interviewed experienced interpersonal violence long before they became involved with the men who fathered their children. Most of the women reported that they had been physically abused during childhood. Out of 40 women, 23 talked about having survived sexual abuse as children; 16 of those 23 had been sexually abused by their parents (Oberman & Meyer, 2008). Thus, from an early age, these women tended to experience sex, violence, and love as intimately connected. As they grew into adolescence, they repeated the violent patterns of their childhood in their romantic relationships. Indeed, one woman recounted feeling this way, telling us, "I thought that if a man didn't hurt you that wasn't what it was supposed to be like."

Of the 40 women we interviewed, the majority did not even discuss their relationships with the men who fathered their children—a silence that is, in itself, revealing. But sixteen of the seventeen who discussed their relationships with romantic partners spoke of being hit, beaten, yelled at, and intimidated.

We were not surprised to learn that violence marked the relationships these women had with their partners. The high rates of abuse in this sample are consistent with a mountain of research documenting this pattern among incarcerated women (Browne, Miller & Maguin, 1999; Gilfus, 2002; Harlow, 1999). What surprised and fascinated us were the ways in which these violent relationships contributed to the deaths of these women's children.

Although all of the relationships discussed below involved violence, they were different on many other dimensions. As we listened more closely to the stories told by the women we interviewed, we were struck not only by the common experience of violence, but also by the differences, both subtle and grand, in how these women experienced their violent relationships. It seemed increasingly clear to us that there was a broad spectrum of ways in which these women experienced and responded to violence. Below, we articulate this spectrum, drawing on stories told by the women in order to illustrate the range of ways in which they experienced and responded to intimate partner violence.

## *Battered Woman's Syndrome and Learned Helplessness*

Several of the women's stories fit the classic description of a "battered woman" as depicted in the literature on intimate partner violence (Walker, 1979). One woman's story is emblematic of the horror of domestic violence and of the insidious manner in which violence can cause a woman's life to unravel. We will call her Cindy to protect her anonymity.

When she was 16, Cindy met a charismatic man of 28, who "swept her off her feet." Within a few months, she was pregnant and they married. After they married, he began emotionally and physically abusing her. Due to her husband's job, they moved constantly, which isolated from her family and friends. Within three years, she had three more children, and her life became a continual struggle to protect her children and herself from her husband's violence. She explained:

> I still have more nightmares about my ex than my crime … Dealing with his alcoholism as a teenager—I didn't know how to keep my body between him and the kids. There were times I felt weak and insignificant but when I look back on them now, I was brave. He was a big man. And when he was angry, his anger and size was intimidating. He weighed 300 lbs. I don't know how I did it.

Cindy tried to leave her husband several times before she finally escaped for good. She reached out to her parents, who sent her bus money to return to Ohio. Cindy and her children ran away from her husband, taking a long bus ride from Florida to Ohio. After their escape, Cindy and her children lived with her parents, and she began the process of pulling her life together.

Over the course of the ensuing years, Cindy was able to come to terms with the terror and trauma that was the legacy of this terrible relationship. She said: "Once I stopped being responsible for my husband, even my nightmares about him are not frequent or traumatic. [In my dreams] I am in control of him— I ask him to leave."

Unfortunately, though, the trauma she endured continued to lie just beneath the surface of her life. One night, after Cindy had succeeded in finding work and moving on with her life, she was raped at gunpoint. This trauma triggered an intense depression. She felt helpless, and despaired over her inability to protect herself or her children. She decided to kill herself and determined that, since her children were an extension of her, she needed to take them with her in death. Ultimately, her suicide attempt failed, but she succeeded in killing her children. Cindy is serving life in prison for their deaths.

Cindy's story resonated with us because it is, in some respects, similar to other accounts from the domestic violence literature. For women in 2015, the estimated lifetime prevalence of physical violence by an intimate partner is 31.5% (Breiding, Smith, Basile, Walters, Chen, & Merrick, 2014). Unfortunately, this number is likely to be an underestimate, because many incidents are not reported. Intimate partner violence is so common that society is inured to it. Consider the 2014 controversy surrounding the National Football League's lenient responses to professional football players accused of having beaten their wives and girlfriends.

The story Cindy told is consistent with the way in which advocates and activists have discussed the problem of domestic violence as well as the way in which many women can be trapped by violent relationships. In her 1979 book, psychologist Lenore Walker coined the term "Battered Woman Syndrome" to describe the effects of intimate partner violence on women. She was one of the early pioneers in the field and established many of the frameworks still used to discuss IPV today. Although later researchers have critiqued and refined Walker's theories, her articulation of the key concepts of the Cycle Theory of Violence remains a powerful descriptor of how intimate partner violence begins and is maintained.

The Cycle of Violence Theory asserts that domestic violence does not occur at a single constant level of intensity, but instead is characterized by three stages, which occur in rotation (Walker, 1979). During the first or tension-building phase, comparatively minor or mildly abusive incidents, such as pinching, slapping, and verbal abuse occur. After this, the woman is likely to become an acute observer of her abuser and try to modify her behavior to keep him calm.

The second part of the cycle is the violent outburst, in which the woman experiences a threat of or actual violence at the hands of her abuser. During the third, or "honeymoon" phase, the batterer expresses remorse and makes loving promises never to hurt her again. The length of the cycle varies over time and across different relationships. The third phase may last for an extended period of time. However, it is important to note the way in which coercion or emotional abuse may occur even during the honeymoon phase. The threat of violence, especially once realized, shapes subsequent interactions. One of the women described the cycle like this:

> People need to be more aware of what's going on in the home. It's hard to know where to go and why. I wasn't educated and I had not seen it with my mom. There's nothing wrong with standing a kid in a corner, but when it's too long then something's wrong. There's a gradual escalation of violence. It doesn't start with someone dying. It doesn't start as violent as it ends up. Women need to be more aware. They say, "Well, he's had a bad day or week."

Battered women generally "walk on eggshells" around their partners, attempting to predict and prevent future abuse. However, research indicates that most women cannot predict the timing of abuse. Indeed, batterers are thought to intentionally behave unpredictably as a means of increasing their power and control within the relationship (Barnett & LaViolette, 2000). The vast majority of abusive men have been abusive in multiple relationships, further indicating that the abuse is not a response to problems within their relationships, but rather results from the abusers' preexisting problems (Walker, 1979).

Walker suggests that as the violence repeats itself, the women come to understand that they have no control over when and whether their partners will attack them. Although they lose the ability to predict whether anything that they do will help to pacify or please their abusers, they continue to experience joy and pleasure during the "good times" with their partners. In contrast, their partners may threaten them if they make efforts to leave. The pleasure of the good times in combination with the escalation of threats and danger when a woman tries to leave are powerful behavioral reinforcers that work in concert to trap many women in abusive relationships.

Another hallmark of the classical cycle of violence is the perpetrator's deliberate isolation of the victim from support systems that may intercede on her behalf. We saw this in Cindy's case, where frequent moves left her unable to maintain, let alone to forge new connections with friends or neighbors.

The isolation is not necessarily explicitly violent in nature. On the surface, it may even seem quite loving. For example, the abuser may say, "Don't spend time with your family today, I will miss you. Spend time with me, instead." On the other hand, he may also take a more active role. One woman we interviewed described her partner's resistance to her forming friendships. She recalled her isolation: "I had a few friends at the time. Because he was an abuser he chased them away. Some of them walked away and they could not do much. He went to one woman's house and knocked her door in. He pretty much chased them away." Another of our interviewees said, "Don threatened me in front of my family and in church. People I had to confide in—there was no one. A couple of people from the hospital, they testified in my defense. No friends, nobody."

Sometimes family members are so invested in the relationship between the victim and her partner that they exacerbate the situation. Consider the following case: "When I would leave my boyfriend and hide, my mother would tell my boyfriend where I was at. I had nowhere to turn. I had to stay in the relationship—where would I go with two kids and no job? I had to stay with him. Nowhere else to go."

Alternatively, friends and family may begin to see the problematic nature of the relationship, and urge a woman to leave. If she fails to leave, her family and friends may lose patience and over time, these relationships can become strained. This is all the more true if her partner is isolating her, so that she is not spending time with them. In the end, the fractured relationships contribute to the woman's belief that she truly has nowhere to go.

This sense of being trapped leads to a feeling of futility, a common feature of the cycle theory of intimate partner violence. The "Learned Helplessness Theory," developed by Seligman and Maier (1967), can help to explain how this feeling of futility effectively prevents victims of abusive relationships from leaving. As such, it supplements the Cycle Theory, offering an additional explanation for why a woman might stay in a violent relationship. Seligman found that both animals and people who could not escape from painful stimuli failed to take action to avoid painful stimuli in subsequent situations— even if they could escape it. This suggests that the combination of pain and inability to avoid it found in abusive relationships can be emotionally and behaviorally paralyzing, essentially teaching women that they cannot escape their situation or stop living in fear (Walker,1979).

One of the women we interviewed described her situation as follows: "Even though I know he can't put his hands on me anymore, I am still scared. When I was in county, I would hide in the corner. After we were captured, I told everything and then a note was passed by the trustee that said if I told any more he [my partner] was going to kill my kids."

Ample research shows that abused women often are trapped by more than this cycle of violence, or by their fear of severe physical beatings or death threats. Women sometimes stay with an abusive partner for social reasons or because they lack the education or job skills needed to care for themselves and their children (Zink, Regan Jacobson, & Pabst, 2003). Children, communal property, and an abuser's intimate knowledge of the woman's daily routine—basic details like the woman's place of employment, the children's school, family members' homes and mutual friends—often restrict a woman's options for escape. Leaving her abuser often requires a woman to completely abandon her current life, moving herself and her children into an unknown and uncertain future.

Women also are inhibited by their relationships with others. They may fear even more violence, whether to themselves or to family members, if they do try to escape. This fear is not unfounded. In fact, one team of researchers found that more than a third of the intimate partner violence survivors they interviewed were assaulted by an ex-partner during the course of a single study! (Fleury, Sullivan, & Bybee, 2015). In addition, a significant portion of women killed in the context of intimate relationships die after attempting to exit the relationship (Kasperkevic, 2014).

Finally, women may stay because they fear losing custody of their children if they leave. One woman said, "I had to move from my husband because I was abused—he was stalking me, making threatening calls, ran me off the road … Everything of value was taken from me. He tried to slander me by claiming adultery. I was working and he would call the police on me, call children's services on me. When the lady looked around, I told her I knew why she was there. He was trying to get to me."

Theories such as Walker's and Seligman's, as well as stories such as Cindy's, helped us to understand why the women with whom we spoke tended to stay through their partners' abusive behavior. Next we will explore how this backdrop of violence may have played a role in the deaths of some of these women's children.

# Characteristics of Women in the Assisted-Coerced Category

As we stated earlier, most women who kill their children act alone. However, women in the assisted-coerced category either actively or passively participated in the death of their children and their partner was also involved in the children's death. In this section, you will meet two women, "Maddy" and

"Sally." Maddy and her husband had abused their toddler since his birth. Eventually their actions resulted in his death. Sally was not home when her child was killed, but she knew her husband had been abusing the child. These stories will help us illustrate the differences and similarities between women in the assisted-coerced category who had either active or passive involvement in the death of their child.

Maddy's father was an alcoholic. As she describes it, "my mother and father were always in arguments and everything and I was scared, really scared. When my mother and father got a divorce, I was living with my mother and one day she went off on me and smacked me on my ear. Me and my mother didn't get along when I was a teenager and I rushed into marriage, which I shouldn't have."

Maddy and her husband had four children together. They both abused drugs and alcohol. Maddy's husband also abused her and their youngest child. Maddy claims that the three older children were never abused. However, they would cry "whenever their daddy was around." Her husband believed that the youngest son was not his child but the product of an affair. Maddy tried multiple times to leave her abusive husband, but he would take the spark plugs out of the car. Although her brother, mother, and sister encouraged her to leave her husband, Maddy was afraid she would lose her children.

One night, Maddy left her son, who was sick with pneumonia, with her husband and his friend while she went to go visit family. After a night of drinking, she returned. Her drunken husband told her that the coffee table had fallen on their son. Her son was also very congested and coughing, so Maddy began to hit him on his back to "break up the congestion," a technique that she told us the hospital had suggested.

Maddy contends that when she put the child down for bed, he fell between the bed and the wall and she pulled him up by his arm. Eventually he became unresponsive, and she took him to the emergency room. There she learned that over the last few months the child had been repeatedly raped, he had other bruises, and that a "vein near his heart [had] ripped." With regard to the rape charges, Maddy said she was surprised, but came to believe that her husband did it since he pleaded no contest. She said, "I do think that he did it. He thought it wasn't his baby and was doing drugs the night my son passed away." Her husband contended that Maddy held the child down while he raped him.

When we asked Maddy what could have been done to prevent this tragedy, she said, "leaving my husband because I was depressed most of the time with him. He would come in late and started yelling and them babies didn't need that. I would take them in the back bedroom and he would just follow me and yell and scare the babies. If I would have left him when ______ was an infant.… But I can't change the past." Maddy claims no responsibility for the child's death.

The controversy over paternity in Maddy's story calls attention to another common feature of the cases falling into the assisted-coerced category. Most of the partners were not (or believed that they were not) biologically related to the children killed. This is congruent with other literature which suggests that children are more at risk of being harmed by caretakers who are not biologically related to them (Barth & Hodorowicz, 2011). Researchers theorize that the presence of a child who is not biologically their own triggers jealousy for some men, with the child serving as an ongoing reminder that their female partner had previously been involved with another man. The women in this category may have been expected to abuse the child as well, as a way of proving loyalty to the abuser. Some women may even have abused their child in order to spare the child more severe abuse from her partner (Coohey, 2004).

Several other notable aspects of this category are social context, method of death, and age of the child. The majority of women in this sample were experiencing multiple social stressors, including poverty and the presence of many other children in the home. All of the children in this sample were physically abused; the majority of the deaths resulted from beatings. Children in this sample were an average of 27.8 months old when they were killed. Maddy's child was 22 months old.

According to maternal filicide literature, young children are more likely than older children to be killed by their mothers. Half of all abuse or neglect-related deaths involve children younger than age one (Gellert, Maxwell, Durfee, & Wagner, 1995). One possible reason that younger children are more likely to become victims is due to the physical demands and resultant frustration associated with parenting young children. Unlike older children, infants are too young to understand rules or instructions, may cry for no apparent reason, and require a large investment of energy and time simply to take care of their most basic needs. Additionally, young children progress through numerous developmental stages (e.g., toilet training, "terrible twos") that may be frustrating for parents. Another possible reason that younger children may be more likely to be killed is that they are more vulnerable to injury than older children. The physical abuse required to kill an infant is likely to be much less than that needed to kill an older child. Parents may not be aware of this vulnerability. Consider the problem of shaken baby syndrome, in which parents accidentally cause brain injury or death when attempting to quiet their crying infant by shaking it (Smithey, 1998).

Next, we turn to a second category of partner-involved maternal filicide: those cases in which the woman did not play an active role in her child's death.

Like mothers in the active category, the "passive" cases involve women living with abusive partners and their children were beaten to death. What distinguishes these cases is that the women were not themselves abusive, or even present when their partners killed their children. In some cases, the partners' abuse was triggered by an overly harsh attempt to discipline the child. In others, though, there was an ongoing pattern of beatings and humiliation.

We believe the patterns underlying these cases are exemplified in the story of one of the women that the second and third authors interviewed in Ohio. We will call her Sally. Sally was institutionalized in a number of state settings starting at the age of 14. As she told us, she was considered incorrigible. Her mother was a barmaid and her stepfather was a long-distance truck driver. According to Sally, her mother was not a good parent. As a result, Sally admits that she did not know how to raise a child. When her boyfriend (and biological father of the child) left her, she decided to become a "truckstop hooker." She said that she was kidnapped "a couple of times" and lost custody of her children.

Her description of her family life reveals the extent to which she sees herself as a victim who was unable to protect her children from her violent partner:

> One of the requirements of Children's Services Bureau (CSB) was to get my life together. My ex-husband was the one who was going to be my knight in shining armor. He was the one who was going to be stable. He was a truck driver with a regular job and no police record. He was going to come and get everything together. I got my kids back, we moved in together, and it went good for a month and a half and then he stopped taking his medication and would self-medicate. He was manic-depressive. I was going to stop the relationship with him, but I was afraid CSB would say that I would lose my kids again. I tried to lock him out. My mother said to go back to him. He was the best thing.

The situation began to get out of control. Her husband became stricter and the punishments he meted out to the children became longer. Sally decided to leave. When her husband went on a weeklong business trip, she went to the bank to obtain some cash. Unfortunately, he doubled back and caught her in the act. Although Sally did not know it, the next morning he beat her seven-year-old son before sending him to school. Later that day, the school called and told Sally her son was sick. Her son would not tell her what had happened, but ultimately died from internal injuries caused by the beating.

When she talked to us, she reported her ex-husband may soon be paroled, and said, "That was a scary thought. He'd be out and be able to involve himself with another troubled family. I never thought about it before but why would he want to step in and be the knight in shining armor? I've never thought that before but now I do…. It's at the end. There's no more. It's behind me, in the past. I take responsibility. I see things that I could have done, should have done, and that's going to have to be enough 'cause I can't do it over. It'll be all right."

A second woman, Nadine, described her life in ways which were surprisingly similar to Sally's situation. Most striking about our conversation was the extent to which she continued to feel emotionally involved with the man who killed her child. She said,

> There was a time that [there] was a good man who lived in that heart, I don't know where he went. People asked how I could stay in contact with him. I do it to keep up with the girls. I wrote him a letter in March and let him have it. I wrote there was once a day I would have died for you, now you have to die for yourself. He kept sending me copies of our marriage license and saying that it was a promise. I'll get divorced when I leave. Yes, I love him. He gave me two beautiful children. I can't erase that. If I could, I would erase some other spots.

When we interviewed Nadine about her wishes for the future regarding love, she had this to say about the lack of support she received during her relationship:

> The neighbors heard things, but they turned a deaf ear. Everyone knew about the calls. The girls told me that there was no way they'd stay. I wasn't from there. There was no help for battered women and anyway, it would do no good. Even his mother knew. She told me that every ass-whipping I get, I deserve. She wanted me to sign T_____ over to her and the car to him. She didn't believe that J_____ was (her husband's child) that's why he is in another home. I'm wife number five and when we moved to Ohio I listened to horror stories of how he stalked one through four. I brought my family into living hell. I know it does no good to second-guess yourself after everything is done.

The stories of these women whose cases fell into in the passive partner-assisted filicide category are consistent with the domestic violence literature. There are similarities between these women and the women in the active partner-assisted category; however, women in this category did not abuse their children. Rather, they were unable to prevent their partner from harming one or more of their children.

We have previously discussed the myriad factors preventing women from leaving battering relationships—factors that may be intensified when there are children involved. Nonetheless, when children die at the hands of women's violent partners, as a culture, we tend to blame the mothers for failing to protect them. We see women who "allow" their children to be hurt as having failed at their most fundamental responsibility (Meyer & Proano-Raps, 2012). Given what we know about intimate partner violence and the way in which it can isolate and disempower its victims, there is little reason to believe we might deter these violent crimes by punishing mothers for failing to protect their children from their abusive partners. This victim blaming is related to the "Just World" hypothesis and may serve a secondary purpose. The Just World hypothesis is the idea that only good things happen to good people and bad things only happen to bad people (Lerner, 1980). By blaming the victim, we can continue to believe that we are safe from such atrocities. By holding these mothers accountable, we gain psychological distance from the nightmare of their lives. If we do things the "right" way, we will never be burglarized, or raped, or abused. Believing that the world is just, that people get what they deserve, allows us to exclude ourselves and our loved ones from the possibility of tragedy (Lerner & Miller, 1978). In the next sections of the chapter, we describe the criminal justice system's reaction to cases of maternal filicide as well as related policy issues.

# Criminal Justice System's Response

One of the most striking features in these cases involves the patterns of conviction and sentencing for these women. The data for women from the partner-involved category illustrate the extent to which the criminal justice system judges mothers and fathers by separate standards. By sentencing these women, courts tend to display a lack of understanding of the dynamics inherent in relationships marked by ongoing battering.

In many of these cases, women were held responsible for their child's death not because they killed their child, but rather, because they failed to prevent their partner from killing their child. Indeed, some of the women in this sample were not even present when their child was killed, yet they were blamed for not preventing the child's death. For example, consider the punishment received by Ivy Lynn Martin, who was not home when her partner killed her son, yet she received 25 years to life for murder.

The literature suggests that it is not unusual for women who fit into the passive category to be harshly convicted and sentenced, even when they were not present when the crime was committed (Jacobs, 1998). Consider the Illinois Supreme Court's decision upholding the murder convictions of two women whose boyfriends killed their children on the grounds that the women allowed the abuse to occur and therefore, they were responsible (Grady, 1992; People v. Stanciel, 1992). Defense attorneys stated that the women were not aware of the abuse; pointing out that Barbara Peters was not present when her child was killed and arguing that Violetta Burgos did not see signs of abuse because she is legally blind. Nonetheless, Peters received 30 years in prison and Burgos received 60 (Grady, 1992; People v. Stanciel, 1992).

Consider a similar situation in which a father left his mentally unstable wife with his children. After the birth of her fourth child, Andrea Yates suffered from severe postpartum depression. Despite repeated hospitalizations, and warnings by medical personnel that if she were to become pregnant again she would suffer the same fate, she and her husband had unprotected sexual intercourse. Andrea became pregnant and gave birth to her fifth child. Following childbirth, Andrea descended into postpartum psychosis. She became suicidal, was again hospitalized, and nearly choked their infant daughter by feeding her solid foods.

Upon her last discharge from the hospital, Andrea's psychiatrist told Rusty, her husband, that she should not be left unsupervised with the children. Nonetheless, Rusty left Andrea alone with the children and, in the short span of one hour, she drowned all five children in the bathtub.

There is no doubt that Rusty knew the risk he was taking in leaving his wife alone with the children. And yet, Rusty has never been charged with any crime, not even child endangerment or neglect. On the contrary, Rusty Yates became a media celebrity, appearing regularly in court during her trial in the deaths of their children, and receiving sympathy from the public. Given that there is clear documentation that he was informed not to leave his children with his wife by a medical professional, and that there is no evidence that Barbara or Violetta ever received this type of information, it is astounding that they were charged and convicted and he was not.

Clearly, the criminal justice system has different expectations for fathers and mothers. Although fathers and mothers have the same legal duty to protect their children, gender-role expectations lead to higher standards for women with regard to the care and protection of children. Consider this quote attributed to Tom DeLay, former United States House of Representatives Majority Leader: "A woman can take care of the family. It takes a man to provide structure. To provide stability." This double standard falls particularly harshly on the shoulders of some of the most marginalized women who appear in our nation's courts—those who are involved in violent and abusive relationships. Although one can sympathize with the outrage felt by jurors and judges in such cases, this fury is of little practical use and, upon closer examination, may be morally misguided, as well. A woman who is unable to protect her child is accused of making her relationship with her partner a higher priority than her duty to protect her child (Melner, 1997). As discussed throughout this chapter, many of these women try to protect their children from their abusive partners, and may even feel that they need to stay in these relationships in order to keep their children.

# Policy Implications

It is tempting, yet far too simplistic, to discount women who kill their children as evil or sick. There are, in these cases, larger cultural and societal influences at play. To the extent that we wish to prevent future cases like these, we must look to the context from which they arise. First there is a general observation to be made; the mothers in these cases were astonishingly isolated. They were attempting to parent their children without even the most basic support from family or friends. Such circumstances are not ideal even for the most resilient of mothers. And the lives led by these mothers were far from ideal. Most of them experienced too little love and nurturing in their own childhoods; most became mothers so young that they were little more than children themselves.

If we want to prevent other children from dying in similar ways, we will need to re-examine and reject the myths of motherhood: that altruism comes naturally to good mothers, that it is easy to take care of babies, that good mothers are always happy, patient, caring, and nurturing, and derive intrinsic pleasure from the tasks of cooking, cleaning, and raising children. Instead, we must acknowledge the pressures associated in caring for babies and small children—pressures that are greatly intensified by isolation. By normalizing the struggles many women experience in early motherhood, and naming isolation as a problem, we can make it less shameful for women to ask for help.

Second, we must expand our awareness of the risk factors that predispose certain mothers for challenges in parenting. In retrospect, it should not surprise us that the mothers in these cases struggled. It is easy to recognize the presence of multiple social stressors in their lives, long before their children's demise. This is not to say that these women are blameless. Many of the women we met readily acknowledge ways in which they should have responded differently given the circumstances in which they found themselves. Nonetheless, if we are to have any chance of successfully responding to the problem of maternal filicide, we must shift the focus from blaming the individual to asking what might have been done to support her in her struggles *before* the tragic death of a child.

Toward this end, it is vital to note how these cases reflect system-wide failures: any number of individuals or structures might have made the difference between life and death for the children in these cases: family, neighbors, doctors, babysitters, state child welfare agencies, domestic violence shelters, and most of all, the children's fathers. Although child protection workers and even physicians may be trained to recognize the extent to which factors such as young maternal age, poor socio-economic situation, and parental substance use may place a child at risk, few recognize that the presence of an abusive partner can be an even larger risk factor. Data from the sample used in this chapter indicate that the presence of a male partner who is violent toward their mother is a serious risk factor for children, particularly when he is not biologically related to them.

Some professionals are beginning to take a preventive approach by working to recognize risk factors such as the presence of multiple social stressors. A few have even created prevention programs based on these risk factors. But more professionals must be made aware of these risk factors and should be educated about the nature of domestic violence in general. Physicians must be made aware of the risk that a mother's violent partner poses for her children. Women and their children are likely to visit a physician, even if infrequently; so these health providers may be one of the most important groups to target with information about risk factors. Teachers and day care providers are other groups of people who have frequent contact with mothers and their children. Social service workers, too, should be aware of the extent to which the relationship between a mother and her partner affects the children, and should screen for the presence of intimate partner violence.

It is not enough to simply identify mothers who are struggling with a violent relationship; we must find ways to support these women so that they can exit these relationships. Professionals must be trained not only to increase awareness of the dynamics of domestic violence, but also to identify resources available to women seeking to exit violent relationships. Devising an exit strategy is not a simple matter; it takes detailed knowledge and awareness of the factors that keep women tied to their violent households, a sympathetic ear to earn the trust of those women who fear leaving, and accurate knowledge of the precise resources available within a given community to ensure that she and her children will be safe once they leave.

The cases in this chapter are truly tragedies. What is vitally important is that we recognize the ways in which the endings might have been different. The solution lies in taking a deep look at the circumstances surrounding the mothers' lives. When we do so, we can recognize the extent to which the absence of a supportive partner, trusted families, close friends and economic resources combined to place not only the women, *but also their children*, at greater risk of harm. These cases are outliers—the harm that came to pass was the worst imaginable sort of tragedy. But truly, we cannot say that the outcome occurred randomly and there were no warning signs. To prevent similar tragedies, we must anticipate and work to address the full spectrum of problems that arise at the intersection of motherhood, violence, and isolation.

As a society, we need to recognize that there are four common and often co-occurring parental risk factors for child abuse—parental substance abuse, parental mental illness, intimate partner violence, and child conduct problems (Barth, 2009) and build prevention programs to address these issues before tragedy occurs. Child abuse prevention programs often directly focus on improving parenting skills, but they must also directly address these risk factors to improve outcomes. Mental health professionals are starting to recognize this need and look for programs that work to impact these risk factors. However, more remains to be done. In a review of interventions for the prevention of the physical abuse of children, only one program was determined to be efficacious: the Positive Parenting Program (Triple P; Poole, Seale, & Taylor, 2014). The Triple P program aims to prevent severe behavioral, emotional and developmental problems of children from birth to age 16 years as well as child maltreatment by parents. It works to increase the protective factors and reduce risk factors associated with child maltreatment by enhancing the knowledge, skills, confidence, self-sufficiency, coping skills, and resourcefulness of parents. This program has five levels of intervention of increasing strength (Sanders, 1999). At the strongest level, Enhanced Triple P targets parents who are experiencing partner conflict by targeting specific concerns and risk factors, such as partner relationships and communication as well as personal coping strategies of the parents. Programs such as Triple P may prevent conflict in at-risk relationships from escalating into intimate partner violence and child abuse. Unfortunately, there is little research examining the efficacy of these interventions when a mother is an abuse victim herself, even though this is a clear risk factor for child abuse (Barth, 2009).

Given our knowledge of the complex nature of intimate partner violence, it is important for the public, as well as the criminal justice system, to consider alternative responses to blaming battered women when their partners abuse their children. If the aim of such punishment is to protect children, the result is unlikely to succeed. Punishing battered women has not, and cannot, increase safety for children. To protect children, we as a society must take into consideration the underlying problem of intimate partner violence. Partner-assisted maternal filicide is an extreme example of how violence wreaks havoc on relationships in a family context, but it is hardly the only way that it does so.

Clearly, this chapter illustrates that the complex problem of partner-involved filicide cannot be solved by merely blaming and punishing mothers. Rather, professionals and community members must work together to build resources to address the larger problem of intimate partner violence and child abuse, in addition to working to reduce the isolation of mothers and children who are vulnerable to such violence.

# References


Barnett, O. W., & LaViolette, A. D. (2000). *It could happen to anyone: Why battered women stay.* Thousand Oaks, CA: Sage.

Barth, R. P. (2009). Preventing child abuse and neglect with parent training: Evidence and opportunities. *The Future of Children, 19,* 95–118. doi:10.1353/foc.0.0031.

Barth, R., & Hodorowicz, M. (2011). Foster and adopted children who die from filicide: What can we learn and what can we do? *Adoption Quarterly, 14,* 85–106. doi:10.1080/10926755.2011.560783.

Breiding, M. J., Smith, S. G., Basile, K. C., Walters, M. L., Chen, J. C., & Merrick, M. T. (2014). Prevalence and characteristics of sexual violence, stalking, and intimate partner violence victimization—National Intimate Partner and Sexual Violence Survey. *Morbidity and Mortality Weekly Report, 63,* 1–18.

Browne, A., Miller, B., & Maguin, E. (1999). Prevalence and severity of lifetime physical and sexual victimization among incarcerated women. *International Journal of Law and Psychiatry, 22,* 301–322. doi:10.1016/S0160-2527(99)00011-4.

Casanueva, C., Martin, S. L., Runyan, D. K., Barth, R. P., & Bradley, R. H. (2008). Quality of maternal parenting among intimate-partner violence victims involved with the child welfare system. *Journal of Family Violence, 6,* 413–427. doi:10.1007/s10896-008-9167-6.

Coohey, C. (2004). Battered mothers who physically abuse their children. *Journal of Interpersonal Violence, 19,* 943–952.

Fleury, R. E., Sullivan, C. M., & Bybee, D. I. (2000). When ending the relationship does not end the violence: Women's experiences of violence by former partners. *Violence against Women, 6,* 1363–1383.

Gellert, G. A., Maxwell, R. M., Durfee, M. J., & Wagner, G. A. (1995). Fatalities assessed by the Orange County child death review team, 1989 to 1991. *Child Abuse and Neglect, 19,* 875–83.

Gilfus, M. (2002). *Women's experiences of abuse as a risk factor for incarceration.* Harrisburg, PA: VAWnet, a project of the National Resource Center on Domestic Violence/Pennsylvania Coalition Against Domestic Violence. www.vawnet.org.

Grady, W. (1992, November 19). Murder convictions upheld, despite presence of judge's wife on jury. *Chicago Daily Law Bulletin,* p. 3.

Harlow, C. W. (1999). *Prior abuse reported by inmates and probationers.* Retrieved from http://www.bjs.gov/index.cfm?ty=pbdetail&iid=837.

Jacobs, M. S. (1998). Requiring battered women die: Murder liability for mothers under failure to protect statutes. *Journal of Criminal Law and Criminology, 8,* 579–660.

Kasperkevic, J. (2014, October 20). Private violence: Up to 75% of abused women who are murdered are killed after they leave their partners. *The Guardian,* http://www.theguardian.com/money/us-money-blog/2014/oct/20/domestic-private-violence-women-men-abuse-hbo-ray-rice.

Lerner, M.J. (1980). *The belief in a just world.* New York: Plenum Press.

Lerner, M. J. & Miller, D. T. (1978) Just world research and the attribution process: Looking back and ahead. *Psychological Bulletin, 85,* 1030–1051. http://dx.doi.org/10.1037/0033-2909.85.5.1030.

Melner, A. R. (1997). Rights of abused mothers versus best interest of abused children: Courts' termination of battered women's parental rights due to failure to protect their children from abuse. *Southern California Review of Law and Women's Studies, 7,* p. 299–328.

Meyer, C. L. & Oberman, M. (2001). Mothers who kill their children: Understanding the acts of moms from Susan Smith to the "Prom Mom." New York: New York University Press.

Meyer, C. & Proano-Raps, T. (2012). Postpartum Syndromes and the Legal System, In R. Muraskin, (Ed.), *It's a crime: Women and justice.* Upper Saddle River, NJ: Pearson. pp. 103–126.

Oberman, M. & Meyer, C. L. (2008). When mothers kill: Interviews from prison. New York: New York University Press.

People v. Stanciel, 606 N.E.2d 1201, 153 Ill. 2d 218, 180 Ill. Dec. 124 (1992).

Poole, M. K., Seal, D. W., & Taylor, C. A. (2014). A systematic review of universal campaigns targeting child physical abuse prevention. *Health Education Research, 29,* 388–432. doi:10.1093/her/cyu012.

Resnick, P. J. (1970). Murder of the newborn: A psychiatric review of neonaticide.*American Journal of Psychiatry, 126,* 1414–1420.

Sanders M. R. (1999). The Triple P-Positive parenting programme: Towards an empirically validated multilevel parenting and family support strategy for the prevention of behavior and emotional problems in children. *Clinical Child and Family Psychology Review, 2*, 71–90.

Seligman, M. E. P., & Maier, S. F. (1967). Failure to escape traumatic shock. *Journal of Experimental Psychology*, *74*, 1–9. doi:10.1037/h0024514. PMID 6032570.

Smithey, M. (1998). Infant homicide: Victim/offender relationship and causes of death. *Journal of Family Violence, 13*, 285–297.

Walker, L. (1979). *The battered woman.* New York: Springer.

Zink, T., Regan, S., Jacobson, C. J., & Pabst, S. (2003). Cohort, Period, and Aging Effects: A Qualitative Study of Older Women's Reasons for Remaining in Abusive Relationships. *Violence Against Women, 9*, 1429–1441. doi:10.1177/1077801203259231.

# Chapter 6

# Dancing, Stripping and Escorting: Women's Experiences of Money, Drugs, and Prostitution in the Legal Sex Work Industry[1]

*Gail A. Caputo, Ph.D.*

## Introduction

A large body of scholarship on the legal sex work industry—dancing, escorting, stripping, go-go bars, strip clubs, peep shows and related sex-focused establishments—covers a broad range of subjects like the social milieu of establishments (Forsyth & Deshotels, 1997; Lewis, 2006; Maticka-Tyndale, Lewis, Clark, Zubick, & Young, 2000; Mesternacher & Roberti, 2004), reasons women choose the work, how workers manage clients, as well as social stigma and emotional wellbeing (Barton, 2007; Bell, Sloan, & Strickling, 1998; Bradley-Engen & Ulmer, 2009; Bruckert, Parent, & Robitaille, 2003; Peretti & O'Connor, 1989; Ronai & Ellis, 1989; Thompson & Harred, 1992; Thompson, Harred, & Burks, 2003; Trautner, 2005; Wood, 2000). Other research considers relationships and the personal lives of dancers (Bradley, 2007; Murphy, 2003; Philaretou 2006), strip club bouncers (DeMichele & Tewksbury, 2004) and the characteristics and motives of patrons (Egan, 2005; Erickson & Tewksbury,

---

1. **Author's Note:** Some material comes from: Caputo, G. (2008). *Out in the storm: Drug-addicted women living as shoplifters and sex workers.* Boston: Northeastern University Press.

2000; Frank, 2002, 2003; Schweitzer, 2000; Wosick-Correa, 2008). While this body of literature is quite diverse, what is missing is an understanding of how women drug users and criminal offenders experience the industry and how the expectations and normative routines of the job influence women's lives and future occupational choices. Using data from an ethnographic study of women drug users in a large northeastern urban area, this chapter builds upon the ideas of sex work as occupational and offers a contextual look inside the world of adult entertainment from the perspective of women drug users who call it work.

## Stripping, Dancing, and Escorting as Work

According to research, women who take up work in the industry come from a range of cultural, social, and economic backgrounds and their motivation to take on jobs as strippers, escorts, and dancers is chiefly financial. Women select the adult entertainment industry as a job quite simply because it pays. Rather than a last resort, women see the industry as a viable alternative to other forms of work, legal and illegal (Bouclin, 2006; Bradley-Engen & Ulmer, 2009; Enck & Preston, 1988; Forsyth & Deshotels, 1996; Ronai & Ellis, 1989; Skipper & McCaghy, 1970); but see Barton, 2002, 2006). For instance, Canadian researchers learned from workers in strip clubs that it was "neither duress nor despair that lead these women to make this choice, but rather reasons very much like those motivating the choice to enter other professions" (Bruckert, Parent, & Robitaille, 2003, p. 15). Women who select this work see other benefits in it. No doubt, women in these occupations may have very troubled lives and victimization experiences, but as Sweet and Tewksbury (2000b) report, women may even select the work for its entertainment, to practice the art of dance, to remain physically fit. In other words, women are making thoughtful choices and are driven more by those rewards and much less often for reasons related to unresolved trauma of childhood even while they may have been raised in alcohol- and drug-abusing homes and were victims of child abuse.

Like workers in other jobs, women in the adult entertainment industry tend to define themselves as workers and their position as skilled work (Bott, 2006; Price, 2008). Wahab (2004) reported of Washington women working in the adult entertainment industry that the women selected the work after evaluating benefits and drawbacks of various forms of work and factors like job flexibility, financial rewards, and work environment. Women in Barton's research also explained their decision to work as dancers and strippers a thoughtful evaluation of alternative options (Barton, 2002, 2006). Unlike nine-to-five jobs, dancing and stripping affords women more free time because the work schedule is so flexible, but most importantly the pay is better than other available work and this is especially important for women who see themselves as having little promise for professional careers. Another Canadian project found of escorts that their choices to enter the job outweighed benefits of alternatives. It provided more flexibility in schedules, social entertainment, and popularity within social networks while alternative low paying jobs would constrain their independence, sense of worth, and income (Jeffrey & MacDonald, 2006).

These benefits of getting involved in the work often keep women engaged even when they would otherwise have chosen to exit the industry. Money earned as strippers and dancers as well as perceived lack of alternatives often means that women stay as they struggle to manage stigma associated with the work, the sexual exploitation and degradation inherent in the job, and demands of clients to expand sexual boundaries (Barton, 2006; Bradley-Engen & Ulmer, 2009; Forsyth & Deshotels, 1997; Pasko, 2002). This does not mean that women workers are powerless actors in their work. As Price (2008:369) puts it, "strippers are neither heroes nor victims but preserving agents struggling against demanding patrols, gender inequalities, and cultural stigma." Workers in the legal sex work industry just as workers in other professions typically find ways to manage constraints and resist the most harmful aspects of their profession (Bouclin, 2006; Bruckert, 2002; Ronai & Cross, 1988; Ronai & Ellis, 1989; Thompson, Harred, & Burks, 2003; Wesely, 2002), even maintaining pleasure and reward in their participation (Bradley-Engen & Ulmer, 2009). Workers often exit the industry when constraints of the work outweigh benefits, that is when the work takes a toll, when women experience job burnout. According to some research, women seek other income generating options when drawbacks of the work create psychological harm, a toll of stress, sexual exploitation, and stigma that affects not only their ability to do the work, but their personal relationships and wellbeing (Barton, 2006; Sweet & Tewksbury, 2000a; Thompson, Harred, & Burks, 2003; Weitzer, 2009).

Taking this scholarship a step further, this chapter describes the lure of the adult entertainment industry for women drug users in an urban setting, illustrates how women experience the work while on the job, and discusses reasons for departure from the work.

## Method and Sample

The data were gathered as part of an ethnographic study of women drug users in the neighboring cities Philadelphia and Camden between 2003 and

2006 that made a variety of comparisons between women earning incomes through shoplifting and others through sex work (street-level prostitution) (See Caputo, 2008). The women were recruited primarily by word of mouth directly from the city streets, from a local jail, and a nearby prisoner halfway house. Snowball sampling helped to bring the study size to 38 women. This author conducted lengthy open-ended life history interviews that were audio recorded and transcribed into text. Multiple interviews were conducted on many of the women who were eager to share their stories. Topics covered in the interviews included early life trauma, pathways to drug addiction and crime, sources of income, involvement in work, and how women manage criminal careers. The objective of the interviews was to encourage women to tell their stories in their own words, because women themselves are experts about their lives. This interview schema resulted in rich data that allows for an unusually comprehensive analysis into these women's lives. Here, data come from the interviews with 18 women who were selected for their experience as sex workers, who earlier in their careers worked as strippers, dancers, escorts and other positions in go-go bars, strip clubs, peep shows and other settings that I refer to here as the legal work sex industry. These interviews were examined around issues related to this work, such as motivations for involvement, the sociology of work, and how participation influenced their criminal careers.

As to sample characteristics, the women in the study can be described as having lived overwhelmingly distressed lives as girls and young women and this is consistent with scholarship on women's backgrounds before drug abuse and criminality. Typically, the women were raised in the poorest, most disordered neighborhoods in the Camden and Philadelphia area; sixteen say they were raised very poor though two described their childhood home environments as working or middle class. The women report physical abuse (72% of the women), sexual abuse (44%), and emotional abuse (72%) inside the childhood home as well as neglect and abandonment by caretakers (38%). They also report childhood traumas in the form of exposure to alcoholism (100%), drug abuse (67%), and domestic violence in the childhood home (78%) as well as rape outside the home (33%). On average, the women in this sample began drinking alcohol in the home at age 11 and at the time of our interviews, they identify as serious drug users (cocaine, crack, heroin, PCP, crank, marijuana, and alcohol). Their troubles with hard drug use normally began in late adolescence and early adulthood. Asked when they first entered the legal sex work industry as workers, one reports being just 13 years old and the oldest was 24; women began stripping, dancing, and escorting at an average age of 18. Before their entry into the industry, every one of them lived as a runaway in the "fast life" on the streets; all but one is a high school dropout. The women's tenure as workers in this trade was usually 4 or 5 years.

# Findings

> Go-go dancing was in and everybody [girls and women] was there to get their money to do drugs. The drugs was in the club, the go-go dancing was there, the men was there, the prostitution was there, everything was there, so it was just a big circle. *LaToya*

Interviews with the women in this study reveal several themes. First, women selected the work primarily for its financial benefit as it provides a direct and source of earnings to finance drug use. The "life" of dancing and stripping was commonplace in their neighborhoods and among girls and women they admired. Work inside the club offered other benefits beyond money they earned, such as excitement and even power. Second, work inside the club fostered increased drug use, which began to take a toll on their lives, as well as prostitution. Third, women talk of leaving the "life" of dancing, stripping, and escorting not because they grew tired of the work or felt psychologically or socially harmed as other scholars have noted, but because their lives began to unravel in addiction and the work became a less profitable source of earnings.

## *Good Money, Easy Money*

With no prerequisite for employment, no experience necessary, and usually no audition or interview required, the legal sex work industry is an inviting place for young women who have broken free of their tortured home life to the fast life on the streets. Some of the women in this study took on jobs as escorts first at escort agencies and then as entrepreneurs on their own, most began directly as strippers and dancers in peep shows, bars and clubs, and some even as her "own boss" catering to private male parties. The women did not actively seek out this form of work to earn money. Rather, every one of them was introduced to the "life" by girls and women they knew in their home neighborhoods and social networks who were already working as strippers, escorts, and dancers. The lure of "easy money," "fast money," excitement, and drugs was so appealing to them, their decisions to become involved were so quickly made. Then a young runaway and school dropout from a poor city neighborhood, LaToya began dancing at age 16. She had always known that dancing was the "in thing" in her neighborhood. She says:

> It was on the block. It was in the neighborhood. You could tell, girls ran with stilettos and stuff on their way to the go-go clubs, which was about three, four blocks away from where I lived. I always knew they was around, but I never had the courage to do it until I got the drugs in me, then I was like whatever. So you just go down and say, "Hey, can I dance or whatever?" All you do is kind of look sexy, put a little bit of makeup on, go down there, and whoever the owner is of the club ask them can you dance?, ya know, it was never no audition before you get on stage; it was nothing like that.

Like so many of the others, LaToya felt the work to be socially acceptable, since so many other girls and women "on the block" in her neighborhood were dancing for money and many men she knew from the neighborhood frequented the clubs and bars. While she might have needed a few drinks to get over her nervousness on the first night, LaToya enjoyed the immediate payoff in money and attention. Money, say the women, was the number one reason they became involved. Pauline, 24, explains why she selected stripping over other occupational choices:

> When I turned twenty, that's when I didn't have no job and I started stripping. You get paid on time. You don't have to worry about yourself. I had a little job so I could pay my rent. I didn't want to get out there and sell drugs because I didn't want to go to jail so that was the fastest way I could make money. I was in a position to work [at other types of jobs] but I thought the money was too slow. There were a couple of girls that I knew that were already doing it and they told me how the money was coming in … I made two or three Gs [thousands] a night. You get paid by the club, you do three dances a night and you work around roulette dances and stuff and you get paid for that. Plus you get paid for you working on the stage.

Pauline, like the others, knew dancing is a "fast" way to make money. She would not have to wait for a weekly paycheck as she would have in most other occupations, did not have to worry about the risk of criminal sanctions as she would if she chose to sell drugs, and the potential earnings from stripping and dancing made the choice of conventional work even less desirable. It was also a safe environment for her.

With bars and clubs situated in and around the high drug and crime areas where many of the women had called home, the legal sex work industry was a smart occupational choice, they explain. All it really took was to "look sexy" and dance the women say. With little or no training for conventional forms of work and with drug use becoming a daily habit, the women knew they were unlikely to earn as much money in a more traditional line of work.

Of dancing says Jarena, "I like dancing, the attention, drugs, and the money, and being on the stage. It was exciting." Dancing and stripping provided the women more than just a means to finance their drug use. Here, Shirelle describes what she experienced as power in the sexual nature of the work and the control and manipulation she felt over men, a finding reported in other research of strippers and dancers (See Bradley-Engen & Ulmer, 2009; Pasko, 2000). She says:

> I wanted to be accepted into my society, like the older girls. I liked the lifestyle, staying out all night, being able to drink in the bars, you know, use drugs, have different men lust over my body. You know, it was just, I don't know, it just felt kinda good ... I'm telling you, you'll make all this money ... It was just like, I just wanted their money. I wanted to play them for their money, get what I could get and go.

Added benefits of the work was excitement of being on stage, conning men, the social outlet, and what other scholars refer to as psychological benefits of the work (Barton, 2002; Bell 1995; Chapkis, 1997; Frank, 2002; Lerum, 1998; Weitzer, 2000a).

## *Drugs, Drugs, Drugs*

Not only could the woman find excitement and cash flow working as strippers and dancers, they could also get drugs and use drugs in a safe and socially alluring atmosphere (for more on drugs in such establishments, see Bott, 2006; Lavin, 2013; Sweet & Tewksbury, 2000a). Research consistently reports that hustling for cash to support continued drug use is often a daily objective for drug users (Goldstein, 1985; Johnson, Goldstein, Preble, Schmeidler, Lipton, Spunt, & Miller, 1985; and more recently, Bennett, Holloway, and Farrington, 2008; Manzoni, Brochu, Fischer, & Rehm, 2006). As the women in this study have found, a lot of "fast" money in the legal sex work industry is one "hustle" that can meet that need (See also Bradley-Engen & Ulmer, 2009).

The strip clubs and other settings of the legal sex work industry according to the women's accounts were the perfect settings for heavy drug use. Quenelle's narrative captures the experiences of the group. She was drinking and smoking marijuana before she started dancing and liked that she could continue at "work." Soon, however, her use of hard drugs escalated at the go-go bar. There she began smoking "bowls" or "moodies," which is marijuana laced with cocaine and then "turbos," which is marijuana mixed with crack cocaine. I asked her to elaborate on the connection between drug use and work. She replies:

Dancin' at a go-go bar, yeah, that's where it all began. Mind you we was already drinking and smoking dope. They was lacing the pot with coke; it was called bowls or moodies and then there's turbos that's like the marijuana or weed mixture with crack. I became addicted to the weed, cocaine, turbos, and crack and now along with the alcohol it just topped it off. But Philadelphia, see the thing about the go-go clubs in Philly it's not like you have to go outside to smoke your weed or nothing like that; it's always in the club. So when we dancing and we givin' them a lap dance, he already smoking weed or whatever he smoking, he could be turbos, bowls, moodies or whatever, passin' something, and you want to fit in and you want to get in with the crowd, you gonna tell him to pass you whatever he got, and along with the money you takin' the drugs too, so you smoking while you're doin' whatever you're doing. So that's what I meant when I said everything came at once; it wasn't like a separate time that I just started smoking, it all came at once.

Quenelle, like the other women were using hard drugs like heroin and cocaine prior to their entry into adult entertainment and they stayed because the "money was good," but they also continued to work in these establishments because they felt free to use drugs even while they were performing their work. They did not have to hide their drug use; smoking marijuana and snorting lines of cocaine was done out in the open in the clubs and bars where these women worked their dancing and stripping. The more money they made, the more they used. An added benefit of getting up in the morning to do it all over again was that when they were at work, they rarely needed to use their own drugs because patrons usually shared their own drugs with the women. This availability and freedom to use drugs on the inside of clubs and bars during work was another factor keeping them in the "life."

"It all came at once," says Quenelle's in the above narrative — the dancing, the drugs, and prostitution. When she said "while you're doin' whatever you're doing," she was referring to more than just using drugs while performing a lap dance. Quenelle was having actual sexual contact with the customer.

## *Sex and Illegal Sex Work*

Work in the legal sex work industry is a form of sex work. Sex sells through displays of a sexual nature, sexual performances on stage, and for the women in this research, sex with other workers on stage and sex with patrons both inside and outside of establishments. How women earn money depends on the type of establishment. For example at peep shows where no physical contact is ever made between the patron and the dancer, women perform behind a curtain that opens to individual patrons waiting in a booth when money is paid. When a certain amount of time has passed, the curtain closes shielding the patron's view until more money is paid. At 15, Shirelle worked at a peep show in Philadelphia located below an adult bookstore and on the same block as a go-go bar, all located just around the corner from her home. She never really had to "do that much," she says but enjoyed finding different ways to entice patrons to deposit more money and watch her longer. Here, she explains the strategy she learned to earn as much money as she could:

> I used to work … at a peep show, down on 13th and Arch. There was a bookstore on top and if you go downstairs, they have live girls. I worked in a booth, my name used to be Champagne. I used to work in this booth and a guy would put two dollars in my thing [timer]. Once I saw the two dollars come down I would push the button and the screen would come up and I would just sit there in a sexy pose, you know, talk, play with my pussy…. whatever he wanted me to do. The window would stay up for like maybe 2 minutes and then it would go back down. I would try to get them to put more money in.

Peep shows can offer only so many opportunities to earn money. The women say they preferred bars and clubs where women can earn money dancing on stage or on "the pole" or even better yet, when making physical contact with patrons lap dancing. As Bouclin (2006:106) says, the lap dances present a conflict between personal boundaries (sexual exploitation) and need for women to earn more money through imaginative ways, to "up the ante." Earning the "good money" means to push the boundaries of performance, moving from displays of dance and desire to sex acts (See also Pasko, 2000). The types of clubs and bars where the women in this study worked are what Bradley-Engen and Ulmer (2009:40) call "hustle clubs" where patrons and workers understand that the interactions between them are "blatant and explicitly sexual" (see also Trautner, 2005.) One strategy the women used to increase profit is to engage in sex with another female dancer on stage before patrons (see also Bott, 2006). Dancers make personal agreements to the sex performances on stage and the money it brings. Being chosen is often a competitive process among dancers and women often expect commitment in the partnerships, but the sex is strictly about business without relational ties off stage. While it might be tolerated (Bradley-Engen & Ulmer, 2009), to what extent this strategy is commonplace among workers in the legal sex work industry elsewhere is not known. Every one of the women in my research worked this strategy because it earned them "good money" and many said they enjoyed doing it. Quenelle explains how this works:

> She be eating your pussy or you eatin' hers. Up on the stage, they throw you more money if you do that, yes. They throw you more money, yes, you get more money. Whenever we dance and I feel as though I need to make some extra money or if I want to be with you, then that's how I'm gonna do it, actually they'll get mad if you're dancing with somebody else. Yeah, Shanika dances with me. If she dances with me this week, if I go down on her and she's allowing me and her to dance, if she's allowing me and her to be together on stage, 24/7, then if she get on stage with Tasha, me and Shanika gonna go at it after we leave out of here. Because I mean you know now, you've been dancing with me for three weeks, who are you to go get somebody else and dance with them. It's just that she's mine when it comes to be on stage, she's mine. It's about the money.

Quenelle will have to share money earned with Shanika when they dance together. In some cases, she would also have to pay a fee to the "house." This is a common practice in most of the establishments where the women in this study worked. Women agree to share money earned from patrons with management for providing the work environment (the music, atmosphere, patrons). In other establishments, a worker would pay an entrance fee at the entrance to the establishment (similar to a cover charge patrons would pay) and work independently of the establishment, keeping all money she earns (See also Bradley-Engen & Ulmer, 2009; Jeffreys, 2008).

As a teenager, Shirelle started her work in the industry at a go-go bar "down the block" from her residence. Just days after taking on the work, Shirelle was introduced by a patron to a new way of increasing her earnings. In this narrative, she describes her first involvement in sex work.

> The first time I slept with a guy for money was at the bar. This guy offered me money, and I thought he was joking. He said to me, "Hey, I want that." I said, "You ain't got the money to pay for it." I said, "$150." He said, "Here, I'm gonna give you the hundred now and I'll give you fifty when we get out there." He put $100 in my hand. I wasn't gonna pass that money up. We went to his car, and it was over in like five minutes. Five minutes I had $150 bucks. That's when I started dating, which is trickin'. You're in a bar and a guy says, "Can I get a shot of that?" And they offer you like $50, you go right up the street

to the room, 10 minutes it's over and you got $50 in your pocket.... And it worked out pretty good. I could sell the drugs and I could still work and still get paid off the drugs and still get paid off my dancing and trickin'. I was in love with it.

Selling sex is more than selling sexual arousal. For women in this study, taking on the job of stripper or dancer, escort or peep show worker meant she would come face to face with the decision to sell her sex for money. Without exception, the women willingly made that decision, prostituting with patrons inside these settings during lap dances and exhibitions, but more frequently outside, in rooming houses that accommodated prostitution or in cars, even in rental rooms connected to the club or bar that were run by the establishment and available specifically for sex work. Just a few (about four) of women had sold sex or traded sex before they were every involved in this industry, when they were girls and wanted drugs or place to sleep. For the majority of the women in this study, the legal sex work industry was the stepping off point for street sex work. The women were "put out" or "brought into the game" of sex work. In their experiences, prostitution and the legal sex work industry of strip clubs and go-go bars go hand in hand. LaToya's description of the industry as a business of sex work and drugs highlights this theme.

They [establishments] get their money from the door [cover charge] and from the alcohol, and from the rooms, like if you want to rent a room [in the building for prostitution with a customer]. Most of the profits is from the prostitution. The doormen usually sell weed [marijuana], but it's everything you want, if you want weed, coke, if you want weed, crack, heroin, snorting powder [cocaine], and alcohol is always at the bar. If you get high, you're all right. You won't worry. They sell just about everything in the bars. You ain't got to worry about what you want, like a little world where you get everything you need. That was my little world. It wasn't like I had to go on the outside of the world. I tested my waters when I got into the go-go life before [prostituting on] the street. I just experiment. It don't come with no rule book; you just go with the flow and then as you go on, you just know the tricks of the trade of their lifestyle. You just know. You do this and make $450, like, because he ain't never felt like that before. You know I made him feel something special so he paid me $100 more. You know? They [bar owners who owned other clubs in New Jersey] even came and picked me up at a certain time, like 12:00 at McDonald's on Broad and Girard, and take me to Jersey to go in them clubs.

> They had a special bus to pick you up and 12:00 at Broad and Girard
> at McDonalds.

Val gives a similar account of sex work inside the clubs. Selling sex is profitable, immediately accessible, and facilitated by sex industry establishments where the women worked. She says:

> I give you a lap dance and then you can whisper in my ear and tell me
> whether or not you want to date.... Then we go upstairs and you pay
> off the owner of the go-go club and you got the night, or you got the
> room for half an hour or whatever but if you want me for the night
> then you got to pay me for the night.... For a blow job I would say probably $50 to rent the room, right but you payin $100 total 'cause you
> can't pay a girl no less or no more than what you're payin to do her.
> You got to give them $50 for the blowjob or $100 for the blowjob and
> get another $50. So if some guys would give you $50 more than what
> you're supposed to have or $50 less, that's if you want to take that easy
> money, but you don't have to because you know that these guys are in
> there spending money for the night. Sex [intercourse] was $200 or
> $150 at times. Sometimes we would luck up and get a $200 day for
> sex. That was good money, every day, all day.

Knowing sex work is so profitable and in high demand, Bernadette offered a menu of options for sexual services at different rates of pay:

> When I was dancing, the guys were coming to take the girls, once they
> pick who they want to see, if they want to pick me and it was a few
> dollars for a show without touching and it was $10, it was $20 to come
> in my booth with me and it was $50 for a hand massage, $100 for a
> blow job and $200 for sex so those were the options. I was bringing
> home about $1,500 a week.

Most of the discussion of drugs and sex has focused on bars and clubs, but the women in the sample who escorted describe similar experiences with excessive drug use and sex for sale. In escorting, however, money is normally made in ancillary goods and services women provide their male patrons. To be a good conversationalist, listener, or pseudo-therapist helps to increase earnings, but the best money comes from sex work. Zeleste explains:

> Sex was just business. When I'm in a relationship I'm very faithful to
> them.... and it sounds very hypocritical but honestly you know I believe in that faithfulness even in my marriage, I would never, it would

never even cross my mind to be unfaithful. If I am with somebody and I love them, I'm exclusive to them and that's it. It's a monogamous relationship. I am not even trying to think about anybody else and I would expect the same back and here I am down here doing this. So I'm thinking, well, it's just business.

Kelly also worked outside of bars and clubs and like Zeleste, understood it as occupational. Driven by need for drugs, Kelly's description of her sex work in the legal sex work industry illustrates her agency. Kelly lived in a middle-class New Jersey suburb of Philadelphia, leaving home just before her 16th birthday. Her own alcohol abuse and troubled family life contributed to her deepening drug use and desire to turn to the adult entertainment industry for fast cash. Introduced years earlier to the "life" by a sexually sadistic former husband, Kelly sought out work as a dancer and then as an escort. For more money, she would occasionally use her apartment as a place for sex with the clients rather than work under the auspices of the escort agency. This way she would keep the entire fee paid by the clients. Here, she describes activities she used to increase her cash stream.

Then I started getting really greedy for money and I started doing home calls, letting them come to my apartment. I learned about that from the girls; they would say, "You don't have to spend the money in gas and all; just let them come to you." Then I get to keep it all…. I'd go down Atlantic City where the guys could call with their credit card and do phone sex. Not that I liked it, but I could sit and drink, pop pills, enjoy my day…. And I would go out to the bars, drink, and make some more money, like I would get $20 bucks to go in the car and give a blow job…. On a good day, I'd make sometimes $300 to $400 sometimes a day.

Moving from sexual performance to selling sex helped the women in this study to meet increasing financial demands of their drug addictions. They do not talk about their sex work in any negative light, do not suggest they were forced or felt stigma. The women make it clear that their choices then, though sometimes regretted, were thoughtful ones that met their drug use needs. For months and years they lived and worked in two parallel economies, one legal (dancing, stripping, escorting) and one criminal (prostitution). Once deeply entrenched in the illegal sex work culture and seriously drug dependent, every one of the women would turn away from legitimate employment to criminal work.

## *From the Pole to the Street*

Without exception, all of the women working as strippers, dancers, and escorts began to incorporate a business of sex work on the streets with their business of sex work inside as they worked as dancers and strippers. Earning money on the inside and then outside, the women embraced "the best of both worlds," at least financially. Selling their sex outside of work on the streets was morally acceptable, many of them reason, because working as dancers even while prostituting there still meant they were entertainers.

At some point in their careers as escorts, dancers, and strippers, the women in this study made decisions to leave the occupation. All of them left to become street-level sex workers. Extant research suggests women exit jobs like stripping and dancing when they have found an alternative source of income or when the burdens of the job (like stigma, control, and other harms) outweigh the financial benefits they enjoy. Here, women leave the industry in when what was once a benefit would become a burden. The women quit the jobs when going to work got in the way of their drug use. With money so easily earned on the street by selling sex, going to a workplace is not necessarily that important, some say. First a dancer, then escort, Zeleste took sex work to the streets just two years after she was introduced to dancing, explaining:

> After a while, I was doing the escorting with a little bit of the street thing [street prostitution]. Then after things started deteriorating [from addiction to crack], I wasn't escorting at all and I was just doing the street thing. Why? Because of my addiction and I needed money for crack and it was an easy quick thing … The money with the escorting was the way to go, but this was the easy way out when you put yourself in a position when you had no drugs left, no money, especially if you were put out there late and you needed to get some money quick.

Zeleste, like many of the other women, was making "good money" in the legal sex work industry and would substitute that money with "quick money" that would come from more dangerous and usually lower-paying street level prostitution. With her drug use becoming more costly, Jarena was living "really bad." She remembers thinking that doing the escorting work took just too much effort. Desperate for drugs, she began "tricking" full time on the streets because it was so much simpler and "easier." So easy, she says, she never had to wait long on the streets for a "date." "Cars were coming all the time," she says. Since those years ago, Jarena has remained a sex worker.

The neighborhoods of the peep shows, go-go bars, and strip clubs are also the same areas where the women would buy and use drugs. Most of them also call those areas home. They quickly learn that they are able to gain access to customers with little effort because it seems that "customers are everywhere." The women had simple and direct access to income obtained through street sex work, which made financial earnings through sex work convenient. While some of the women say they enjoyed even greater profits by prostituting outside of the bars and clubs (because they did not have to give up any of their earnings to the bar or club), most did not. Eventually when their addictions became their primary objective, as it did for the women in this study, dancing and stripping had to end. LaToya remarked, "When you mix the high into [the dancing] that was never going to work because then you're getting high; that lifestyle is one job by itself."

All of the women who worked as dancers, strippers, and escorts supplemented their incomes with sex work until they decided finally to leave the agency, club, or bar work environment and work entirely as sex workers on the streets. There were no exceptions. All of the women who made the decision to work in the adult entertainment industry followed this path. As dependable, daily access to cash was their primary objective, the women saw street sex work as a more sensible alternative to sex work in the confines of a club, escort agency, or bar. With drugs on their mind, they became their own agents, creating a new financial enterprise for themselves in street sex work where many of them remained.

# Discussion

The women in this study are a special group; they are drug users who have financed their lives through deviance and crime. Consistent with scholarship on women and girls in drugs and crime, they suffered a significant amount of trauma during their childhood and adolescent years in the form of child abuse (Acoca, 1999; Belknap and Holsinger, 1998, 2006; Bloom, Owen, Rosenbaum, Piper Deschenes, 2003; Chesney-Lind and Rodriguez, 1983; Daly, 1992), parental substance abuse (Kramer & Berg, 2003; Peugh & Belenko, 1999; Windle, 1996, 1998), and domestic violence in the home (Carlson, 2000; Fergusson & Horwood, 1998; Fleming, Mullen, and Bammer, 1997). Furthermore, the places where women in the study worked as dancers, strippers, and escorts are located in and around poor and disordered neighborhoods, along adjacent highways and near trucking destinations in Philadelphia and Camden. They were in neighborhoods where the drug culture thrives. As young women living as part of that drug culture, they understood the legal sex work industry to be an income option open to them. They did not actively seek out the work but were enticed by excitement, drugs, and were drawn in by the money. Strip clubs, go-go bars, peep shows, and escort services represent a lucrative and exciting occupational alternative for troubled girls and young women with limited capital and opportunity. Living the "fast life," especially as runaways and dropouts, they knew their sexuality could earn them money they needed. Their selection of this work as an occupational choice best suited to their personal and social situations and more appealing and profitable than other forms of work, legal and illegal illustrates their agency, or ability to exercise choice.

Their work may be seen as a dichotomy—in the "life"—where they used their bodies to earn money doing gender in the most sexist of ways yet exhibiting power, control, and agency as they negotiate profits in the work. Pasko (2002) refers to this as a "confidence game" where strippers move for male desire yet they exert power and maintain control over the interactions with customers. Taking a similar position that women in these settings are not oppressed, but act as agents in their own economic and occupational lives, Wood (2000) study of strippers revealed that women working in the industry see themselves as active participants in the work rather than as controlled, entrapped objects of sex. Though limited by their personal and social situations, the women were versatile in the various strategies they controlled to increase profits, including moving through different jobs in the industry and working for themselves on the side. Moving from one role or job in the industry to others, what Escoffier refers to as "diversifying sexual repertoire" (2007, p. 174), was a common means for the women to earn additional money.

From the stage to the street, all of the women sold sex during their employment in the legal sex work industry, mixed street sex work with the legal employment of the legal sex work industry, and then turned fully to street sex work. The environment of the strip club and go-go bar, the peep show and escort scene that initially drew them in with the promise of good money, excitement, and drugs use contributed to their worsening drug addictions and entry into prostitution. These findings seem to be new to the literature as research on sex work by women working as dancers and strippers suggests sex for sale is taboo and unwanted by women themselves (Raphael & Shapiro, 2004; Ronai & Ellis, 1989; but see O'Connell Davidson, 1998). Of women in this study after time, the legal sex work industry was just too restrictive for the women to finance their addictions—the women needed full-time access to drugs and money and they found it with street-level prostitution. Their decision to take it to the street was heavily influenced by their increasing dependence on drugs, but also by the seemingly straightforward and simple access to street-level sex work in the neighborhoods they called home. This shows that working in the legal sex work industry was not simply a precipitating factor for their involvement in sex work on the streets. It was a clear pathway to street sex work. To be sure, the women were not passive agents in these settings. They wanted to earn good money and learned just how to do it; they knew how to hustle.

# References


Acoca, L. (1999). Investing in girls: A 21st century strategy. *Juvenile Justice, VI, Number 1*. Washington DC: U.S. Department of Justice, Office of Justice Programs, Office of Juvenile Justice and Delinquency Prevention.

Barton, B. (2002). Dancing on the Möbius Strip: Challenging the sex war paradigm. *Gender & Society, 16*, 585–602.

Barton, B. (2006). *Stripped: Inside the lives of exotic dancers.* New York: New York University Press.

Barton, B. (2007). *Managing the toll of stripping. Journal of Contemporary Ethnography, 36*, 571–596.

Bell, H., Sloan, L, & Strickling, C. (1998). Exploiter or exploited: Topless dancers reflect on their experiences. *Journal of Women & Social Work, 13*, 352–368.

Bell, S. (1995). *Whore Carnival.* New York: Autonomedia.

Belknap, J., & Holsinger, K. (1998). An overview of delinquent girls: How theory and practice have failed and the need for innovative changes. In R. T. Zaplin (Ed.), *Female offenders: Critical perspectives and effective interventions.* (pp. 31–64). Gaithersburg, MD: Aspen Publishers.

Belknap, J., & Holsinger, K. (2006). The gendered nature of risk factors for delinquency. *Feminist Criminology, 1*, 48–71.

Bennett, T., Holloway, K., & Farrington, D. (2008). The statistical association between drug misuse and crime: A meta-analysis. *Aggression and Violent Behavior, 13*(2), 107–118.

Bloom, B., Owen, B., Rosenbaum, J., & Piper Deschenes, E. (2003). Focusing on girls and young women: A gendered perspective on female delinquency, *Women & Criminal Justice, 4*, 117—136.

Bouclin, S. (2006). Dancers empowering (some) dancers: The intersection of race, class, and gender in organizing erotic labourers? *Race, Gender & Class, 13*, 98–129.

Bradley, M. (2007). Girlfriends, wives, and strippers: Managing stigma in exotic dancer romantic relationships. *Deviant Behavior, 28*, 379–406.

Bradley-Engen, M. & Ulmer, J.T. (2009). Social worlds of stripping: The processual orders of exotic dance. *Sociological Quarterly, 50*, 29–60.

Bruckert, C. (2002). *Taking it off, putting it on: Women in the strip trade.* Toronto: Women's Press.

Bruckert, C., Parent, C., & Robitaille, P. (2003) *Erotic service/erotic dance establishments: Two types of marginalized Labour.* Ottawa: Law Commission of Canada.

Carlson, B. E. (2000). Children exposed to intimate partner violence. *Trauma, Violence, & Abuse, 1,* 321–342.

Chapkis, Wendy. 1997. *Live Sex Acts: Women Performing Erotic Labor.* New York: Routledge.

Chesney-Lind. M., & Rodriguez, N. (1983). Women under lock and key. *The Prison Journal, 63,* 47–65.

Daly, K. (1992). Women's pathways to felony court: Feminist theories of lawbreaking and problems of representation. *Southern California Review of Law and Women's Studies, 2,*11–52.

DeMichele, M. T. and Tewksbury, R. (2004). Sociological explorations in site-specific social control: The role of the strip club bouncer. *Deviant Behavior, 25,* 537–558.

Egan, R. D. (2005). Emotional consumption: Mapping love and masochism in an exotic dance club. *Body Society, 11,* 87–108.

Enck, G. E., & Preston, J. D. (1998). Counterfeit intimacy: A dramaturgical analysis of an erotic performance. *Deviant Behavior, 9,* 369–381.

Erickson, D. J., & Tewksbury, R. (2000). The gentlemen in the club: A typology of strip club patrons. *Deviant Behavior, 21,* 271–293.

Escoffier, J. (2007). Porn star/stripper/escort: Economic and sexual dynamics in a sex work career. *Journal of Homosexuality, 53,* 173–200.

Fergusson D.M., & Horwood L.J. (1998). Exposure to interparental violence in childhood and psychosocial adjustment in young adulthood. *Child Abuse & Neglect, 22,* 339–357.

Fleming, J., Mullen, P., & Bammer, G. (1997). A study of potential risk-factors for sexual abuse in children. *Child Abuse and Neglect, 21,* 49–58.

Forsyth, C. J. & Deshotels, T. H. (1996). A sociological profile of the nude dancer. *International Review of Modern Sociology, 26,* 111–120.

Forsyth, C.J., & Deshotels, T.H. (1997). The occupational milieu of the nude dancer. *Deviant behavior, 18,* 125–42.

Frank, K. (2002). *G-strings and sympathy: Strip club regulars and male desire.* Durham, NC: Duke University Press.

Frank, K. (2003). "Just trying to relax": Masculinity, masculinizing practices, and strip club regulars. *Journal of Sex Research, 40,* 61–75.

Goldstein, P. J. (1985). The drugs/violence nexus: A tripartite conceptual framework. *Journal of Drug Issues, 15*(4), 493–506.

Jeffreys, S. (2008). Keeping women down and out: The strip club boom and the reinforcement of male dominance. *Signs, 34,* 151–173.

Jeffrey, L.A., & MacDonald, G. (2006). It's the money honey: The economy of sex work in the Maritimes. *Canadian Review of Sociology and Anthropology, 43,* 313–327.

Johnson, B. D., Goldstein, P. J., Preble, E., Schmeidler, J., Lipton, D. S., Spunt, B., & Miller, T. (1985). *Taking care of business: The economics of crime by heroin abusers.* Lexington, MA: Lexington Books.

Kramer, L.A. & Berg, E.C. (2003). A survival analysis of timing of entry into prostitution: The differential impact of race, educational level, and childhood/adolescent risk factors. *Sociological Inquiry, 73,* 511–528.

Lavin, M. (2013). Rule-making and rule-breaking: Strip club social control regarding alcohol and other drugs. Deviant Behavior, 34, 361–383.

Lerum, K. (1998). Twelve-step feminism makes sex workers sick: How the state and the recovery movement turn radical women into 'useless citizens.' *Sexuality in Culture, 2,* 7–36.

Lewis, J. (2006). I'll scratch your back if you'll scratch mine: The role of reciprocity, power and autonomy in the strip club. *The Canadian Review of Sociology and Anthropology, 43,* 297–311.

Manzoni, P., Brochu, S., Fischer, B., & Rehm, J. (2006). Determinants of property crime among illicit opiate users outside of treatment across Canada. *Deviant Behavior, 27*(3), 351–376.

Maticka-Tyndale, E., Lewis, J., Clark, J., Zubick, J., and Young, S. (2000). Exotic dancing and health. *Women & Health, 31,* 87–108.

Mesternacher, R. & Roberti, J. W. (2004). Qualitative analysis of vocational choice: A collective case study of strippers. *Deviant Behavior, 25,* 43–65.

Murphy, A. (2003). The dialectical gaze. *Journal of Contemporary Ethnography, 32,* 305–335.

O'Connell Davidson, J. (1988). Prostitution, power, and freedom. Cambridge: Polity Press.

Pasko, L. (2002). Naked power: The practice of stripping as a confidence game. *Sexualities, 5,* 49–66.

Peretti, P.O. & O'Connor, P. (1989). Effects of incongruence between the perceived self and the ideal self on emotional stability of stripteasers. *Social Behavior and Personality, 17,* 81–92.

Peugh, J., & Belenko, S. (1999). Substance-involved women inmates: Challenges to providing effective treatment. *The Prison Journal, 79,* 23–44.

Philaretou, A. G. (2006). Female exotic dancers: Intrapersonal and interpersonal perspectives, *Sexual Addiction & Compulsivity, 13,* 41–52.

Price, K. (2008). Keeping the dancers in check: The gendered organization of stripping work in the lion's den. *Gender & Society, 22,* 367–389.

Raphael, J., & Shapiro, D.L. (2004). Violence in indoor and outdoor prostitution venues, *Violence Against Women, 10,* 126–139.

Ronai, C. R. & Cross, R. (1988). Dancing with identity: Narrative resistance of male and female stripteasers. *Deviant Behavior: An Interdisciplinary Journal, 19,* 99–119.

Ronai, C. R., & Ellis. C. (1989). Turn-ons for money: Interactional strategies of the table dancer. *Journal of Contemporary Ethnography, 18,* 271–298.

Schweitzer, D. (2000). Striptease: The art of spectacle and transgression. *Journal of Popular Culture, 34,* 65–75.

Scott, D. (1996). *Behind the g-string.* Jefferson, NC: McFarland.

Skipper, Jr., J. A., & McCaghy, C. H. (1970). Stripteasers: The anatomy and career contingencies of a deviant occupation. *Social Problems, 19*(3), 391–405.

Sweet, N., & Tewksbury, R. (2000a). Entry, maintenance, and departure from a career in the sex industry: Strippers' experiences of the occupational costs and rewards. *Humanity & Society, 24,* 136–61.

Sweet, N., & Tewksbury, R. (2000b). What's a nice girl like you doing in a place like this? Pathways to a career in stripping. *Sociological Spectrum, 20,* 325–343.

Thompson, W. E., & Harred, J. L. (1992). Topless Dancers: Managing stigma in a deviant occupation. *Deviant behavior, 13,* 291–311.

Thompson, W. E., Harred, J. L., & Burks, B. E. (2003). Managing the stigma of topless dancing: A decade later. *Deviant behavior, 24,* 551–570.

Trautner, M. N. (2005). Doing gender, doing class: The performance of sexuality in exotic dance clubs. *Gender Society, 19,* 771–788.

Wahab, S. (2004). Tricks of the trade: What social workers can learn about sex workers through dialogue. *Qualitative Social Work, 3,* 139–160.

Weitzer, R. (2009). Sociology of sex work. *Annual Review of Sociology, 35,* 213–234.

Weitzer, R. (2000a). *Sex for Sale: Prostitution, Pornography, and the Sex Industry.* New York: Routledge.

Windle, M. (1996). On the discriminative validity of a Family History or Problem Drinking Index with a national sample of young adults. *Journal of Studies on Alcohol, 57,* 378–386.

Windle, M. (1998). Substance use and abuse among adolescent runaways: A four-year follow-up study. *Journal of Youth and Adolescence, 18,* 331–344.

Wood, E. A. (2000). Working in the fantasy factor: The attention hypothesis and the enacting of masculine power in strip clubs. *Journal of Contemporary Ethnography, 29,* 5–31.

Wosick-Correa, K. J. (2008). Sexy ladies sexing ladies: Women as consumers in strip clubs. *Journal of Sex Research*, 45, 201–216.

Chapter 7

# "I'll hook you up": Women's Experiences Selling and Trading Methamphetamine

*Robert Jenkot, Ph.D.*

The common public conception regarding the motivation for selling illicit drugs is economics. In short, drug dealers want money. This chapter adds support to the idea that economic motivations are common, yet when women are involved with illicit drug sales additional motivations are uncovered. It is important to fully understand the variety of motivations that lead women to illicit drug sales if we are to construct effective policy to combat illicit drug sales, divert women from future involvement, and provide for effective rehabilitation and reintegration of these offenders.

This chapter focuses on women who sell methamphetamine. This drug has captured the media's attention and has spread from the West Coast to the East Coast of America with surprising speed. The low cost and easy manufacture of the drug results in the combination of availability with the strong possibility for addiction. The presence of dependence or an addiction to a cheap and readily available drug is the perfect market for a drug dealer. Women entering into this realm face all of the risks of men, plus an additional or increased risk of personal security. Today, the drug's popularity among users is highest in rural communities in many Midwestern states, and use rates in the South and on the East Coast are rising. Yet little is known about how the methamphetamine-centered groups function and the way that gender interacts within those transactions.

## Women Involved with Drug Dealing

Blum et al. (1972) provide us with an in-depth look at drug dealing behavior. While their study is wide-ranging from junior high school dealers to drug using communities, they did not differentiate between male and female dealers (Blum and Associates, 1972). Arguably, it was not until the 1980s when crack cocaine became popular that researchers sought to differentiate between male and female experiences with illicit drugs.

Investigations into women's involvement with dealing illicit drugs centered on crack cocaine and to a lesser extent powder cocaine and heroin (Maher & Daly, 1996; Fagan, 1995; Fagan, 1994; Mieczkowski, 1994; Dunlap, Johnson, & Manwar, 1994). These researchers found that women were clearly involved in drug dealing for two main reasons: financial gain/financial independence, and supporting an addiction to drugs (Maher & Daly, 1996; Mieczkowski, 1994; Dunlap et al., 1994; Fagan, 1994).

Morgan and Joe (1996) expanded on the previous researchers by examining women involved in methamphetamine sales along the West Coast and in Hawaii. Their research supports the idea that economics play a role in women's involvement in drug dealing; however, they add the idea of lifestyle contexts to our understanding of this behavior (Morgan & Joe, 1996, pp. 128–9). The organizing principle of lifestyle contexts is that these women's drug selling behavior is shaped by their lifestyle along a continuum from citizen to outlaw (Morgan & Joe, 1996). A "citizen lifestyle context" allows the female methamphetamine dealer to remain located in an apparently conformist lifestyle/community while taking part in the criminal activity (Morgan & Joe, 1996). Alternately, an "outlaw lifestyle context" locates the methamphetamine dealer in a marginalized community where her drug dealing "fits" with expectations of the community members (Morgan & Joe, 1996).

Even though women are involved with illicit drug sales, males are still considered the dominant actors in drug sales phenomena. Therefore, the position of women as illicit drug dealers is uncommon. Most illicit drug selling activity is very gendered (Denton & O'Malley, 1999; Williams, 1992, Williams, 1989; Johnson, Hamid, & Morales, 1990; Johnson et al., 1985; Adler, 1985; Preble & Casey, 1969). The findings reported in this chapter are important because it provides insight into the uncommon behavior of women regularly distributing methamphetamine over an extended period.

## Theoretical Frame

Since gender is a central part of this research, the gendered pathways perspective is employed to provide us with the context in which the drug transactions take place. As Belknap (2001) explains, gendered pathways:

> [a]ttempt to examine girls' and womens' (and sometimes men's and
> boys') histories, allowing them, when possible, "voice" in order to un-
> derstand the link between childhood and adult events and traumas
> and the likelihood of subsequent offending. (61)

Using this approach, this chapter is able to determine key factors in each
person's attempts at dealing methamphetamine, as well as their method of
dealing. For example, if a woman grew up in a household with alcoholics she
might be more or less likely to use alcohol in excess. These experiences should
also carry over to any other group that woman would associate with. This study
relies on the women themselves to explain in their own words why they deal
methamphetamine, and what methods they use. While there have been several
studies that have employed the gendered pathways perspective, each has focused on at least one of several key elements. The varieties of pathways used
are conflated into several categories below.

1. *The Lack of Conforming Parental Guidance and/or Abuse at Home*: Multiple authors have found that a woman's domestic situation, whether as a child
   or adult, can be a linkage to future deviant and/or criminal behavior (Evans,
   Forsyth & Gauthier, 2002; Belknap, 2001; Richie, 2000; Richie, 1996;
   Maher & Daly, 1996; Daly, 1992). The types of domestic situations that have
   been found that may lead to deviant and/or criminal behavior include
   poverty, strained relations with parents and significant others, as well as
   physical, emotional, and sexual abuse.
2. *The Double-Edged Sword of Sexual Relations*: Several authors have noted a
   connection between sexual activity, whether consental, abusive, or as an
   assault as possibly leading to future deviant and/or criminal behavior
   (Evans, Forsyth & Gauthier, 2002; Belknap, 2001; Richie, 1996; Daly,
   1992). A woman's choice to take part in sexual behavior is often referred
   to as a double-edged sword. On the one hand, taking part in sex can be
   perceived as a necessary part of lasting relationships building trust and intimacy. However, that same behavior can result in the woman being negatively labeled (Schur, 1984). Refusing to take part in sex leads to yet other
   negative labels, or compromising their commitment to a relationship or
   group. Women who decide to take part in sexual behavior, in light of the
   repercussions for not taking part, may be more likely to take part in other
   behaviors that they would not do without such an "initiation" to potentially
   deviant behavior.
3. *Sexual Abuse and/or Sexual Assault:* The connection between being a victim and survivor of sexual abuse and/or assault and future deviant or criminal behavior has also been noted (Evans, Forsyth & Gauthier, 2002;

Belknap, 2001; Richie, 1996; Schur, 1984). While the rationale for this connection varies, the central idea is that once a woman is victimized, degraded, or abused, she may have a lowered self-esteem and deviant or criminal behavior becomes a realistic alternative to conforming behavior. Such a connection is all the more clear when the abuse takes place in the home, traditionally a place of safety. Magnifying the effects of sexual abuse and assault may occur when the perpetrator is also a family member, again negating the expectation of safety within the home. The lack of a safe home life may call into question much of the woman's socialization. If the home is not considered a safe place, then perhaps the conceptions of right and wrong may also be in question.

4. *Economics Pushing Toward a Behavior and/or Drug Addiction*: Women's involvement in criminal activity is also linked to economic motives (Evans, Forsyth & Gauthier, 2002; Belknap, 2001; Denton & O'Malley, 1999; Richie, 1996; Maher & Daly, 1996; Fagan 1995; Fagan, 1994; Daly, 1992). The need to acquire money to maintain a household and/or a lifestyle, raise children, or to simply maintain a drug habit can instigate the decision to take part in an underground economy.

Akin to the push-pull theory of immigration, the pressures and strain of a domestic situation (as child, partner, or parent) can "push" a person to mitigate issues of economic strife. Whether running away from home as a child, heading a single parent household, or responding to the desire for material goods, additional income is appealing. It is well known that illicit drug sales are a method for making money quickly. As such, we can consider drug sales a "pull" that can provide the money necessary to limit/mitigate that same pressure and/or strain.

5. *Health & Mental Health*: Linked with the life situations noted in items 1-3 above, a woman's physical and emotional health can be linked to future behavior (Belknap, 2001; Richie, 1996; Daly, 1992; Schur, 1984). As a situation of domestic violence continues over time, a woman's sense of self-worth and confidence is affected. From this situation a form of criminal behavior or deviance may be viewed as an opportunity, for good or ill. Obviously, a woman's health and mental health is affected by their current relationship and any abuse linked with that relationship.

6. *Relationships:* The final social situation that can affect a woman's path through life is the relationships that they are in (Evans, Forsyth & Gauthier, 2002; Belknap, 2001; Denton & O'Malley, 1999; Richie, 1996; Maher & Daly, 1996; Fagan, 1995; Fagan, 1994; Daly, 1992; Schur 1984). For example, as a child, the woman may live in a poor home or have endured abuse. As an

adult the woman may still live in a condition of poverty, may still be enduring abuse, or have to negotiate living with a partner whose behavior borders on abuse of any variety. Further as an adult the woman may also have to deal with children as a single parent or within a domestic arrangement. The inclusion of children in the equation can result in a greater "push" to maintain some degree of economic solvency. Additionally, the push to maintain such solvency may lead to greater and greater acts of deviance and/or criminality in order to mitigate the pressure caused—in part—by the relationship she is in. Alternately, the relationship a woman is a part of may instigate association with her partner's friends. These "new" friends may be involved with deviant and/or criminal behavior. Therefore, the relationship may lead to the opportunity to take part in deviant and/or criminal behavior.

These six social situations that have been shown to affect a woman's choice (perceived diminished choices or diminished ability to choose) can be conflated into four categories. The four categories are: relationships, economics, gender norms, and abuse. The rationale for conflating the six pathways into four is due to the overlapping aspects of several of the categories. For example, being in an abusive relationship may be tied to a woman's economic situation and any further abuse she may endure.

The category of relationships involves those aspects of a woman's life where she is connected to family, children, and significant others. The category of economics relates to the women's economic status, their relationship to wealth, and their wealth-making capacity. Gender norms as a category reflect those aspects of a woman's life where conformity to, or deviation from gender norms affects their lives and/or livelihood. The final category, abuse, focuses on those aspects of women's lives where any abuse they have endured may affect future behaviors. It should be noted that any woman's life may include aspects of all four pathways, or any combination of them. These pathways are not mutually exclusive.

The gendered pathway perspective is applied with knowledge of Maher's (1996) critique. Maher (1996) states that much research and theory dichotomizes women's agency as either "passive victims" or "active subjects" (p. 1). This project attempts to include the context of the women's lives and maintain a connection with their agency within their lives. The amount of agency will vary among women, and will include a subjective self-assessment that guides their behavior. If a woman believes that she is powerless, we can expect her behavior to reflect that belief. Similarly, if a woman perceives herself to have some degree of control over her life, this too should be evident.

Using the women's own voices to understand their social behavior avoids Maher's critique because it does not polarize women's experiences. Instead, it will allow women to illustrate where they fall on the continuum between the two extremes. Using such an understanding of women's lives, this chapter uncovers how women can operate as illicit drug dealers within a structure historically dominated my male operators. While this study examines a sample of women in the Midwest who have dealt methamphetamine, it may shed light on female drug dealers more generally and will add to our understanding of the illicit drug trade and what role gender can and does play in that trade.

# Methods

This project is part of a larger qualitative examination of women in Missouri and Arkansas and their involvement with methamphetamine. The population is limited to those women who have been charged with drug related offenses in Missouri and Arkansas, and the sample for this study was drawn from multiple site visits to the county jails in Perry and Jefferson counties in Missouri, and Pulaski County, Arkansas. The sample for this study, then, was 31 women incarcerated in county jails in Missouri and Arkansas who were charged with drug related offenses.

The location of the interviews were multi-purpose rooms located either in the cell-pod complex themselves, or in the visitor section of the facilities. The rooms consisted of cinder block walls painted gray with molded plastic furniture. Each room had an opaque window in the door for security reasons, although no correctional staff ever looked in.

The interviews were semi-structured allowing the women to expand/explain their experiences as they saw fit. The interview schedule was employed to insure all of the relevant topics were fully covered. Each woman was interviewed one time as they may have been transferred or made bail upon subsequent visits to the jail. Each interview lasted at least one (1) hour, but some were as long as three and one-half (3.5) hours. Each woman selected a pseudonym to allow for confidentiality. This project was approved by the Human Subjects Committee at Southern Illinois University.

## *Demographics of the Sample*

The average age of my sample was 36 years old, with a range of 18 to 48 years old. One woman was 18 years old. Seven women were between 21 and 29 years old, twelve women were between 30 and 39 years old, and eleven women were between 40 and 49 years old. The sample consisted of 28 white women, 1 African American woman, and 2 Hispanic women. The majority of my sample, 19 women, were single at the time of their interview, 4 women were married, 4 women were separated, and 4 women were divorced.

Every woman interviewed was employed prior to incarceration; however, their employment status varied considerably. Fifteen women had regular legitimate occupations (e.g., restaurant managers, retail clerks, and fast food cooks), eleven women were employed in seasonal or family operated businesses (e.g., drywall installers, roofing companies, and house painters), and the remaining five women drifted between low level minimum wage jobs and/or maintained illegitimate occupations (e.g., methamphetamine production, prostitution).

With regard to educational attainment, 26 women had a high school diploma or a GED and the remaining 5 women possessed an Associates Degrees, Bachelors Degrees, or some form of post-secondary education (e.g., Med-Tech training, Paramedic Training).

The combination of educational attainment and occupation can be considered hallmarks of class standing. The women in this sample can be considered largely lower- to working-class individuals. Many, if not most, had illegitimate income in addition to income derived from their occupations (e.g., illicit drug sales and/or prostitution). The result is that many reported indicators of wealth (e.g., multiple new automobiles, high grade stereo equipment, and cash on hand), yet none of the women reported assets that are normally associated with the wealthy (e.g., real estate, stocks, etc.). The demographic data provided can be used to illustrate that a typical woman in this study would be a single white woman in her mid-thirties employed in either a service sector job or manual labor position. She would also hold a high school diploma, living comfortably but financially would have little to no net worth.

Realizing that my personal presence as a large white male can be intimidating, I relied upon the idea of assuming the role of an "acceptable incompetent" (Lofland & Lofland, 1984; Lofland, Snow, Anderson, & Lofland, 2006). In this way I was able to minimize my potentially intimidating persona, and rely upon the women to "teach" me what they knew and relate their experiences. Using this method also shows my deference to their knowledge and experience. It should also be noted that, due to my personal presence, the women were not expected to discuss issues of abuse to a great degree. After all, the vast majority of women are abused by men, and any rapport I was able to build over a short time may not be strong enough to break through an emotional issue as intense as abuse.

## *The Gendered Distribution of Methamphetamine*

The discussion regarding the gendered distribution of methamphetamine is divided into four parts that reflect the major themes uncovered in the data. The themes are: identity as a dealer, selling versus trading, reciprocity, and sex for drugs.

The following accounts reveal that all respondents (with the exception of the sole African American woman) either sold methamphetamine for money or traded the drug for some other item of value at least one time. It should be stressed that when the women were queried about selling methamphetamine, even one instance of transferring the drug for money or some other item of value qualified as selling.

## *Identification as a Dealer*

The women in this study had an overall negative reaction to the identity of being a drug dealer. While all of the women in this study (except for one) had exchanged methamphetamine for some item of value, only eighteen of the women in this study when asked specifically if they sold methamphetamine stated that they had "dealt" methamphetamine at least once. This difference reflects a single behavior (drug sales) being perceived by the actors in different ways. The first way is to have taken part in this behavior, yet not consider oneself to be a "dealer." The second perception acknowledges engaging in the behavior and self-identifying as a drug dealer. The difference is worth noting as both groups technically have sold the drug, but only the admitted dealers define their behavior as dealing.

Margie would often trade drugs instead of selling them outright. Margie (a 23-year-old white woman) is 5'5" tall with brown hair and is very healthy-looking. She is a very talkative and engaging person. As she would answer questions she would easily get off track and begin talking about any subject with great relish. Margie is single and has no children. She has been cooking methamphetamine for several years and enjoyed the camaraderie that she felt with her group. At the conclusion of the interview she said that many of the questions have given her cause to think about the group she was with and reevaluate what she will do once out of jail. Margie was arrested while she and other members of her group were cooking methamphetamine. A former methamphetamine user turned them in as part of their plea bargain. She did not like the stigma of being a drug dealer. She explains:

> I'd get all kinds of stuff for meth, like once I got a pound of pot for
> an ounce of meth. It was easier than holding cash. I coulda sold meth

for cash, I mean ain't no thing, right. But I always think of dealers as
scummy. I don't want to be thought of as scummy…. Shit, I'd trade
for anything. There was this Shell station [gasoline retailer] and the
guys there would fill my tank for some meth! I'd always get full service! Ha!

Margie's comments illustrate the value placed on methamphetamine by
users of the drug. Dealers of other drugs were willing to trade a pound of marijuana for one ounce of methamphetamine. Even so, sales remained secondary. Trading items of value rather than receiving cash were desirable because
should law enforcement officials attempt to arrest her, items of value other
than cash would be more difficult to link her to drug selling activity. Margie
stated that she did not need to sell methamphetamine to earn money, "I work,
you know, always have. My family has a painting business. So I didn't have to
sell. I coulda, but why?" Her decision not to sell as a means of personal support is twofold. First, she had legitimate employment and stated that she did
not need additional money. Second, she stated that there was a stigma attached
to selling drugs. Margie did not want to be thought of as "scummy." For Margie
there was a negative reaction to being a methamphetamine dealer in the technical sense, but she could avoid this label if she traded the drug for other items.

Kathryn also thought of dealers negatively: "Never met a good one, so I never
dealt." Kathryn (a 48-year-old white woman) is 5'7" tall, long brown hair, married, and she has no children. Kathryn appeared to be in good health, but
seemed either bored or tired. She would respond to questions, but she also took
time to consider her answers. Her situation is unique in that her husband did
not use any illicit drugs, nor did she until recently. Her arrest came when she
was at the home of a methamphetamine cook that was raided by the police.

When probed further about dealing Kathryn replied, "Oh, sure, I sold some
to friends or I'd trade off for it. Like I got a stereo once for meth … that was
cool." While Kathryn did not define herself as a dealer, she did take part in
drug-dealing behavior, but only to friends and often for items of value other
than cash. Perhaps indicating initially, "I never dealt," is reflective of how dealers are seen by methamphetamine users. Trading drugs for items of value is perhaps less stigmatizing.

While methamphetamine sales have been reported by the women in this
study, 13 women reported that they never sold the drug. However when the
data were analyzed, all but one of the women had traded methamphetamine
for something of value. The decision not to self-report as a dealer may involve
the women's attempts to negate the stigma associated with drug dealing. The
women do not appear to equate trading items of value (electronics, gasoline,

other drugs, vehicles) for drugs with drug-dealing. Such a disassociation with being a drug dealer may be a facet of this particular drug subculture. In the drug subculture there may be a sort of camaraderie where trading is positive, yet drug-dealing carries a negative connotation.

Aside from the usual user–dealer relationships, some women have turned to alternative methods to obtain methamphetamine; these methods include theft, forgery, and trading other items of value for the drug. An important aspect related to using alternate means to obtain drugs is the perception of stigma attached to drug dealers. So long as a person does not sell drugs in the usual way (e.g., street-corner sales), they can avoid perceiving themselves as dealers and avoid the stigma of being "scummy."

## Selling versus Trading

Mickey (a 31-year-old white woman) is 5'5" tall with dark brown hair and she appears very healthy in spite of being incarcerated for several years. She was recently released from prison, only to be arrested again. Mickey is very talkative and open about her experiences with illicit drugs. As she is interviewed, she reclines in the chair and uses her hands to help express herself. When she was originally arrested in Arkansas, she was in the process of cooking a batch of methamphetamine as the police raided her home. Mickey sums up methamphetamine sales, "Ya want some? If I got extra I'll hook you up [pause] so long as I know you. Ain't no big deal." Mickey's comment shows the necessity of being involved in the drug subculture and being involved in her network for her to sell the drugs to anyone provided she has more than is needed for personal consumption. In this case, drug selling or trading is not perceived to be problematic.

Methamphetamine sales, according to these women, were never a concerted effort or goal. For Mickey, methamphetamine sales are almost an afterthought. In this instance, the sale of methamphetamine is largely an unintended consequence of being involved in this lifestyle. Annie agrees with Mickey: "I sold some meth, no biggie, it was only a 'G' [gram] here or there." Annie (a 32-year-old white woman) is 5'2" tall, blonde, currently separated from her second husband, and has three children. She appears to be in good health and claims that the jail food has "bulked" her up. Annie has a long sentence yet appears in good humor. She has earned a college degree and worked as a Registered Nurse and has had paramedic training. Her second husband began sexually molesting her oldest child from her first marriage; she has since separated from him. She stated that the stress of the abuse of her child, combined with being alone, caused her to gain weight. Annie reported that her weight ballooned to 285 pounds. Annie stated that her existing stress was compounded by her self-image as being "fat." It was at this point in her life that she contacted an old friend from high school that she used to use drugs with. This high school friend offered Annie methamphetamine as a means to control her weight and feel better about herself. Annie was captured by a bounty hunter due to outstanding warrants for drugs. Upon her arrival at the jail, she was found to have both methamphetamine and marijuana in her possession. Annie's statement reiterates the conception of methamphetamine sales as something not out of the ordinary and an indication that drug selling is not something that she does regularly but only on occasion. The opportunity to sell methamphetamine therefore occurs within the context of the group each of these women was associated with. Incidental drug sales, according to these women, appear to be part of the lifestyle of methamphetamine-using groups.

The women's reports of methamphetamine sales repeatedly show a lack of focus on the selling behavior. The sales of methamphetamine can be characterized as an idea of accommodation. The women report that they do sell methamphetamine as long as they have an excess supply to part with and if they know the buyer. If a person does not have the excess supply of the drug, they will not sell any.

There are several benefits associated with dealing methamphetamine; however, many of the women did not sell methamphetamine for cash but traded the drug for other items of value as the following will demonstrate. Drug dealers are commonly referred to as people who exchange drugs for money. Marybeth demonstrates that methamphetamine dealing can involve cash transactions, but also includes trading other items of value for drugs. Marybeth (a 30-year-old white woman) is 5'11" tall with dark brown hair. She appeared very healthy. She was very evasive in answering questions posed to her. Even after some probing, she would rarely give more than a single word response. During the duration of the interview, she sat back in the chair with her arms crossed. She has three children who have always been in her custody, unless she is in prison or jail. The children were with Marybeth's mother at the time of the interview. Her latest arrest came during a traffic stop, and the police found a pipe used to smoke illicit drugs in her possession. Marybeth states, "I don't remember when exactly, but I always had some kind of pills. People knew it. So at some point I traded some downers for meth." She had obviously defined positively that drug trading (for money or other drugs) is acceptable. Further, the group she was associated with was aware that she often possessed pills.

The same benefits (i.e., easy money and obtaining material goods) others use as their rationale to sell methamphetamine are also valued by the women in this study. The next woman tells of a wide variety of valuable objects traded for drugs. In her case the material possessions were enticing benefits of methamphetamine sales. As Bea relates,

> Did I have all the nice things? Hell yeah! Shit I have a Boss Mustang, a beautiful dark blue [Ford] Explorer, I have a JBL and Kenwood stereo system, big screen TV, all that shit. I got it all from selling my crystal. Some of it I got traded for dope, I got a fuckin' computer in trade for an eight-ball [1/8 of an ounce], not that I know how to use the damn thing [laughs].

Bea (a 41-year-old Hispanic woman), a homemaker in a suburban community with a GED, is 5'3" tall with long blonde hair and is apparently healthy. While some people appear to be younger than their actual age, Bea was the opposite; she appeared to be much older than she actually was. Bea is married, and her husband was also in the jail for unrelated charges. She has no children but would have liked to have had some. Bea has been a methamphetamine user since the 1970s. She was very willing to discuss every aspect of her involvement with methamphetamine. At times, her explanations sounded almost canned, as if she had been telling people about her experiences for years. She wanted to help with the research so much she was about to provide names, phone numbers, and addresses of active methamphetamine cooks—but then thought better and did not. Bea was arrested for possession of methamphetamine during the course of a traffic stop. Bea's statement reflects her desire to possess high-quality material goods and she used methamphetamine dealing (both trading for items and sales for cash) as a means to reach this goal. Once again, the drug has become the currency and an economic pathway is evident.

This is not to say that these women did not sell methamphetamine in the usual sense of the term. Bea's experience provides a link between trading methamphetamine and selling it for cash. However the sales interaction is interesting to examine. Bea relates how she would deal methamphetamine,

> … it's like not a big deal. You want some? Stop by. We'll do a line, party for a while and I'll sell you some. I never done it for money, but the cash is nice. I never had to sell to keep the lights on or buy food, no, never. But after a while I got a decent stack of cash. So many people want dope, you can't help but make money.

Bea states that potential methamphetamine buyers would first "party" with her for a while (using drugs) indicating a social aspect to the methamphetamine sales interaction where the buyer enters (or re-enters) Bea's group. Additionally, by sharing her drugs with the potential buyer, two things are accomplished. First, the buyer can obtain a "taste" of the product he/she will be buying. This allows the buyer to determine the quality of the methamphetamine. Second, the buyer is introduced to the norms of Bea's methamphetamine related group. The buyer may be taught how Bea likes to conduct an exchange, or what norm of drug use is used (i.e., smoking versus snorting or intravenously).

Bea's explanation of methamphetamine sales differs from our knowledge of the sale of other drugs. For example, the sale of crack cocaine and powder cocaine is often driven by the money that can be made. In the case of methamphetamine, economic gain is almost an afterthought, a bonus to the methamphetamine dealer (who might also be a methamphetamine producer). In many cases, due to the bartering of methamphetamine for other goods and services, methamphetamine can be considered a form of currency itself. Under these circumstances, money would only be useful for interactions with the dominant society (e.g., the power company, grocery stores, etc.). Bea also intimates how a user might be lured into a sale by the free use of the drug, which performs three functions. First, it initiates the user into the norms of that particular drug's use and the communal sharing aspect. Secondly, when high a user might be less able to determine if the amount purchased is correct, which can provide the unscrupulous dealer an easy means to exploit more money from an unknowing neophyte. For example, the user might pay for a gram, but only receive three-fourths of a gram or the dealer might simply raise the price. Third, if the user is new to the drug scene, the free drugs might bring him/her in more deeply into the group, thus assuring the dealer of a new and/or repeat client.

Tracy (a 38-year-old white woman) is 5'4" tall, blonde, has been divorced several times and has two children (both are now adults). Her appearance is almost skeletal, dirty and unkempt. Several of her front teeth are missing. Tracy was also very upbeat and talkative, even though she stated that she was facing up to 20 years in prison if convicted. She has been in and out of jail many times, so many that she could not provide a number. Her use of drugs began at an early age. She stated that as a child she would "rock" cocaine for her mother to smoke because her mother would often have hand tremors and could not do it herself. Her most recent arrest was due to her attempt to help a friend from jail. Tracy offered her friend a place to live; the two had stopped using drugs but once together they began to use again. Her friend was arrested and told the police that Tracy had methamphetamine in her house, and Tracy was then arrested. Tracy also stated that she made money from methamphetamine sales, but that she did not try to, "It just happens." She expanded on this by stating, "Someone stops by, you sell a gram or two. Next day somebody else, another gram or two. So in two days you make like $400." Tracy's statements reveal that she made money from methamphetamine sales, but that it was largely unintended. Tracy's sales were the result of a network of associates who came to her group to buy and potentially use methamphetamine. Additionally, norms of behavior are conformed to, for example, quantities to buy. Notice that Tracy did not mention people trying to buy a single hit of methamphetamine, or one and a half grams. The buyers conformed to the standard weights used in her group.

Selling methamphetamine is a common occurrence among the women in this study; however, these women characterize the behavior of selling in two different ways. First, drug dealing, as it is commonly understood, exchanges drugs for cash. The second way that women characterize drug-selling behavior is as a medium for exchange. These women have learned that the drug has a value. In these cases, drugs are exchanged for material goods.

These women have been taught that selling to strangers poses a risk to the woman and the group. Those women who do take part in methamphetamine sales, either admittedly or technically, say they will only sell when they have an excess supply. These women will not endanger their own supply of the drug to satisfy another person. This amounts to methamphetamine sales as secondary to possession of the drug. These women noted that selling the drug was a "perk" of being involved in the lifestyle of methamphetamine users. Selling the drug was not the focus, nor the goal of these women's involvement with the drug. However, several women (especially Bea) noted the array of material goods they were able to obtain from selling and trading methamphetamine. Lastly, methamphetamine sales are unlike the sales of crack cocaine and other drugs that are regularly sold to strangers (e.g., on street corners).

The following section focuses on one form of the trade in methamphetamine. It has been noted above that sharing is used within methamphetamine-related groups. Integral to the idea of sharing is for all parties involved to share communally. The communal aspect of methamphetamine use and distribution can be termed reciprocity.

## *Reciprocity*

This sharing of one's drugs with others in the group carries the expectation that the behavior will be reciprocated. Bea's statement regarding how she sold methamphetamine refers to a "party" where she readily shares her supply of the drug. In this subculture it would be expected that other partygoers would share their supply as well, regardless of the drug possessed. The sharing behavior reaffirms the norm of reciprocity that surrounds methamphetamine using groups. Each time a person shares her/his supply of drugs the norm is reinforced. Within the methamphetamine using group the drug is often offered free of charge to group members with the expectation that they will be afforded the same treatment when they are a visitor in another member's home.

Still, dealing methamphetamine does have its benefits, most notably money and valued goods. Additionally, the dealer of methamphetamine (like any drug) will be able to maintain a supply of the drug for their own personal consumption. Closely linked with the idea of maintaining a personal supply is the norm of reciprocity. Even if the dealer is not able to maintain a personal supply she/he will be associated with other people who may have excess methamphetamine (and possibly other drugs) to sell. Further, the accumulation of material goods has long been recognized an American cultural goal as well as a sign of success (Messner & Rosenfeld, 2001).

One additional item of value that is often traded for drugs is the human body in the form of sexual relations. We are very familiar with the phenomena of crack cocaine addicts trading sex for drugs. The following section explores the possibility of women trading sex for methamphetamine.

## Sex for Drugs

It is important to note that none of the women in this study reported that they traded sex for drugs. However several of the women did report being asked to perform sexual acts in exchange for drugs. Every woman stated that they rejected these proposals.

Several women noted the connection between sex work and methamphetamine transactions. Sidetrack (a 36-year-old white woman) is 5'6" tall with brown hair with blonde streaks. She appears older than her years. She is currently homeless and works as a prostitute at a truck stop along the interstate. She has an affable personality and is very willing to discuss her life and her experience with methamphetamine. During the interview, the jail's Bible discussion group begins their meeting across the hall; this minor distraction causes Sidetrack to lose her train of thought and constantly begin talking about being a "good Samaritan" and "returning to Jesus." It takes a lot of effort to maintain her focus on the interview. As she said, "That's why they call me Sidetrack!" She was arrested for prostitution, and the arresting officer found a pipe used to smoke various drugs in her possession. Sidetrack's entrance into methamphetamine use occurred at a truck stop while was engaged in sex work. She was asked by a "John" to find methamphetamine for him. She was able to get the drug for her client, yet she considered it "facilitating" her work. She explained that the client would seek her out if she could offer more services than only sex. Interestingly, Sidetrack's facilitating behavior can be viewed as helping her clients, or perhaps even caring for her clients.

Dealing methamphetamine has very gendered behaviors associated with it. The power that dealers have over users is reported to be used by males to coerce women to trade sex for drugs. This power differential is mitigated when women are able to eliminate the dealer and produce for their own consumption. This fact is supported by the women's rationale not to sell because producing methamphetamine is so simple.

In any discussion of illicit drug dealing we must note the key element of power differentials. The dealer clearly has power over the user. This becomes especially clear when we add drug dependence and addiction to the interaction. As we consider this power relationship and add gender as a contributing factor, we quickly see the establishment of the social construction of gender in a patriarchal system. The women were quick to report that dealers wanted to trade drugs for sex. This behavior would reinforce the male's sense of their own masculinity. Further, this behavior reaffirms the idea of compulsory heterosexuality. Women who choose a pathway into deviance that includes dealing with illicit drug dealers must defer to such behaviors, purchase the desired amount, or begin to produce their own methamphetamine.

## Gendered Pathways

The four pathways identified as central to understanding the context from which women take part in the distribution of methamphetamine are considered individually. While gendered pathways are central to this study, aspects of stigma, strain, and differential association are apparent. The additional theoretical links are not developed in this study, but they may provide for future research integrating the theoretical positions.

The general pathway can be understood as gendered in so far as women report the role that gender plays in their own involvement with methamphetamine sales. The following theoretical linkages are divided among three pathways identified: the relationship pathway, the economic pathway, and the gendered norms pathway. Regarding the fourth gendered pathway, abuse, the women provided no reports of abuse being involved with their involvement with methamphetamine distribution. It should be noted that the lack of reports of abuse may be attributed to the differences in sex between the women and the interviewer. As Williams and Heikes (1993) discuss, an interviewer's gender can limit responses depending upon the topic under consideration. Therefore, it cannot be said that these women have not endured abuse, nor that they have, only that no abuse was reported in this study.

*The relationships pathway:* None of the women in this study made any intimation that they were coerced to sell the drug. Instead the opposite was true; sales were an added bonus that some women took advantage of. However, the evidence that was reported by the women in this study point to the centrality of being in a relationship affecting whether they took part in methamphetamine sales. As several authors have noted, women taking part in criminal behavior are less threatening than male counterparts (Denton & O'Malley, 1999; Miller, 1998; Fleisher, 1998). Using this expectation of non-violence (or manageable violence) people would feel at ease exchanging items for methamphetamine with these women. It is not expected that men would enjoy similar success as men are expected to be violent and request sex from women in exchange for drugs.

Through their involvement with a group of fellow methamphetamine users, and most probably dealers/traders, these women learned the norms of the group behavior. Further, Bea is, in effect, teaching the buyers the informal norms of her methamphetamine group in her home. Part of Bea's informal instruction is teaching the newcomer the techniques of buying the drug. Experienced buyers will have learned the technical details of determining quality and quantity when buying methamphetamine. Tracy takes her deviant education and couples it with the expectation of a female dealer as "safe." The arrival of methamphetamine-using associates at her home created the opportunity for her to take part in illicit drug sales. She did not seek out potential buyers for her drugs; they came to her.

*The economic pathway:* A cash-based economic pathway may not be useful in fully understanding women's involvement in methamphetamine. However, if we allow that methamphetamine can be substituted for cash, then the economic pathway into methamphetamine sales can be understood as a substitute for low-wage employment at the least. Lacking cash for various transactions, these women report following an economic pathway through methamphetamine sales where the drug is the currency.

The transition from methamphetamine user to trader (sales) for women appears to result in their gaining agency through following an economic pathway. I believe that men would find similar freedom following this same pathway through methamphetamine trading (sales), but the data do not include men and cannot confirm that conclusion. The key to understanding this relationship is minimizing money as the medium for exchange and maximizing methamphetamine as the currency for exchange. The exchange of methamphetamine for other products and/or services can serve the group as well as the individual. Further, the women's desire to sell only to known others is tied to the desire to minimize risk and maximize gain. The gain can be in the form of money or simply bargains traded for.

In both the relationship pathway and the economic pathway there have been references to the gendered nature of the interactions. The next section focuses on gender norms and how these norms effect women's involvement in methamphetamine distribution.

*The gender norms pathway:* The apparent revulsion that these women have with being labeled a "dealer" reflects their desire to maintain the facade of a construction of a "traditional woman." The desire to avoid the stigma of being labeled a dealer is also in line with the idea of gendered regimes where women are often tied to traditional gender roles (Connell, 1987). These women have identified dealers as "scummy"; such a label runs contrary to traditional conceptions of women and the behavioral roles they are "supposed" to take part in (Connell, 1987). This is especially true for white women who are often upheld as "pure" and representatives of the "cult of true womanhood" (Schur, 1984; Welter, 1966). Reactions to the constructed ideal for women have led these women to rationalize their own drug-selling behavior.

These women avoid the stigma of "scummy" dealer by trading the drug and helping friends and known others when they need drugs. Such a rationalization fits neatly with a traditional conception of a woman's role; in effect these women are taking on some characteristics of motherhood (e.g., care-giving). It is only through a rationalization process that a "mother figure" could provide help through the supply of illicit drugs.

# Limitations

The two clearest limitations of this study regard the issue of abuse the women endured (if any), and the generalizability of the findings. Past or present abuse is a recurring theme in much of the literature surrounding women involved with criminal behavior. The present study was not able to uncover evidence of abuse suffered by the women interviewed. Future researchers may be able to shed greater light on the effects of abuse on female methamphetamine dealers. The second limitation of this study is the generalizability of the findings. This study focused on women in two states. It is hoped that future studies can add to these findings and expand our understanding of women involved with drug dealing on the larger social scene, and especially women who trade in methamphetamine.

# Conclusions

Based upon the four themes reported by the women in this study, there are clear connections with the gendered pathways into and through methamphetamine distribution. While this study was unable to uncover any evidence of abuse or sex-for-drugs linked with the women's reports of their own drug sales, it has exposed several unique characteristics of women's involvement with methamphetamine distribution.

The women report that they were concerned about being labeled as a "dealer" which connected with the traditional construction of gender and the gendered pathways of the relationships they were involved with and gender norms. While women have often been constructed as secondary players in the illegitimate economy, to take on the role of drug dealer complicates that construction. However, further research is needed to focus on behaviors that are part of the illegitimate economy yet are not "fully involved" as dealers but are consistently involved as facilitators and regular distributors of drugs.

However strong the label of "dealer" is for the women, economics appear to play an important role in their decision to take part in methamphetamine distribution. It should be made clear that economic gain is not a central rationale for taking part in the behavior. Instead, economic and material gains are byproducts of behavior that is akin to care-giving. By facilitating the use patterns of methamphetamine users, these women framed their sales as helping, perhaps even caring about fellow drug users. Through the course of their care-giving/facilitating behavior, the women were able to accumulate material goods and cash money. Through the economic gain, these women largely reproduced the traditional constructions of gender roles seen in the larger society.

The conclusions drawn from this study provide evidence that women's roles in methamphetamine transactions are broader than previously conceived. Additionally, as we continue to develop policy to limit the use, sales, and production of methamphetamine, we must understand that the actors taking part in these behaviors are not simply users seeking a steady supply for themselves. Indeed, women's involvement with methamphetamine transactions is multi-faceted involving the relationships they are in, the economics of domestic life, and the structure of American constructions of gender.

# References


Adler, P.A. (1985). *Wheeling and dealing: An Ethnography of an upper-level dealing and smuggling community.* New York: Columbia University Press.

Belknap, J. (2001). *The invisible woman: Gender, crime, and justice* (2nd ed.). Belmont, CA: Wadsworth.

Blum, R.H., and Associates. (1972). *The dream sellers: perspectives on drug dealers.* San Francisco, CA: Jossey-Bass Inc.

Connell, R. W. (1987). *Gender and power: Society, the person and sexual politics.* Oxford, UK: Polity Press.

Daly, K. (1992). "Women's pathways to felony court: Feminist theories of law-breaking and problems of representation." *Southern California Review of Law and Women's Studies* (formerly *Review of Law and Women's Studies),* 2, 11–52.

Denton, B. & O'Malley, P. (1999). Gender, trust, and business: Women drug dealers in the illicit economy." *The British Journal of Criminology, 39,* 513–30.

Evan, R.D., Forsyth, C.J. & Gauthier, D.K. (2002). Gendered pathways into and experiences within crack cultures outside of the inner city. *Deviant Behavior, 23,* 483–510.

Dunlop, E., Johnson, B.D., & Manwar, A. (1994). A successful female crack dealer: case study of a deviant career." *Deviant Behavior, 15,* 1–25.

Fagan, J. 1995. Women's careers in drug use and drug selling. *Current Perspectives on Aging and the Life Cycle, 4,* 155–90.

______. 1994. "Women and drugs revisited: Female participation in the cocaine economy. *Journal of Drug Issues, 24(1),* 179–227.

Fleisher, M.S. (1998). *Dead end kids: Gang girls and the boys they know.* Madison, WI: University of Wisconsin Press.

Johnson, B.D., Goldstein, P.J., Preble, E., Schmeidler, J., Lipton, D.B., Spunt, B. & Miller, T. (1985). *Taking care of business: The economic lives of crime by heroin users.* Lexington, MA: Lexington Books.

Johnson, B.D., Hamid, A. & Morales, E. (1990). Emerging models of crack distribution. Pp. 9–68 in *Drugs and crime: A reader* (ed. T. Mieczkowski). Boston: Allyn-Bacon.

Lofland, J. & Lofland, L. (1984). *Guide to qualitative observation and analysis* (2nd ed.). Belmont, CA: Wadsworth.

Lofland, J., Snow, D.A., Anderson, L., & Lofland, L.H. (2006). *Analyzing social settings: A guide to qualitative observation and analysis* (4th ed.). Belmont, CA: Wadsworth.

Maher, L. (1997). *Sexed work: Gender, race, and resistance in a Brooklyn drug market*. New York: Oxford.

Maher, L. & Daly, K. (1996). Women in the street level drug economy: Continuity or change? *Criminology, 34(4)*, 465–91.

Messner, S.F. & Rosenfeld, R. (1997). *Crime and the American dream* (2nd ed.). Belmont, Ca: Wadsworth.

Mieczkowski, T. (1994). *The experiences of women who sell crack: some descriptive data from the Detroit Crack Ethnography Project. Journal of Drug Issues, 24*, 227–48.

Miller, J. (1998). Up it up: Gender and the accomplishment of street robbery. *Criminology, 36*, 37–65.

Morgan, P. & Joe, K.A. (1996). Citizens and outlaws: The Private Lives and Public Lifestyles of Women In the Illicit Drug Economy. *Journal of Drug Issues, 26(1)*, 125–43.

Preble, E & Casey, J.J., Jr. (1969). Taking care of business: The heroin user's life on the street. *International Journal of Addictions, 4*, 1–24.

Richie, B.E. (2000). Exploring the link between violence against women and women's involvement in illegal activity. Pp. 1–14 in *Research on women and girls in the justice system* (ed. J.E. Samuels). Washington D.C.: National Institute of Justice.

______. (1996). *Compelled to crime: The gender entrapment of battered black women*. New York: Routledge.

Schur, E.M. (1984). *Labeling women deviant: Gender, stigma, and social control*. New York: McGraw Hill.

Welter, B. (1966). The cult of true womanhood: 1820–1860. *American Quarterly, 18*, 151–74.

Williams, C.L. & Heikes, E.J. (1993). The importance of researcher's gender in the in-depth interview: Evidence from two case studies of male nurses. *Gender & Society, 7(2)*, 280–91.

Williams, T. (1992). *Crackhouse*. Reading, MA: Addison Wesley.

______. (1989). *Cocaine kids*. Reading, MA: Addison Wesley.

# Chapter 8

# Terrorism and the Female Suicide Bomber

*Vesna Markovic, Ph.D.*

Women have not generally been the focus of criminological research in offending, with a few exceptions (Renzetti, et al., 2003). This holds true for research on women's participation in unconventional warfare, including insurgencies, guerilla warfare, and terrorism. Traditional gender roles view women as nurturers, the gentler sex, thus making them much less susceptible to violence than men (Alvanou, 2006; Markovic, 2009). Women were labeled as only holding peripheral roles in terrorist organizations as opposed to actively participating in the terrorist acts. There is a tendency to use stereotypical explanations when women engage in acts such as political violence or other acts that are inherently male (Nacos, 2005). This stereotypical view makes it important to examine women's roles in violent terrorist organizations, particularly as suicide bombers. For the purpose of this chapter, a suicide bomber is a person who takes their own life during the commission of the terrorist act by using some form of explosive, which differs from a suicide attacker (Markovic, 2009). The following chapter will give a brief history of women's participation in terrorist organizations, a historical account of suicide terrorism, and an examination of the use of female kamikazes.

Although women are viewed as the gentler sex and having a lower propensity towards violence, there are examples throughout history of women participating in conventional warfare. An early example of this is A'ishah, a favored wife of Mohammed. In November 656 A.D., after the Prophet Mohammed's death, she led troops in the Battle of Jamal (Camel), also known as the battle of Basra (Wadud, 2002; Al-Oraimi, 2008). In the 1400s, Joan of Arc led French troops in battle during the Hundred Years' War. Catherine II of Russia, also known as Catherine the Great, led the Russians in war against the Ottoman Turks in the 1700s. More recently, women in the Indian National Army (INA) fought against the British in the 1940s (Cunningham, 2003). A more extreme example occurred in Rwanda during the 1990s. Pauline Nyiramasuhuko, the

Minister for the Family and Women's Development, was arrested in 1997 in Nairobi and charged in the International Criminal Tribunal (ICT) for Rwanda with crimes against humanity, including rape and genocide (Ness, 2007). In June 2011, Nyiramasuhuko and her son received life sentences from the ICT for Rwanda located in Arusha, Tanzania (Simons, 2011).

# Women and Terrorism

Over the years, women have been involved in terrorist organizations to varying degrees. In some cases, they have only been involved in peripheral roles. There are, however, many examples that show women taking a lead role in various terrorist groups as well as participating in violent actions. Women have participated within nationalist conflicts in many areas including Algeria, Palestine, Lebanon, and Turkey. Muslim women participating in religiously motivated violence is not a new phenomenon either, although this is a more recent phenomenon. Such participation by Muslim women began during the Iranian revolution and was amplified in Chechnya and Palestine (Cunningham, 2008). In Dhaka, for example, an estimated 50,000 females, some who studied in Madrassas, were linked to Islamic extremist organizations, helping them carry messages, explosives and weapons, and in some cases, sabotage (Ahmed, 2007).

Early examples of women's involvement in terrorist groups can be seen in the late nineteenth century. Women have taken on different roles including leadership roles in various conflicts. Vera Nikolayevna Figner, who had become a leader of the revolutionary group *Narodnaya Volya* (People's Will), often times participated in committing violent acts (Crenshaw, 1981), including involvement in the planning of Czar Alexander II assassination in 1881. Sophia Perovskaya, another female member of the group, also participated in the planning of the assassination. These are just some of the early examples of women's participation in carrying out violent terrorist attacks.

Between 1954 and 1962, the Front de Libération Nationale (FLN), an Algerian resistance movement, fought for liberation from French colonialists by employing terrorist tactics. Terrorism was used as a tool in obtaining public support (Crenshaw, 1981). The FLN saw the need to use women in this struggle. In this case, women were not part of the command structure, but were generally mobilized in support roles which fit the traditional gender roles in the society (Gonzalez-Perez, 2008). Official records estimated that there were 205 women active in the FLN, with only 2 percent of these women participating as active combatants (Gonzalez-Perez, 2008). Although women were not used extensively, the late 1960s and 70s would mark the turning point in women's participation in various groups.

In the 1960s women began to take more participatory roles in terrorist organizations. In some cases the women held prominent positions and leadership roles within the groups. Other women took a more active role in carrying out terrorist actions, such as Randa Nablusi and more notably Leila Khaled, a member of the Popular Front for the Liberation of Palestine (PFLP). Nablusi was convicted in 1969 for planting a bomb in a Jerusalem supermarket (Cunningham, 2003). On August 29, 1969, Leila Khaled and Salim Issawi, calling themselves the Che Guevara Commando Unit of the PFLP, hijacked a TWA flight from Rome, Italy, to Athens, Greece, forcing the flight to land in Damascus, Syria (Cronin, 2002). On September 6, 1970, members of PFLP hijacked four aircrafts, including an El Al flight from Amsterdam to New York, that was seized by Khaled and Patrick Arguello (PBS, 2006). The flight made an emergency landing in London where Arguello was shot and killed by a sky marshal, and Khaled was arrested but later released in a prisoner exchange (PBS, 2006).

In 1971, Fusako Shigenobu founded the Japanese Red Army (JRA) and was its leader until her arrest in November 2000 (Ness, 2005). One of the major attacks carried out by the JRA was the Lod Airport Massacre in Tel Aviv, Israel.[1] On May 30, 1972, three members of the JRA opened fire inside the airport, killing twenty-five civilians and injuring seventy-six (Sloan, 2006). The JRA acted as hired guns, even carrying out attacks against the Japanese, Canadian, and U.S. embassies in Jakarta, Indonesia; the U.S. embassy in Rome in 1987; and a U.S. Servicemen's club in Rome in 1988 (Sloan, 2006). Shigenobu was not the only female to help establish a terrorist organization. Ulreike Meinhof helped co-found the Baader-Meinhof Group in Germany, which eventually evolved into the Red Army Faction (*Rote Armee Fraktion*—RAF). The number of female members of RAF outnumbered their male counterparts (de Cataldo Neuberger & Valentini, 1996).

Various other terrorist organizations also had a large female presence in their membership. The Red Brigades (*Brigate Rosse*—BR), a left-wing terrorist group in Italy, also had a large number of female members. Susanna Ronconi, for example, entered the Red Brigades in 1974 after having been involved in the feminist movement in Italy for many years (Jamieson, 2000). She was believed to be a founder and leader of the Front Line (*La Prima Linea*), a Red Brigade ally, and was charged in connection with the Red Brigades kidnapping and murder of former Premier Aldo Moro in the late 1970s ("Italian Police," 1980). Among the various Italian groups, however, the Communists

---

1. The airport is now known as Ben Gurion.

Organized for the Liberation of the Proletariat (*Comunisti Organizzati per la Liberazione del Proletariato*—COPL) had the highest percentage of female members, as well as a strong presence of females in their command structure (de Cataldo Neuberger & Valentini, 1996).

During this period, other groups also had female contingents. Many women belonged to groups such as the Symbionese Liberation Army (SLA) and Weather Underground in the U.S., the Puerto Rican group Armed Forces of National Liberation (*Fuerzas Armadas de Liberación Nacional*—FALN), and in the Irish Republican Army (IRA) (Ness, 2005). Women also participate in the Basque Fatherland and Liberty (*Euskadi ta Askatasuna*—ETA) in Spain and numerous other leftist groups. Other groups, such as the *Farabundo Martí Front for National Liberation (FMLN)* and the Democratic Revolutionary Front (FDR) in El Salvador, often recruited females offering them the chance to improve their status (Gonzalez-Perez, 2008). The National Liberation Movement of Tupamaros in Uruguay also urged female involvement not only in peripheral roles, but as active participants as well (Gonzalez-Perez, 2008).

Many secular ethnic and separatist groups during the 1980s and '90s recruited female militants in large numbers (Ness, 2005). These groups include the Kurdistan Workers' Party (*Partiya Karkerên Kurdistan*—PKK) in Turkey, the Liberation Tigers of Tamil Eelam (LTTE) in Sri Lanka, the Shining Path (*Sendero Luminoso*—SL) in Peru, and the Revolutionary Armed Forces of Colombia (*Fuerzas Armadas Revolucionarias de Colombia*—FARC) (Markovic, 2009). Right wing groups, such as the Ku Klux Klan (KKK), Aryan Nation, and the World Church of the Creator (WCOC) in the U.S., as well as the single interest groups Animal Liberation Front (ALF) and the Earth Liberation Front (ELF), all have a female contingent (Cunningham, 2003). The levels of involvement by women vary from group to group from peripheral roles to, in some cases, leadership roles.

## *History of Suicide Terrorism*

Early examples of suicide terrorism date back to the first century. During the Roman occupation of Judea, Sicarii used short daggers called *sica* to kill those who they viewed as traitors (Burgess, 2003). When the Roman general Flavius took siege in Masada, the Sicarii committed suicide, rather than being captured (Zeitlin, 1965). The Zealots murdered Greeks and Romans, killing their targets in broad daylight, giving them little chance to escape their own death (Burgess, 2003), thus these attacks were considered to be suicide missions. In the 11th Century, the *Nizari Isma'ilis* used tactics similar to those of the Zealots and Sicarii. This group, led by Hasan ibn Sabbah, was a breakaway Muslim Shi'a sect that battled against Sunni Muslims and later Christians, during the Crusades (Burman, 1987). In the 18th century, extremists in various countries realized the usefulness of using suicide attackers as well.

## Modern Suicide Bombings

One of the first modern suicide attacks occurred during the Iranian Revolution. Mohammad Hossein Famideh, a 13-year-old Iranian, became a martyr by throwing himself in front of an Iraqi tank and detonating a grenade in 1980 (Baer, 2005). Later the following year, a suicide car bombing took place outside the Iraqi Embassy in Beirut on December 15, killing 24 and injuring over 500 and destroying the five story embassy, marking the beginning of the modern era of suicide bombings. It wasn't until 1983 that suicide bombings were carried out against U.S. interests abroad. In April 1983 the U.S. Embassy in Beirut was targeted, followed by the massive attacks against the U.S. Marine barracks and French Paratrooper barracks in October of that year, killing nearly 300 in the simultaneous suicide truck bombings. This large-scale attack brought worldwide attention to suicide bombings, and caused the U.S. and French to pull their troops out of Lebanon, proving that the tactic was useful to terrorist groups.

## The Advent of the Female Suicide Bomber

Contrary to popular reporting about the advent of this new tactic, female suicide bombers are not a new concept. The first female suicide bomber was used less than four years after the first modern suicide bombing which took place in Lebanon. The Syrian Socialist Nationalist Party (SSNP/PPS) dispatched Sana'a Mehaidli, a seventeen-year-old girl, on April 9, 1985. She drove a Peugeot into an Israeli military convoy in Badr al Shouf, Lebanon, killing two Israeli soldiers. According to a video will she left behind, her motivation was simple: she was carrying out the attack as a duty to her people (Moore, 1985). The Syrian PPS used females in five of their twelve suicide bombing attacks (Schweitzer, 2000). Since then, several groups have adapted these female kamikazes as part of their arsenal, and the numbers continue to grow.

## Personal Motivations

There are various personal reasons why women carry out suicide bombings; however, it is often times difficult to gain insight on the motivations for these attacks. Although psychological disorders are not a likely motivator, media accounts on the reasons may vary, as can the personal accounts given by friends and family (Patkin, 2004). Even when interviewing a failed female bomber, the motivations given may change from one interview or interrogation to the next. Rania Ibrahim, a 15-year-old would-be suicide bomber arrested in Iraq on August 24, 2008, gave varying accounts as to why she was driven to carrying out the attack. She initially told police that she was not aware she was carrying a suicide bomb and that her mother gave her a vest to help with back pain (A.H. Hashimi, Iraqi police, personal communication, April 28, 2010). In interviews with McClatchy, she said she was given juice which made her dizzy (Fadel, 2008). She later changed her story again telling police that she knew it was an explosive, and that her father and husband were both affiliated with Al Qaeda in Iraq. She told officers that her husband had told her that she would go to paradise and not to remarry there, but to wait for him instead (A.H. Hashimi, Iraqi police, personal communication, April 28, 2010).

Because women are viewed as the gentler sex, and not particularly violence-prone, reasons for carrying out attacks can become stereotyped. Berko et. al. (2010) conducted research on Palestinian women and found that the suicide bombers were not pursuing "women's liberation" or rebelling against gender oppression. Interviews with Palestinian would-be suicide bombers reveals that the women were motivated by nationalism, religion, and revenge as a main reason, rather than the view that they were "damaged goods," although in some cases that also was a contributing factor (Schweitzer, 2008). Revenge is a factor which is also seen in Chechnya, where many of the female suicide bombers had lost their fathers and/or brothers in fighting, hence the term "black widows," which is used to describe them. One of the female suicide bombers in the Dubrovka Theater siege, which occurred in Moscow in October 2002, shared her thoughts in a letter stating that with the death of her brother, she did not have much reason to live either (Nivat, 2008). In other cases, women (and girls) are simply exploited.

Kimhi and Even's (2003) typology of suicide bombers include the *religious fanatic*, the *nationalist fanatic*, the *avenger*, and the *exploited*. Although this research focused on Palestinian suicide bombers, the typologies also apply to other regions of the world as well. The religious fanatic is deeply religious and has received some type of indoctrination. This can be witnessed in the video wills left behind by suicide bombers, who oftentimes give religious reasons for carrying out their attack. The nationalist fanatic is involved attempting to liberate their land. Sana'a Mehaidli, the first female suicide bomber, stated in her video will that she was carrying out the attack as a duty to her people (Moore, 1985). The avenger's prime motivation is revenge. For example, Chechen Black Widows are driven by revenge because of their sense of loss.

The exploited include those with weak personalities, or children, who are easily swayed or pressured into carrying out an attack. For example, Leyla Kaplan, a female suicide bomber for the PKK in Turkey, witnessed Turkan Adiyaman get executed for declining to carry out a suicide bombing (Ergil, 2000). A more recent example is the use of child suicide bombers. On January 5, 2014, a 10-year-old girl named Spozhmay was detained in Helmand Province. She stated her brother and his friend forced her to wear a suicide vest and detonate it at a checkpoint ("Afghan Police Probe," 2014). Girls as young as ten have also been used as suicide bombers in Nigeria. One 13-year-old girl in Nigeria stated that she was forced to become a suicide bomber, but she escaped. Her father was a Boko Haram member and allegedly asked her if she wanted to "go to Heaven." When she responded, she was told the only way to achieve that was to carry out the suicide bombing, and if she attempted to run they were going to kill her (Abubakr & Almasy, 2015).

Conflicts at the local level play a significant role in motivating suicide bombers. Each of these local conflicts must be viewed independently due to the fact that each region has its own historical context that provided the groundwork for conflict (Ali, 2006). From the nationalist/separatist disputes to the conflict areas, numerous studies have come up with motivational factors in the decision of women to participate in suicide bombings. It is important to note that an organization cannot create a person's willingness to die, but can identify women who are more predisposed to sacrificing their life (Merari, 2004). Rosendorff and Sandler state that the suicide bomber will believe that "the expected utility of their sacrificial act" will exceed their "expected utility of living" (2010, p. 8). Regardless of the personal motivation, most bombers are not viewed as insane, or having severe psychological disorders (Sprinzak, 2000; Gunawardena, 2006).

The Liberation Tigers of Tamil Eelam (LTTE), a nationalist/separatist group, have a suicide squad called the Black Tigers. As with other organizations, there is no evidence that points to psychological disorders in those that carry out suicide bombings. There is, however, evidence to suggest that "societal and peer pressure, social stigma by the dishonor brought about by the refusal to become one, the social conditioning of Tamil society, and even economic reasons" were found to be motivating factors in volunteering to become a suicide bomber (Gunawardena, 2006, p. 82). In Iraq, there was a large increase in female suicide bombers between 2007 and 2008, many of them coming from Baquba, the capital of Diyala Province. The women came from isolated communities which had a large presence of extremists, some lost their brothers and fathers in the war, and, for the most part, were unable to make decisions about their own lives (Rubin, 2009).

## *Organizational Motivations*

Whatever the personal motivations of female suicide bombers, it is extremely rare that a female or male would carry out an attack of his or her own accord. Groups will also use ideology, religion, and other discourse to justify their use of using suicide bombings (Hafez, 2007). Evidence has shown that "gender clichés influence the tactical considerations and decisions of terrorist groups and the behavior of female terrorists" (Nacos, 2005, p. 436). Groups dictate the use of this tactic and find willing participants to carry out these attacks.[2] Therefore, just like any other form of terrorism, using suicide bombings is a way to achieve a groups stated goals when they feel that other tactics are not effective (Pedahzur, 2005). When security measures targeting male suicide bombers became successful, groups in Iraq turned to women, as was the case in Israel. A female dressed in the traditional abaya would not only draw less attention from security forces, but would also have the ability to conceal a large amount of explosives.

Terrorist organizations use suicide bombers because they cause high casualties for a relatively low cost, among other reasons. With increased scrutiny of males by security forces, female bombers became an attractive alternative. Female suicide bombers have been used as part of terrorist campaigns all over the world. In Israel, for example, women aroused less suspicion and were able to circumvent security measures implemented to target their male suicide bomber counterparts. Some operatives would feign pregnancy to avoid detection. In Turkey several female suicide bombers pretended to be pregnant, giving them the opportunity to conceal a large amount of explosives and arouse very little suspicion. In Sri Lanka, a female suicide bomber was able to gain entry to a secure military facility by posing as the wife of a ranking military officer. Although she was not successful in carrying out the attack, it showed the usefulness of the female suicide bomber in thwarting security measures.

Traditionally, attacks by females also garnered more media attention, therefore allowing groups to receive worldwide attention for their cause. Muriel Degauque, a Belgian convert to Islam, was on the cover of Time Magazine after carrying out an attack in Iraq in November, 2005, becoming the first Western woman to become a suicide bomber. Another example was the suicide bombing carried out by on a public bus in Volgograd, Russia, on October 21, 2013, killing 6 and wounding 33. The bomber, identified at 30-year-old Naida Asiyalova, carried out the suicide bombing with a suicide belt believed to be constructed by her husband, and containing approximately 500–600 grams of TNT equivalent (Bacchi, 2013). The attack occurred just three and a half months before the start of the Winter Olympics in Sochi, Russia. Video of the

---

2. There has been discussion on the willingness of suicide bombers. Those bombers that are exploited are not considered willing participants, but rather forced into the act.

attack, captured by a motorist travelling behind the bus, was broadcast all around the world.

These attacks also serve as a recruitment tool for the groups. After Wafa Idris became the first Palestinian female suicide bomber,[3] a large number of other Palestinian females followed. Women's active participation can also increase the number of male recruits because it can serve to shame them into participating (Van Knop, 2007). Women who have lost family members in conflicts can also be recruited as suicide bombers. The husband of Dzhennet Abdurrakhmanova, one of the two female suicide bombers in the Moscow subway system in March 2010, was killed in a shootout with Dagestan police on December 31, 2009 (Bates, 2010). These strategic benefits will continue to inspire terrorist groups to continue using female's in suicide bombing campaigns.

One particularly troubling trend is the use of the female suicide bomber by the Nigerian terrorist group Boko Haram. The group was formed in 2002 but did not carry out their first suicide bombing until June 16, 2011, when a male suicide bomber detonated a car bomb targeting Nigerian Police Headquarters in Abuja, Nigeria, killing a policeman. In November 2013, the U.S. Department of State designated Boko Haram as a foreign terrorist organization. They further gained international notoriety in mid-April 2014, when the group kidnapped over 200 school girls from Chibok, Nigeria, in Borno State. Less than two months after the kidnappings, the female suicide bomber appeared in the terrorism landscape in Nigeria. On June 8, 2014, a female bomber carried out a suicide bombing at a military checkpoint in Gombe, Nigeria, killing one soldier and wounding another. In the year that followed this first female suicide bombing, there were 29 other incidents with a total of 35 additional female bombers. In some cases the bombers are as young as 10 years old. Leading up to the election in Nigeria in February 2015, there were more female suicide bombers in that month than ever before, and all occurred in Nigeria.

# Method of Analysis

In order to properly examine female suicide bombers, it is important to look back historically to see patterns and trends in the use of these female

---

3. Some believe that Idris was not a suicide bomber, and was only supposed to carry the bombs into the restaurant and leave them, but got caught in the revolving door, causing the explosives to detonate.

kamikazes. This will help shed light on the use of female bombers over time. Previous research by this author has been conducted on suicide bombings carried out by both males and females worldwide from 1981–2014, capturing the majority of suicide bombings that were carried out during that time period. The incidents were collected using the open-source data collection methodology employed by the Institute for the Study of Violent Groups (ISVG);[4] this methodology uses foreign and domestic news sources, wire reports, books, journal articles, publicly available government reports, and any other reports that are classified as open source or public information (Markovic, 2009).

The dataset was expanded to include the first half of 2015 for female suicide bombers. The benefit of this data collection methodology is the ability to triangulate the data to collect the most accurate information on the bombings themselves, and particularly casualty counts (Markovic, 2009). This dataset includes all suicide bombings carried out by females, and recorded in open sources between the April 1985 and June 12, 2015. The definition of the suicide bombing is also more inclusive, and will therefore include suicide bombings perpetrated not only against non-combatants, but also targeting military and police personnel. The following section will provide descriptive statistics on female suicide bombers between 1985 and 2015.

Figure 8.1 on the following page shows female suicide bombings over time, overlaid with a linear trend line. The use of female suicide bombers fluctuates over time, instead of a steady increase. Between the first observed female suicide bombing, carried out in Lebanon in 1985, and 2001, female bombers comprised 20% of the overall number of suicide bombers in the dataset. Although the total number of female suicide bombers has increased in number, it has not increased at the same pace as male bombers. Between 2002 and 2015 female bombers only comprised less than 4% of the total number of suicide bombers worldwide.

Although the use of suicide bombers has increased at a very high rate, the Figure 8.1 shows the cyclical nature of the use of female suicide bombers. In months 315 (February, 2008) and 320 (July, 2008), there were a total of 5 female suicide bombers for the month, these representing the months in which there were the largest total number of female suicide bombers, until February 2015. As mentioned previously, there were a series of suicide bombings in Nigeria leading up to the presidential elections in that country. In that month (399) there were 7 female suicide bombers, the most in one month ever recorded. Compared to male suicide bombers, this is a very minor fraction of

------

4. ISVG is a research institute at the University of New Haven collecting events on terrorism worldwide. For more information, visit www.isvg.org.

Figure 8.1. Monthly suicide bombing carried out by females,
1985–June 10, 2015.

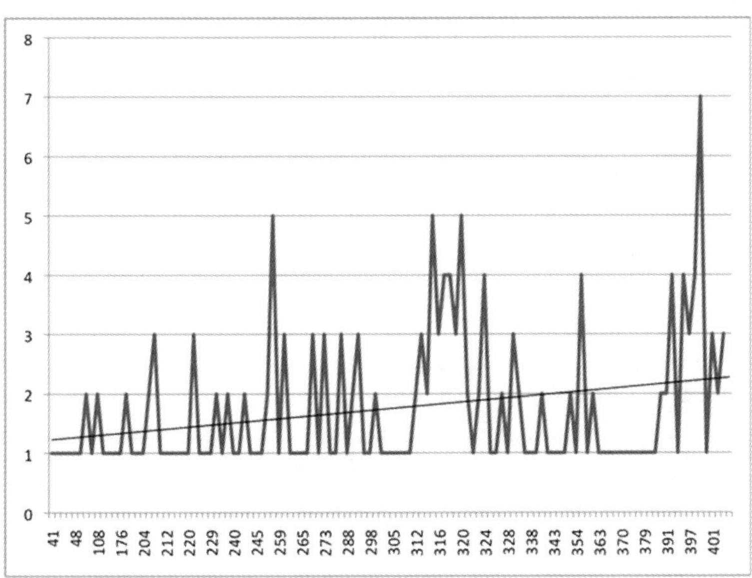

the total. In March 2007, for example, there were no female suicide bombers, while the total number of male bombers for that month totaled 62.

Sixteen countries have experienced at least one attack by a female suicide bomber. Compare that to the 47 countries that have experienced attacks by male suicide bombers. Of the 16 countries that have had female suicide bombers, the country that has experienced the greatest number is Iraq, although the female suicide bomber has all but disappeared from Iraq. They also have the most overall suicide bombings in general, with nearly 2,000 total suicide bombings carried out. Although Iraq, Afghanistan, and Pakistan comprise the majority of all suicide bombings, there are very few female suicide bombers in Afghanistan. Table 8.1 shows the top six countries by total number of suicide bombings carried out by females and males.

When focusing on the six countries with the largest number of overall female suicide bombers, the two deadliest are Iraq and Russia. Until 2014, Nigeria did not even make the list. The number of people killed per attack carried out by female suicide bombers are as follows: Iraq averages nearly 16.5 deaths per female bomber; Russia just under 14.5 deaths; Nigeria with almost 10 deaths; Sri Lanka with nearly 11 deaths; Pakistan almost 10 deaths; Israel with 4 deaths; and Turkey with nearly 2.6 deaths per female suicide bomber. This shows the capability of the female suicide bomber to inflict mass casualties.

**Table 8.1. Top six countries by number of male and
female bombers, 1981–2014.**

|  | Top 6 Countries by Male Suicide Bombers | Top 6 Countries by Female Suicide Bombers |
|---|---|---|
| 1. | Iraq | Iraq |
| 2. | Afghanistan | Russia |
| 3. | Pakistan | Nigeria |
| 4. | Israel | Sri Lanka |
| 5. | Sri Lanka | Turkey |
| 6. | Russia | Israel / Pakistan |

The suicide bomber has been called a "smart bomb" because of the ability of the bomber to change the time and place of detonation at any time. Suicide bombings are also highly effective because of the number of deaths they cause, making them the most lethal form of terrorism. One of the most lethal modern suicide bombings was simultaneous suicide truck bombings carried out in Qahtaniya, Iraq, targeting Yazidi tribes in August 2007. The bombings killed nearly 500 and wounded over 1,500. Although many of the most lethal suicide bombings were carried out by male bombers, the female bombers have also had their share of major casualties. Figure 8.2 on the next page shows the number of people killed by female suicide bombers per month (solid line) and the average number killed per month (dashed line). Some months the lines completely overlap because there was only one suicide bombing.

The month with the largest number of people killed by female suicide bombers is month 315 (February, 2008). In that month, there were two concurrent female suicide bombers in Iraq, detonating in a pet store and a bird market for a total of nearly 100 deaths. The other deadliest months include 273 (August, 2004), 293 (April, 2006), and 329 (April, 2009). In April 2006 and 2009, the major attacks targeted mosques in Iraq both with under 100 deaths. In August of 2004, two female suicide bombers targeting Russian Airlines downed two commercial airliners, killing all those aboard: 44 on the Siberia Air flight, and 46 on the Volga Avia Express flight.

**Figure 8.2. Number of casualties per month with the average number of casualties, 1985–2013.**

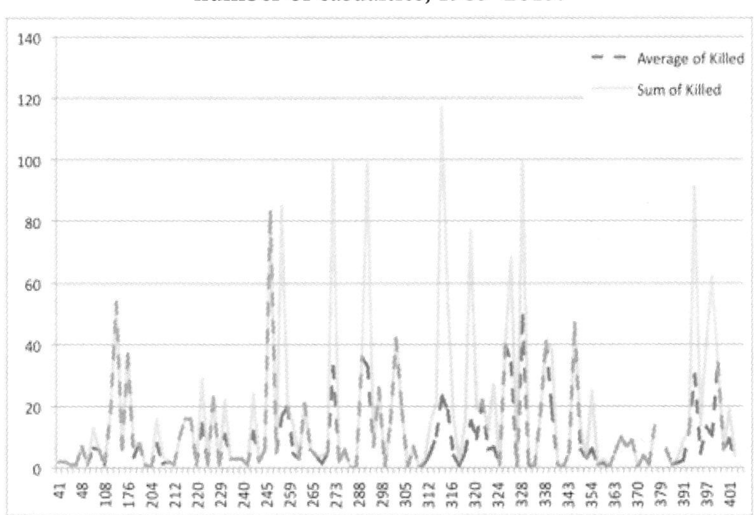


# Conclusion

Women have participated in armed conflict and terrorism throughout history. The female suicide bomber is no exception. Based on the number of female suicide bombers, it does not lend itself to statistical analysis; however, more research needs to be conducted on this phenomenon. Regardless of why these women carry out the attacks, it seems to be dictated by terrorist organizations that employ the tactic. Why terrorist groups use female suicide bombers also needs to be researched in depth. Historically, terrorist groups have adapted to changes by security forces in order to maintain their longevity (Markovic, 2009). By examining tactical aspects as to why and how groups employ suicide bombers, particularly females, governments can be better equipped to fight this phenomenon.

Another area to focus on is why some groups have not employed the female suicide bomber. On June 21, 2010, a female suicide bomber wearing a burqa detonated a suicide vest at a checkpoint in Kunar Province, Afghanistan killing two U.S. soldiers and wounding a dozen others (Abi-Habib and Zahori, 2010). The Taliban claimed responsibility for the attack. In Afghanistan there have been several instances in which males wore a burqa, but to date only five confirmed case of a successful attack involving a female bomber.[5] There are rela-

---

5. There were several attacks thought to be female but after investigation it was found that they were males wearing burqas.

tively few occurrences of female suicide bombers in Pakistan as well, especially compared to groups such as the Syrian PPS, Kurdish PKK, Sri Lankan Tamil Tigers, and Chechen Black Widows, and more recently Boko Haram, who have used female suicide bombers regularly. It is equally important to research the dynamics and context of conflict to explain why some groups are not employing female suicide bombers.

Although the number of female suicide bombers has increased, their percentage of overall attacks has decreased. Between 1985 and 2001, women accounted for approximately twenty percent of the suicide bombings carried out, as compared with the period between 2002 and 2015, during which women accounted for only about four percent of the thousands of total suicide bombings (Markovic, 2009). The trend in the use of female suicide bombers also appears cyclical in nature. Also, despite various reports over the past several years of female suicide squads ready to be deployed, groups use female suicide bombers when necessary. The media attention given to the female kamikazes and their ability to avoid suspicion and circumvent security will lead to their continued use; however, their use will probably continue to follow the same cyclical pattern. It is clear that as long as terrorist organizations employ the tactic of suicide bombings, the threat from female suicide bombers will remain.

# References


Abi-Habib, M. and Zahori, H. (2010, June 22). Two U.S. soldiers killed in Afghan suicide bombing. *The Wall Street Journal.*

Abubakr, A. and Almasy, S. (2015, January 4). Girl, 13: Boko Haram tried to force me to become a suicide bomber. *CNN.* Retrieved from: http://www.cnn.com/2014/12/26/world/africa/nigeria-teenage-girl-suicide-bombing/.

Afghan police probe case of 'suicide attack' girl. (2014, January 10). *Radio Free Europe Radio Liberty (RFE/RL).*

Ahmed, S. (2007, April 7). More than 50,000 women workers of militant organizations active. *Dainik Kortowa Bangladesh.* Retrieved April 7, 2007 from FBIS.

Ali, F. (2006). Ready to detonate: The diverse profiles of female suicide bombers. National Memorial Institute for the Prevention of Terrorism (Eds.), *The MIPT Terrorism Annual.* November 2006, 49–58.

Alvanou, M. (2006). Criminology and the study of female suicide terrorism. In Y. Schweitzer (Eds.), *Female suicide bombers: Dying for equality?* (pp. 91–106). Tel Aviv: Jaffee Center for Strategic Studies.

Al-Oraimi, S.Z. (2008). Defying the prohibited arena: Women in the UAE military. In H. Carreiras and G. Kümmel (Eds), *Women in the military and armed conflict*. VS Verlag für Sozialwissenschaften.

Bacchi, U. (2013, October 22). 'Russia's White Widow': Volgograd bus suicide bomber Naida Asiyalova was 'terminally ill Jihadist." *International Business Times*.

Baer, R. (Writer), Batty, D. (Director, & Toolis, K. (Writer/Director). (2005). *The cult of the suicide bomber* [Documentary]. United Kingdom: Disinformation.

Bates, T. (2010, April 2). Moscow suicide bomber was widowed teen bride. *AOL News*. Retrieved from http://www.aolnews.com/world/article/moscow-suicide-bomber-was-widowed-teen-bride/19424186.

Berko, A., Erez, E. & Globokar, J.L. (2010). Gender, crime and terrorism: The case of Arab/Palestinian women in Israel. *British Journal of Criminology*, April 8, 2010.

Burgess, M. (2003). A brief history of terrorism. *Center for Defense Information*. Retrieved July 2, 2003 from http://www.cdi.org.

Burman, E. (1987). *The Assassins: Holy killers of Islam*. Wellingborough: Borgo Press.

Crenshaw, M. (1981). The causes of terrorism. *Comparative Politics*, *13*(4), pp. 379–399.

Cronin, A.K. (2003). Behind the curve: Globalization and international terrorism. *International Security*, *27*(3), 30–58.

Cunningham, K.J. (2003). Cross-regional trends in female terrorism. *Studies in Conflict and Terrorism*, *26*, 171–195.

Cunningham, K.J. (2008). The evolving participation of Muslim women in Palestine, Chechnya, and the global Jihadi movement. In C. Ness (Eds.), *Female terrorism and militancy: Agency, utility, and organization*. New York: Routledge.

de Cataldo Neuberger, L. and Valentini, T. (1996). *Women and terrorism*. New York: St. Martin's Press.

Ergil, D. (2000). Suicide terrorism in Turkey: The case of the Workers' Party of Kurdistan. *Countering Suicide Terrorism: An International Conference* (73–88). Herzliya, Israel: The International Policy Institute for Counter-Terrorism.

Fadel, L. (2008, August 25). Dazed Iraqi teen suicide bomber says she didn't want to die. McClatchy Newspapers. Retrieved from http://www.mcclatchydc.com/2008/08/25/50681/dazed-iraqi-teen-suicide-bomber.html.

Gonzalez-Perez, M. (2008). *Women and terrorism: Female activity in domestic and international terror groups*. New York: Routledge.

Gunawardena, A. (2006). Female black tigers: A different breed of cat? In Y. Schweitzer (Eds.), *Female suicide bombers: Dying for equality?* (pp. 91–106). Tel Aviv: Jaffee Center for Strategic Studies.

Hafez, M.M. (2007). *Suicide bombers in Iraq: The strategy and ideology of martyrdom.* Washington, D.C.: United States Institute of Peace Press (USIP Press).

In C. Ness (Eds.), *Female terrorism and militancy: Agency, utility, and organization.* New York: Routledge.

Italian police crackdown on Red Brigade strongholds. (1980, December 4). *The Prescott Courier.* Retrieved November 11, 2009 from LexisNexis Academic.

Jamieson, A. (2000). Mafiosi and terrorists: Italian women in violent organizations. *SAIS Review, 20*(2), 51–64.

Kimhi, S., & Even, S. (2003). Who are the Palestinian suicide terrorists? *Strategic Assessment, 6*(2), 7–9.

Markovic, V. (2009). Suicide bombings and lethality: A statistical analysis of tactics, techniques and procedures (Doctoral dissertation, Sam Houston State University, 2009). *ProQuest UMI.*

Merari, A. (2004) Suicide terrorism in the context of the Israeli-Palestinian conflict. *Suicide* Terrorism Research Conference. National Institute of Justice. Washington, D.C. October 26, 2004.

Moore, D. (1985, April 10). Teen kamikaze. *Telegraph.* Retrieved February 5, 2010 from LexisNexis Academic.

Nacos, B.L. (2005). The portrayal of female terrorists in the media: Similar framing patterns in the news coverage of women in politics and terrorism. *Studies in Conflict & Terrorism, 28*(5), 435–451.

Ness, C.D. (2005). In the name of the cause: Women's work in secular and religious terrorism. *Studies in Conflict & Terrorism, 28,* 353–373.

Nivat, A. (2008). The black widows: Chechen women join the fight for independence—and Allah. In C. Ness (Eds.), *Female terrorism and militancy: Agency, utility, and organization.* New York: Routledge.

Patkin, T.T. (2004). Explosive baggage: Female Palestinian suicide bombers and the rhetoric of emotion. *Women and Language, 27*(2), 79–88.

PBS (2006). *Hijacked.* PBS American Experience [Documentary]. Houston: Public Broadcast Service.

Pedahzur, A. (2005). *Suicide terrorism.* Cambridge: Polity Press.

Renzetti, C., Curran, D., & Carr, P.J. (2002) *Theories of Crime: A reader.* Boston: Allyn & Bacon.

Rosendorff, B.P, and Sandler, T. (2010) Suicide terrorism and the backlash effect. Retrieved on March 3, 2010 from http://www.utdallas.edu/~tsandler/website/Rosendorff_Sandler_SuicideMs_DPE2010.pdf.

Rubin, A.J. (2009, August 16). How Baida wanted to die. *The New York Times*, Retrieved from http://www.nytimes.com.

Schweitzer, Y. (2008). Palestinian female suicide bombers: virtuous heroines or damaged goods?

Simons, M. (2011, June 24). Life sentence in Rwanda genocide case. *The New York Times*, retrieved from http://www.nytimes.com.

Sloan, S. (2006). *Terrorism: The present threat in context.* Oxford: Berg Publishers.

Sprinzak, E. (2000). Rational fanatics. *Foreign Policy, 120*, 66–73.

Van Knop, K. (2007). The female Jihad: Al Qaeda's women. *Studies in Conflict & Terrorism, 30*(5), 397–414.

Wadud, A. (2002, May). A'ishah's legacy. *New Internationalist*, Retrieved from http://www.newint.org/features/2002/5/01/aishas-legacy/.

Zeitlin, S. (1965). Masada and the Sicarii. *The Jewish Quarterly Review, 55*(4), pp. 299–317.

# Part III

# The System Responds

# Chapter 9

# Women and Wrongful Conviction: How? Who? Why?

*Michael H. Fox, Ph.D.*

Very little research exists on women and wrongful conviction, and no comprehensive empirical study has yet been published. Most of the literature consists of autobiographical accounts by Tyler (1977), Brown (1990), Jacobs (2007), Moskowitz (2010), and Killian (2012), and third-person narratives, such as Armstrong (2005), Smith (2008), and Sherrer (2010).

In terms of empirical research, there is some evidence about gender and wrongful convictions. For example, Ruesink and Free (2005) have compared wrongful conviction crimes by gender and by race. Likewise, Belknap (2014) describes systemic and individually gendered displays of power in the criminal processing context. Fox (2009) explores vengeful arrests of women who have brought suit for police malfeasance, both in Japan and the USA. Furthermore, Konvisser (2012) examines the psychological effects of wrongful incarceration of women with proposals for aiding psychological recovery. Sharp (2014) shows how law is used to excessively criminalize and incarcerate women for non-violent offenses.

## Introduction

Our world's prisons are filled with women who have been unjustly convicted and excessively sentenced. Many, if not most, are serving time for tangential participation in crimes initiated and committed by men. Guilt by association is enough to lock a good woman away for life.

The struggle for justice is a great theme in American society. In movies and television, the innocent are always vindicated. The public sleeps comfortably believing that the system works. The hard fact is that it often does not. Numerous unjust convictions of women in the USA clearly show the system can be downright dreadful.[1] This chapter will examine "how" women are unjustly convicted. It will also look at "who" gets prosecuted, and make the case that "unfit" women, particularly mothers in non-orthodox lifestyles, are targeted. It will also assert that innocent mothers get convicted due to law enforcement's notion that "good mothers do not let their children die." Lastly, it will boldly tackle the issue of "why," and discuss eugenic control as motive.

The five women described in this paper were all charged with murder. They represent a wide cross section of America, and one case from Japan. The Japanese case will show that the mentality and tactics facilitating unjust convictions of women are hardly endemic to the USA, but are, in fact, a universal problem.

# How?

## *I) How: Guilt by association.*

According to conventional thinking, convicting an innocent defendant is a difficult task. Many non-fiction TV programs such as Forensic Files dramatize the pressure on prosecutors to gather the proper evidence to put away suspected murderers. Gaining conviction even in light of pressing evidence is often deemed difficult.

In fact, the modus operandi for convicting innocent suspects, especially women, is quite simple. Say that Joe and Sam go into a convenience store to buy a six pack. Sally waits in the car. Joe and Sam rob the store, fire a shot, and the cashier later dies. All are caught by the police. Sally had nothing to do with the crime, and knew nothing of the robbery plan.

Joe had the gun and pulled the trigger. He could face the death penalty, and Sam could get life without parole. But the police want to put Sally away too, as an accomplice to murder. After all, good girls do not associate with murderers. She must be punished.

Sally is offered a plea bargain. Testify against the two boys and you will do 10 years. Cross us and go to trial and we will ask for 25 to life. Sally gives much thought to the offer but her conscience rebels. In the end, she cannot assume responsibility for a crime in which she did not participate. The robbery was caught on video, and she was not in the store.

---

1. Different data bases include: http://www.wcjn.org/Data_Base.html (Worldwide Women's Criminal Justice Network); and Justice: Denied! http://forejustice.org/db/women /innocents_women.html.

So what evidence exists to tie her to the perpetrators? The answer: the testimony of Joe and Sam. Both are offered plea bargains to testify against Sally. Joe takes a plea of life imprisonment, Sam agrees to 25 years to life.

Sally goes to court and takes her chances in front of a jury. The judge urges her to accept the ten-year plea bargain. At age 21, she cannot imagine spending 10 years in prison. Joe and Sam testify that Sally was in the store, out of view of the camera, helped procure the handgun, and is lying about her non-participation.

The jury cannot believe both stories. Either she or the men are lying. Sally is out-testified two to one. And the jury will tend to side with the prosecutor. After all, would a respectable, well-dressed public servant who graduated law school go through enormous time and effort to build a case against an innocent? Those sworn to uphold the law would not and could not suborn perjury to win a conviction. Certainly, she must be guilty of something.

End result: Sally is convicted and sentenced to twenty-five years to life.


## II) How: False testimony of the real assailant.

### Case #1 Renee Thomas (Pennsylvania)

The above story may seem too far-fetched to be true. Quite to the contrary, American prisons are full of "Sallys" and even others who have been convicted on less evidence and sentenced to more time.

In May of 1983, 25-year-old Philadelphia resident Renee Thomas confronted a local man to collect a debt. The man suddenly became irate, and knocked her down. Her nearby boyfriend came to the rescue. A fracas ensued, a shot was fired, and the irate man was dead.

At first, Renee attempted to aid the victim. But knowing that the police in Philadelphia try to ensnare anybody tangentially connected to a crime, she left the scene. Knowing the authorities were hot on their trail, she and her boyfriend absconded to California.

On the road, he became controlling and abusive. Their relationship soured and the boyfriend returned to Philadelphia. Renee called the police and gave a true statement implicating her ex-boyfriend in the shooting. Upon return, the boyfriend was arrested.

At first, he assumed complete responsibility for the crime. But after learning of Renee's betrayal, he changed his original story, to implicate Renee in the murder. The police assumed her "guilty by association."

Renee stood trial. No evidence other than the shooter's testimony tied her to the murder. In a "he said, she said" case, Judge Albert Sabo—who later presided over the Mumia trial and was known to unequivocally despise black defendants—sentenced Renee for second degree murder. Second degree murder in Pennsylvania means life without parole, and, currently, no chance of commutation. At the time of this writing, she is in her 30th year of incarceration, under hospice care, and seeking compassionate release.[2]

## *III) How: Failure to protect.*

### Case #2: Miriam Nebot (Pennsylvania)

The 1970s saw legislation passed in many places to, ostensibly, prosecute child abuse. This legislation was rooted in the notion that if a child is abused by one parent, the other parent could, and perhaps should, be held responsible. The laws made "failure to protect" and "enabling child abuse" into felonies.

The end result of these new laws has been to punish women who associate with child abusers. Being married to or associating with male child abusers is often a violation of the criminal code.

Nobody knows this better than Pennsylvania inmate Miriam Nebot. At age 18, Miriam met a guy who was smart, funny and charming. They began to date, and she fell in love, hard and fast. They moved in together, and very soon a baby was on the way. They had little money, but she was happy to be independent and starting a family.

Slowly his "other side" began to show: short tempered, possessive, and controlling. He became abusive, and she started being frightened. Still, she somehow believed this was a show of love—a love that caused emotions to run wild.

After being blessed with the birth of a beautiful girl, the relationship went from bad to worse. Love became black eyes, a busted nose, and cracked ribs. Miriam never called the police or asked for help. Having watched her mother and stepsister suffer the same, this was a state of normality. Instead of venting or defending, she rationalized: "If I do this or that, maybe things will be different."

Her husband's anger went from bad to worse. He found a new target: the baby. First there were bumps and bruises. Then bite marks. Reporting this to the authorities was a possibility, but there might be repercussions. What if they took him to jail? Or took the baby away? Being codependent and trapped, Miriam kept everything inside.

Ultimately, this became "the worst decision in my life." Some six and a half months after giving birth, her beautiful baby was dead. The official cause of death was head trauma.

---

2. Sources for this case are derived from http://www.wcjn.org/Renee_Thomas.html.

Miriam was charged with murder. Before trial, the Lebanon County District Attorney boasted, "Nebot is being charged with homicide not because it is thought she physically caused her daughter's death, but because she failed to prevent it."[3]

The D.A's action is typical of an emerging type of prosecution throughout the country. "Failure to protect," also known as "enabling child abuse," exists on the books in most states. On the surface, it is gender-neutral, but in reality, the targets are nearly all women. In fact, a study on the phenomena noted, "defendants charged and convicted with failure to protect are almost exclusively female" (Fugate 2001). Moreover, it does not seem to matter if the police and D.A. know that the father was the sole abuser. The Fugate study found that "in virtually every case where Dad is the abuser, the Mom is charged with failure to protect."

The net effect: convicting young impoverished women for associating with bad men.

Miriam stood trial in August, 2008. Crippled with guilt, she took an open plea for 3rd degree murder. Expecting a sentence of 6 to 12 years, the presiding judge practically tripled the sentence of this dark-skinned defendant. She is serving 17 to 35.[4]

# Who?

## I) Who: The unfit mother.

### Case #3 Karlyn Eklof (Oregon)

Guilt by association, as illustrated above, is a powerful force in the case of female defendants. While any woman who cavorts with criminals can come become a target, law and order supporters often harbor deep prejudices against particular female profiles. A special wrath is directed at mothers who cavort with criminals.

Motherhood is a sacred societal duty, perhaps the most sacred.[5] Mothers with children who do not live in the traditional nuclear family unit, and who

---

3. "Mom, doctor charged in baby's death." The Patriot-News, Friday July 04, 2008.

4. Sources for this case are derived from http://www.wcjn.org/Miram_Nebot.html.

5. Federal law allows for extreme enhancements for pregnant women who commit crimes. http://advocatesforpregnantwomen.org/blog/2014/12/press_release_challenging_1st.php.

associate with criminal men, are quick to draw suspicion. They are apt to be viewed as unfit to be a mother, a blemish upon society. It is a clear double-standard. Male wolves may stray from the family and prowl in the night; the she-wolf should stay close to the den. Woe to those who live otherwise.

In May of 1993, Karlyn Eklof, a 33-year-old single mother of three children, held a pizza party in Eugene, Oregon, to celebrate her relationship with Jeffrey Tiner, who had just been released from prison in California. Until recently, Karlyn and her children had been homeless and had been sheltered by a local man, James Salmu.

Living conditions in the small house, already cramped by two adults and three children, were further strained when Tiner arrived from California. The night of the pizza party, the two offered Salmu money to go to a motel for the night. When Salmu refused to leave his own house, Tiner shot him three times.

The right thing for Eklof to do would have been to call 911. But a woman starved for love and with three young mouths to feed will not always make the right choice. Instead, she took off with Tiner and the children and headed for California. After being repeatedly beaten and abused, she eventually contacted the police back in Eugene, filed a report, and requested help.

With Eklof's statement describing the murder, it would seem that the crime had been solved, and her involvement was over. But to the contrary, she was targeted as an accomplice: guilt by association. After six full days of interrogation, she confessed to stabbing the decedent with a plastic fork before the shooting.

Such evidence would hardly fill the script of a bad murder drama. But the local prosecutor learned that one of Karlyn's acquaintances in Eugene had been arrested for child sexual abuse. He was offered a generous plea deal in exchange for testimony. He accepted the deal and testified to procuring the handgun used in the crime at Karlyn's, rather than Tiner's, request (Bornstein 2005).[6]

Karlyn was offered a ten-year plea bargain with early release after eight years for good behavior. But the woman who had been beaten and abused most of her life decided to make a stand. She took her chances in front of a jury. The prosecution asked for death. She was found guilty and sentenced to two life terms plus 16 years for a single murder. Had she accepted the plea bargain, she would have been released in 2008. An unmarried mother with three chil-

---

6. At trial, Eklof's attorneys knew nothing of the bargain. It was later uncovered on appeal. Eklof vs Hoefel (2006).

dren, cavorting with a murderer, Karlyn Eklof fits the idealized profile of the "unfit mother."[7]

## II) Who: Mothers of murdered children.

Mothers who get wrongfully convicted suffer double tragedies. They suffer the degradation of prison, and the tragedy of being separated from their children. Yet an even more wretched scenario is the mother who is wrongfully suspected of murdering her own child. Life imprisonment for such "witches" is seen as perhaps too lenient.

### Case #4: Keiko Aoki (Japan)

On a hot, sweltering July day in 1995, Tatsuhiro Boku filled his van with gas and returned to his home in Osaka. He parked in the attached garage which had been added on to house. Shortly after arriving home, he noticed a small fire under the van. He and his wife Keiko Aoki tried to extinguish the fire by pouring water upon the flame.

In a matter of moments, the tiny fire catalyzed into a blaze that engulfed the whole garage. Smoke began pouring into the home. Tatsuhiro, Keiko and their ten-year-old son, managed to escape. Their eleven-year-old daughter, taking a bath at the time, did not. The cause of death was cited as tracheal scalding.

The fire itself did not draw the attention of the authorities, but the family circumstances did. Investigators soon learned that Tatsuhiro and Keiko were not formally married. The two children were from Keiko's previous marriage, and both children had life insurance. The boy was insured for $250,000 and the daughter for $150,000.

To the Westerner, such coverage probably seems excessive and suspicious. In much of Asia, certainly in Japan, life insurance for children is quite common. While Japan is quite Western on the surface, Confucian sensibilities still exert strong influences. In the traditional agrarian social structure, children are expected to take over the fields when parents become infirm and unable to work. Though far fewer people derive livelihoods from rice farming in contemporary society, Confucian sensibilities still run deep. Life insurance for children is rather common.

Some six weeks after the blaze, Boku and Aoki were called in for voluntary questioning. The questioning soon became a brutal interrogation. Boku was

---

7. Sources for this case are derived from http://www.wcjn.org/Karlyn_Eklof.html.

verbally abused, kicked and choked. Aoki was placed in a separate room where two male police officers laid pictures of her naked deceased daughter on the table, put their mouths right up to her ears, and screamed "murderer" in tandem over and over again. In a short time, both ended up signing confessions to murder, arson and insurance fraud.

One lynchpin in this case is ethnic prejudice. What likely disturbed the authorities most of all was that Boku is Korean—Boku being the Japanese pronunciation of the common surname Park. The Koreans are the largest ethnic minority in Japan and continue to face intense discrimination. Since Ms. Aoki, a divorced mother with two children, was domiciling with a Korean, she was likely seen as an unfit mother and guilty by association.

An unmentioned but keenly felt factor in this case is the desire to pin a child's death on the mother. Law enforcement authorities frequently subscribe to the notion that "good mothers do not let their children die." Mothers are expected to sacrifice all to save a child. Certainly, many do. But blinded and choking in a house filled with smoke, the exigencies of saving someone can be impossible.

Arson investigation is a recognized profession in the USA, but not so in Japan. With little evidence to provide in their defense, both Aoki and Boku were found guilty of murder, arson and insurance fraud. Both were sentenced to life imprisonment.[8]

## Case #5: Debra Milke (Arizona)

On December 2, 1989, Debra Milke, a 25-year-old Phoenix mother recently separated from her drug-addicted husband, dressed up her four-year-old son Christopher for a meeting with Santa. Debra had taken shelter with Jim Styers, a 42-year-old disabled Vietnam veteran and father of a young girl. Debra and Jim shared expenses and chores but nothing more. Debra had recently landed a good job and was planning to move into her own place.

Jim, a friend, and little Chris departed to the local mall in the morning. In the early afternoon, Jim called Debra with dreadful news: Chris had gone missing. But the story was a ruse—Jim's friend later lead police out into the desert. The little boy had been shot three times in the head and left there.

Later that night, a detective visited Debra, told her of the murder, and demanded that she confess to planning the murder. The assumed motive was a $5,000 life insurance policy on the boy. Debra refused to confess, and after arrest, even refused to sign the written waiver allowing police to continue questioning.

---

8. Sources for this case are derived from: http://www.jiadep.org/Higashi-Sumiyoshi.html.

Nothing captures media attention more than a femme fatale. The media latched onto the story and treated Debra with the sensitivity a starving cat affords a blind, injured hamster. The only evidence presented in court was testimony by the detective who insisted that Debra confessed. He raised the issue of the insurance money, and testified that she wanted the boy dead out of the fear that he would end up a replica of his drug-addicted father.

Apart from the lone detective's testimony, no evidence of a confession exists. Common criminal procedure mandates that a confession be either signed, recorded or filmed. And at the very least, it should be witnessed by a second observer. None of this occurred. In fact, when ordered to turn in his notes of Debra's interrogation, the detective testified to destroying them after typing up his report (*Milke v. Ryan*, 2013, p. 42).

At trial, neither of the two men who actually carried out the killing, despite promises of leniency from the prosecution, would testify against Debra. The housemate gave statements to the police insisting that "she had nothing to do with the murder" (*Milke v. Ryan*, 2013, p. 54).

Needless to say, Debra Milke was tried in the media even prior to the first hearing in court. It was a simple case of guilt by association. Ludicrous as it may seem, social convention, as mentioned above in the Aoki case, dictates that good mothers do not let their children die, let alone be murdered. The jury found her guilty, and in October 1990, Debra was sentenced to death.

# Why?

Social science often produces complex analyses of pressing problems. But in regard to the cases presented here and studied elsewhere, the reasons "why" certain women get arrested and wrongfully convicted are quite simple, perhaps shockingly so.

## *Reason 1: Women who associate with criminals are guilty by association.*

Four of the cases presented in this paper describe women who came under suspicion for associating with men who committed crimes. "If you run with the wolves, you are guilty of the kill" is the mantra intoned by many law enforcement agencies. Women who associate with criminals are thus guilty of two things: violation of the criminal code, and violation of standards of appropriate womanhood. It is a terrible double standard, but it exists. This may be the least acknowledged and most pernicious factor in the prosecution of women.

For those women who have brought children into the world, the penalties are even more severe. Guilt or innocence is beside the point. Associating with criminals, in addition to violating womanhood, is a violation of motherhood. Those who plead innocent, reject plea bargains, and refuse to acknowledge their sins merit no mercy. They must be separated from their children, and ostracized from society. In short, childless women may have some chance of rehabilitation, but mothers are viewed as incorrigible.

## *Reason 2: Good mothers do not let their children die.*

Of the cases examined in this study, three involve mothers whose children died. One was by accident, two were killed by men. And though none of the women participated nor could predict the deaths, all were charged and convicted of murder.

Gerald Hurst, one of America's premier arson investigators, has long stated, "Where there's a fire and someone dies, the survivors will likely be charged with arson and murder."[9] Likewise, we can infer that if a child dies suspiciously, the mother will likely be suspected of murder. Though this paper has only looked at three cases of women convicted of child murder, much evidence has been gathered to support this phenomenon.[10]

The notion that "good mothers do not let their children die" has propelled many investigations and caused substantial wrongful convictions. This belief has been solidified by laws to indict mothers who "fail to protect" or "enable child abuse." Miriam Nebot is no aberrant case; many women have been convicted under these draconian laws.[11] And the targets are hardly women from the upper strata of society.

## *Reason 3: Eugenic control of undesirable women.*

Of the five women discussed above, all were sentenced to long terms, including death. The shortest sentence, that of Miriam Nebot, was 17 to 35 years.

What significance do these terms have? Do they contain some other ulterior motive, apart from retribution, for crimes against society?

---

9. http://www.nlada.org/forensics/for_lib/Documents/1124468256.56/arson.htm.

10. The Women's Criminal Justice Network maintains a list of women wrongfully convicted of child murder. See http://www.wcjn.org/Chart_Filicide_files/page86_1.html.

11. An investigative report published in 2014 discovered 28 cases of women who have been convicted of child abuse perpetrated by men (Campbell, 2014).

Quite clearly, I believe they do. The motive, difficult to deny, is to seal the wombs of socially undesirable women, and to prevent them from giving birth. In the end, the intention is twofold: to punish and isolate bad women, and to inflict a judicial hysterectomy.

Renee Thomas never gave birth. Her life sentence for second degree murder negated any chance for motherhood. Karlyn Eklof, already a mother of three when she was sentenced at age 34, was offered a plea bargain of ten years. Whether she wanted more children is beside the point; the plea bargain virtually sealed her womb—likewise for Keiko Aoki, a mother of two. Debra Milke was sentenced to death at age 25. Even if her sentence been 25 years to life, the result would have been the same: a judicial hysterectomy.

Miram Nebot's sentence keenly illustrates this point. She pled guilty expecting a sentence of 6 to 12 years. Why did the judge sentence her to 17 to 35 years? Assuming release after 17 years, she would be 39 and still capable of giving birth. But, most women in Pennsylvania serve more than the mandated minimum. Essentially, the judge's sentence, much longer than the prosecution's suggestion, is an outright judicial hysterectomy.

Let those who doubt this motive take notice. In 2005, William J. Bennett, former education secretary under Ronald Reagan and director of drug policy for George H.W. Bush, loudly proclaimed on radio, "[I]f you wanted to reduce crime,—you could abort every black baby in this country, and your crime rate would go down" (McCorkel, 2013).[12]

As shocking as it may sound, Bennett's vision of crime reduction has been practiced for some time. In September of 2014, the state of California acknowledged that women prisoners had been forcibly sterilized and passed legislation prohibiting such treatment in the future (Bhattacharjee, 2014). It is obvious that eugenic control of inadequate women has been an objective of American criminal justice.

## Postscript: Brotherly Love, Sisterly Hate

The purpose of criminological research is to improve society. It is not art for art's sake. All research in this field should contribute to the reform of criminal justice and the improvement of the human condition, both locally and globally.

---

12. Bennett is best known for authoring the 1996 best seller, "The Book of Virtues." In 2003, he admitted to a gambling addiction and the loss of several million dollars to casinos.

Nowhere is the need for reform more dire than in the state of Pennsylvania. Though Philadelphia is called the "City of Brotherly Love," the state of Pennsylvania could also be known as the sphere of sisterly hate. Pennsylvania may be the only place in the developed world where second degree murder—simple tangential participation in a crime—may be punished with life without parole. And the target of this brash, draconian punishment is women, particularly women of color.

Take the case of Avis Lee. On November 1, 1979, the 18-year-old Pittsburgh native agreed to serve as a look-out in a robbery. The crime was to be carried out by her brother and a male friend. The robbery went awry, and shots were fired. After hearing the gunshots, Avis saw her companions flee the scene. She herself boarded a bus, and out of sympathy for the victim, frantically explained the situation to the driver. The driver alerted the police. Unfortunately, the victim later died.

Avis's brother was found guilty of first degree murder, and she was convicted as an accomplice to second degree murder. The third accomplice was released after serving less than two years ("Commute Avis Lee," 2014). Pennsylvania is one of the few places in the universe where the penalty for second degree murder is the same as first—life without parole.

At the time of this writing, Avis has been in prison for 35 years. She has become the poster girl of the criminal justice reform movement in Pennsylvania. On August 27, 2014, various citizens' groups gathered at the state capitol in Harrisburg to support her bid for a commutation before the Board of Pardons. The five member parole board consists of the lieutenant governor, the attorney general, a representative from the Department of Corrections, a psychiatrist, and a single citizen who represents the voice of victims. Three votes are enough to advance the parole request to the second stage, an open public hearing. The board did grant several applications, and quite often by majority rather than unanimous votes. This was her fourth attempt, and Avis was categorically denied by all five voters. The denial likely had a separate ulterior motive: to skewer the ever-growing grassroots activism in the state.

What's the matter with Pennsylvania? Recidivism for commuted lifers is an astonishingly low 1.5%.[13] And this is for men—no women lifers have ever returned to prison. What is the reason for keeping all these women, particularly poor, black women, in prison at great expense to the state? These are women

---

13. History of Commuted Life Sentences http://commutationnow.blogspot.jp/p/history-of-commuted-life-sentences.html.

who are beyond their child bearing years. Such women could become tax payers rather than tax burdens. But unlike men, they are denied the opportunity.

Renee Thomas, the first woman discussed in this paper, was sentenced to life without parole for second degree murder. According to the prosecution (not to her), she was an accomplice to a killing. As such, she received the same sentence as the shooter.

This is an awful phenomenon. But unlike other social problems, the solutions are simple and obvious. First, remove life without parole for second degree murder. Second, restore commutations for all women serving life in Pennsylvania. Depriving women the release opportunities afforded men is capricious and cruel.

# Summary

Women wrongfully convicted and unjustly sentenced is a severe problem, both in the USA and elsewhere. Present research of this phenomenon has barely scratched the surface. Women are easily convicted for tangential participation in crimes instigated and carried out by men. Those who associate with criminals will likely be charged according to the convention of guilt by association: "those who run with the wolves are guilty of the kill." Add the notion of "failure to protect" to the equation, and mothers of children who are abused and killed by men are equally guilty in the eyes of the law.

According to social convention, women who associate with criminals are guilty of two crimes—violating criminal codes, and violating the norms of appropriate womanhood. The case of mothers—women caring for young children—is even more egregious. Motherhood is sacrosanct. Mothers who associate with men who commit murder are seen as "unfit," a threat to children, and a cancer upon society. Rehabilitation is not a real option; long incarceration assures that society will not be further infected.

As dysfunctional as it may seem, criminal justice authorities cling to the notion that "good mothers do not let their children die." If a child is murdered or dies suspiciously, the mother will likely be suspected. And if a case can be built, the lack of evidence is no problem. Associating with a man outside the "tribe" can be sufficient cause for a sentence of life imprisonment. Guilt by association, coupled with media frenzy, is more than enough to convict, enough even for a sentence of death at times.

Society believes that bad women need to be punished and isolated. Since bad women will certainly give birth to bad babies, eugenic control in the form of long incarceration to prevent future pregnancies is necessary. Actual hysterectomies, sometimes carried out unnecessarily and forcibly, ensure the safety of society and a lesser welfare burden on the state.

Repairing the system is the goal of criminological research. Once the severity of wrongful convictions of women is acknowledged, relief will be possible. Of immediate importance is the implementation and restoration of meaningful commutations for all women prisoners.

| Present Status of Cases in This Chapter | |
| --- | --- |
| Case #1 Renee Thomas | Renee was diagnosed with terminal cancer in July 2014. Her petition for compassionate release was denied. She passed away on January 2, 2015. |
| Case #2 Miriam Nebot | Miriam continues to appeal her case. |
| Case #3 Karlyn Eklof | Karlyn continues to appeal her case. |
| Case #4 Keiko Aoki | On March 7, 2012, the Osaka District Court, in a very rare move in Japan, ordered a retrial. The order is currently being appealed. |
| Case #5 Debra Milke | On March 14, 2013, the United States Court of Appeals for the Ninth Circuit overturned Debra's conviction. It held that the prosecution violated Milke's rights by failing to disclose multiple instances of detective misconduct. On December 11, 2014, the Arizona State Appeals Court ruled that retrial in the case of egregious prosecutorial misconduct is barred by double jeopardy. This decision is currently before the Arizona Supreme Court. |
| Case #6 Avis Lee | Avis's 4th petition for commutation was turned down in August 2014. She is now in her 35th year of incarceration. |

# References

Armstrong, E. (2005). *Improper submission: Records of a wrongful conviction.* Dallas, OR: Tanglewood Hill Press.

Belknap, J. (2014). *The Invisible woman: Gender, crime, and justice, 4th edition.* Stamford, CT: Wadsworth Publishing.

Bhattacharjee, R. (2014, Sep 26). California bill bans forced sterilization of female inmates. nbcbayarea.com Retrieved from http://www.nbcbayarea.com/news/local/Gov—Jerry-Brown-Signs-bill-to-End-Forced-Prison-Sterilization—277229702.html.

Brown, J. A. & Gaines, J. (1990). *Justice denied.* Dallas, TX: Mass Inc.

Commute Avis Lee. (2014) Campaign for meaningful commutation. Retrieved from http:/commutationnow.blogspot.jp/p/commute-avis-lee.html.

Campbell, A. (2014, October 3). 28 Mothers were sentenced to at least 10 years for failing to protect their children from a violent partner. Buzzfeed. Retrieved from http://www.buzzfeed.com/alexcampbell/these-mothers-were-sentenced-to-at-least-10-years-for-failin.

Eklof v. Hoefel (2006). Memorandum of law in support of petition for writ of habeas corpus. Civ. No. 04-1141-HA. Retrieved from http://www.wcjn.org/Habeas-Argument.html.

Fox, M.H. (2009). Accusing the accuser: Police malfeasance, women plaintiffs, and vengeful arrests. *Criminal Law Bulletin, 45*(3)., 648–649.

Fugate, J. A. (2001). Who's failing whom? A critical look at failure to protect laws. *New York University Law Review, 76,* 272–308.

Graterfriends, 44, 5. (2013, May). Retrieved from http://www.prisonsociety.org/.

Jacobs, S. (2007). *Stolen time: One woman's inspiring story as an innocent condemned to death.* London: Transworld Publishers.

Jacobsen, C. & Lempert, L.B. (2013, Autumn). Institutional disparities: Considerations of gender in the commutation process for incarcerated women. *Signs, 39*(1), 265–289.

Killian, G. & Kobrin, S. (2012). *Full circle: A true story of murder, lies, and vindication.* New Jersey: Far Hills Press.

Konvisser, Z. D. (2012). Psychological consequences of wrongful conviction in women and the possibility of positive change. *DePaul Journal for Social Justice, 5*(2), 221.

McCorkel Jill A. (2013) *Breaking Women: Gender, Race, and the New Politics of Imprisonment.* New York: New York University Press.

Milke v. Ryan, 711 F.3d 998 (9th Cir. 3013).

Mom, doctor charged in baby's death.(2008, July 04) *The Patriot-News,* pp. 4–5.

Moskowitz, M. (2012). *Phantom spies, phantom justice: How I survived McCarthyism.* Seattle, WA: The Justice Institute.

Pennsylvania Department Of Corrections. (2014, October 31). Monthly institutional profile. Retrieved from https://www.portal.state.pa.us/portal/server.pt/document/915871/monthly_profile_pdf.

Ruesink, M. & Free, M.D. Jr. (2005). Wrongful convictions among women: an exploratory study of a neglected topic. *Women & Criminal Justice, 16*(4).

Sharp, S.F. (2014). *Mean lives, mean laws: Oklahoma's women prisoners.* New Brunswick, NJ: Rutgers University Press.

Sherrer, H. (2010). *Kirstin Blaise Lobato's unreasonable conviction: Possibility of guilt replaces proof beyond a reasonable doubt.* Seattle, WA: The Justice Institute.

Smith, A. (2008) *Case of a lifetime: A criminal defense lawyer's story.* NY: Palgrave Macmillan.

Tyler, M. (1977). *My years in an Indian prison.* London: Littlehampton Book Services.

# Chapter 10

# Women's Experiences with Imprisonment: From Silence to Resistance

*Jodie Michelle Lawston, Ph.D.*

In 1999, long before I started my research on incarceration, I became active in organizations that sought to raise awareness about women's imprisonment. As part of these organizations I communicated with women in prison, who sought to improve the conditions of confinement and communicate with the "outside world." These women were particularly concerned with the ways in which they were treated by staff, and with improving inadequate healthcare in the prison system. As I got to know some of these women they communicated that they wanted a voice; the prison, they explained, works to silence those within it. The theme of voice would come up again and again in my interactions with imprisoned women, and they would always request that I and others "tell society about them" so that they would perhaps be a little less invisible. The desire to be heard was strong among these women, and their courage in and commitment to resisting the silencing effects of prison, through a variety of means, was remarkable. Ten years later, when I speak with women in prison, they still explain that they want a voice. Women in prison are hopeful that in having a voice they will be able to educate the larger society about the conditions of confinement, and potentially foster better understanding about incarcerated women's lives.

In a humble attempt to fulfill incarcerated women's desire to be heard beyond the razor wire, this chapter highlights the voices of both incarcerated and formerly incarcerated women and their responses to and reflections on their experiences with imprisonment. Drawing on qualitative data, I underscore a multitude of quotes provided by women who have experienced, or continue to experience, incarceration. I find that incarcerated and formerly incarcerated women identify feelings of separation, loneliness, lack of control, and silencing as crucial experiences that frame and define their time in prison. I also find that despite these experiences, women find ways to resist, and find a voice in, this oppressive social structure.

# "Incarceration Nation"

In February 2008 a landmark study was released by the Pew Center on the States Public Safety Performance Project. This report showed that 1 in every 99.1 men and women are now incarcerated in U.S. prisons and jails, or 2,319,258 adults. With just five percent of the world's population, the U.S. houses nearly one-quarter of the world's prisoners (Gottschalk, 2006), more than any other industrialized nation. The U.S. incarceration rate of 723 per 100,000 is more than seven times greater than the rates of incarceration in Western Europe, which incarcerates 100 per 100,000 people (Western, 2007; Mack, 2007; Gottschalk, 2006).

Women only constitute seven percent of the prison population, yet since the early 1980s the numbers of women who have been imprisoned have increased at unprecedented rates. Whereas between 1980 and 1997 there was a 294 percent increase in the rates of incarceration for men, the women's state and federal prison population increased by a staggering 573 percent, from 12,300 to 82,800 (Mauer, Potler and Wolf, 1999). Since 1995 the annual growth rate of female prisoners has averaged five percent, in comparison to a growth rate of just over three percent for men (Gottschalk, 2006). More than 200,000 women are now confined in U.S. prisons and jails, in addition to 94,000 women on parole and 958,000 women on probation (Talvi, 2007, p. xv). At least two-thirds of these women are mothers to children under age eighteen (Mumola, 2000).

The process of incarceration—for both women and men—is marked by race and class. Black and Latino men account for nearly two-thirds of the state male prisoner population (Western, 2007). These men are disproportionately poor and undereducated, with an average of fewer than eleven years of schooling; one-third were not working at the time of their arrest, and the remaining men had average salaries that were significantly lower than non-incarcerated men with the same level of education (Western, 2007). Black men in particular are at a heightened risk for imprisonment: occupying just six percent of the U.S. population, they have a 32 percent chance of experiencing incarceration, constitute over 40 percent of the prison population, and are eight times more likely to be incarcerated than white men (Mack, 2007; Western, 2007).

Mirroring the trends we see in men's incarceration, the increase in the imprisonment of women has disproportionately affected those who are of color and poor. Close to 70 percent of women confined in local, state, and federal institutions are Black, Latina, First Nation and Asian (Diaz Cotto, 2006; James, 2005; Johnson, 2003); most are also poor or working class. Black women are four times as likely to be incarcerated as white women, and more than twice as likely to be incarcerated as Latinas (Talvi, 2007, p. 7). According to the Pew study (2008), 1 in 100 black women in their mid- to late 30s are incarcerated. When isolating the economics of those women who get caught up in the criminal justice system, studies show that 37 percent of female prisoners had incomes of less than $600 per month prior to arrest, and approximately 30 percent of female prisoners reported receiving some form of welfare assistance prior to arrest (Greenfeld and Snell, 1999; see also Owen and Bloom, 1995; Covington, 1998; Owen, 1998; Girshick, 1999; Morash and Schram, 2002; Pollock, 2004). Nearly 45 percent of women in local jails and state prisons, and 25 percent of women in federal prisons, have not graduated high school, with between 60 and 70 percent never having attended any college (Greenfeld and Snell, 1999; see also Owen and Bloom, 1995; Owen, 1998; Morash and Schram, 2002).

In addition to experiencing high rates of poverty and low levels of formal education, a very high percentage of imprisoned women have been physically, sexually, and/or psychologically abused. Among women in the general population, 43 percent have experienced either physical or sexual assault at some point in their lives (Walker, Unutzer, Rutter, Gelfand, Saunders, Vonkorff, Koss and Katon, 1999). In contrast, studies show that between 57 percent (BJS, 1999) and 75 percent (Browne, Miller and Maguin, 1999) of respondents report that they have experienced sexual and/or physical violence prior to their confinement; one-third of incarcerated women also report having been raped (Mauer, Potler, and Wolf, 1999; see also Lawston and Schlesinger, forthcoming; Finkelhor and Browne, 1985; Gilfus, 1988; Bloom, Chesney-Lind and Owen, 1994; Owen and Bloom, 1995; Covington, 1998; Haney and Kristianson, 1998; Marcus-Mendoza, Klein-Saffran, and Lutze, 1998; Owen 1998; Morash and Schram, 2002; Pollock, 2004; Marcus-Mendoza and Wright, 2004; Dougherty, 2008; Guevara Urbina, 2008). To cope with the resulting emotional pain of violence and abuse, women often turn to drugs. Through an analysis of incarcerated women's case studies, Zaplin (2008) shows that women report having turned to drugs to "disassociate" and "escape" from the emotional pain they experience as a result of violence and trauma.

# The Continuation of Violence and Abuse in Prison

While a great deal of scholarship shows that incarcerated women have experienced higher rates of both physical and sexual abuse than women in the general population (Cook, Smith, Tusher, and Raiford, 2005; Guevara Urbina, 2008; Greenfeld and Snell, 1999; Browne et al., 1999; BJS, 1999; Singer, Bussey, Song, and Lunghofer, 1995; Bloom, Chesney-Lind, and Owen, 1994), research also shows that once incarcerated, the violence continues. Most of the research on violence and abuse in women's prisons has focused on sexual assault (Human Rights Watch, 1996; Heney and Kristianson, 1998) and medical neglect (Covington, 1998; Amnesty International, 1999) at the hands of prison staff.

Sexual violence at the hands of male correctional staff—which only serves to further terrorize women who experienced such trauma prior to their incarceration—has existed since women were incarcerated in separate wings of men's prisons in the nineteenth century (Freedman, 1981; Covington, 1998; Morash and Schram, 2002; Zaplin, 2008). As researchers have shown, the trauma women experienced on the outside of prison walls is relived in prison—and is conducted in the form of pat-downs, strip searches, and less often, internal body searches—in the name of safety and security (Faith, 1993; Heney and Kristianson, 1998; Dirks, 2004; Guevara Urbina, 2008).

In addition to such day-to-day intrusions, other violations of one's bodily integrity also occur in prison. Both Human Rights Watch (1996) and Amnesty International (1999) released reports that not only document this ongoing abuse but that underscore the ways in which male correctional staff inflict sexual violence with almost total impunity. Human Rights Watch exposed cases of sexual abuse and assault by male correctional officers in women's prisons from Georgia to California; this report found that male guards have subjected women to sexual assault, extortion, groping during body searches, rape, and in some cases, impregnation. Amnesty International (1999) devoted an entire section of its report, "Not Part of My Sentence: Violations of the Human Rights of Women in Custody," to the sexual assault of incarcerated women.

Approximately 25 percent of incarcerated women report sexual abuse while imprisoned (Talvi, 2008). For example, until a class action lawsuit was filed on behalf of women prisoners in Georgia, incarcerated women in this state were fondled and groped by male prison staff, sexually propositioned, coerced into sexual relationships by threat of retaliation or in exchange for contraband, raped, and/or impregnated (Human Rights Watch, 1996). Similarly, in 1997 a U.S. Department of Justice investigation into women's prisons in Arizona found that the prison administration failed to protect women from sexual abuse inflicted by correctional officers and other staff. This abuse included rape, sexual relationships, sexual touching, and close-up viewing during dressing, showering and use of toilet facilities (Amnesty International, 1999). Even medical staff have been found to sexually abuse women in prison. In 1994 several cases were brought to the attention of human rights organizations, of a prison doctor that sexually assaulted women at Central California Women's Facility (CCWF). Women that went to this doctor for common colds or other ailments were subjected to forced gynecological exams and sexual touching (Human Rights Watch, 1996). In a more recent 2008 case in Michigan, women prisoners at Scott Regional Correctional Facility were awarded $15.4 million dollars for the sexual abuse they endured. The prisoners testified about sexual advances, assaults, and rapes by male guards (Lam, 2008).[1] Marcus-Mendoza and Wright (2004, p. 252) argue that such actions produce "a microcosm of patriarchal society inside prison walls and [recreate] dynamics similar to those experienced during prisoners' violent past."

Healthcare, or lack thereof, can also be considered a form of abuse, and runs the gamut from improper medical care administered by untrained and unqualified staff to outright refusal of medical treatment. Although medical care is also problematic in men's institutions, in comparison to men women present "more serious and longstanding health problems" when they enter prisons (Talvi, 2007, p. 87; see also Covington, 1998; Pollock, 2004). Not only do women's reproductive issues, such as pregnancy, present them with unique health concerns, compared to men they have "higher illness rates for infective diseases, respiratory and digestive system conditions, injuries, ear diseases, headaches, genitourinary disorders, and skin and musculoskeletal diseases" (Talvi, 2007, p. 88). One of the biggest complaints of women inside, which is a uniquely female concern, is the general lack of follow-up tests for irregular gynecological exams (Talvi, 2007). Annual and follow-up gynecological exams would help address reproductive health issues early on, yet "gynecological care is treated as a 'specialty service'" (Talvi, 2007, p. 88).

Cases of medical neglect in women's prisons are too numerous to enumerate here, but I will mention a few. In a study of prison healthcare in Florida from 1992 to 1996, a woman prisoner who had a miscarriage waited six to seven hours before medical personnel sent her to the hospital, even though she was bleeding profusely; another pregnant prisoner, who had a history of prior pregnancy problems and was in severe pain, was told that the prison

---

1. The state of Michigan appealed this decision.

does not treat pregnant prisoners (Amnesty International, 1999). In 1998, forty prisoners at the Virginia Correctional Center for Women signed a petition describing delays in getting access to emergency care, doctors, medication, and treatment for chronic illnesses (Amnesty International, 1999). The women explained that the facility did not have a gynecologist on staff; a woman who was bleeding profusely from the rectum was told by staff to elevate her feet, and subsequently bled to death (Amnesty International, 1999). In early June 1996, Debra Gant, a prisoner in Washington, DC, began experiencing vaginal bleeding and abdominal pain. Although she complained to prison staff, she did not receive treatment until one month later, when her pain had become severe and she was semi-conscious; she was taken to a hospital and was diagnosed as having a ruptured ectopic pregnancy. Debra underwent emergency surgery to stop her from bleeding to death, and surgeons had to remove an ovary and her fallopian tube (Amnesty International, 1999).[2] Incidents like these highlight the underlying violence of prisons and the lack of care about and regard for those within them.

# Situating the Current Study

There is a great deal of empirical evidence explaining what occurs in incarcerated women's lives—especially in terms of violence before and during prison (Gilfus, 1988; Bloom, Chesney-Lind and Owen, 1994; Marcus-Mendoza, Klein-Saffran, and Lutze, 1998; Owen, 1998; Covington, 1998; Heney and Kristianson, 1998; Girshick, 1999; Morash and Schram, 2002; Pollock, 2004; Zaplin, 2008). Too, several studies and anthologies have featured imprisoned women's voices and their reflections on their incarceration (Richie, 1996; Hardin and Hill, 1998; Enos, 1998; Morgan, 1998; Boudin, 1998; Tuesday, 1998; Owen, 1998; Girshick, 1999; Pollock, 2002; Block, Wislanka, Pierson, and Fadem, 2008; Johnson, 2003; Lamb, 2004; Sudbury, 2005; Diaz Cotto, 2006; Zaplin, 2008). This is important research, as the women who have experienced imprisonment directly are best able to articulate the ways that incarceration affects them.

This chapter can be situated in, and seeks to contribute to, this rich body of literature. I explore how women who have experienced incarceration, or who are currently experiencing incarceration, make sense of their confinement

---

2. According to the report released by Amnesty International, Debra Gant filed a lawsuit against the District of Columbia in 1997, *Gant v. District of Columbia*, and she received an undisclosed sum of money from the case.

by asking two questions. First, given what we know about prison conditions and women's lives before prison, what do incarcerated and formerly incarcerated women identify as the experiences that *define* their imprisonment? Second, how do incarcerated women *resist* the conditions of confinement and find a voice for themselves? This second question, in particular, has been less studied and gives us an idea of the types of strategies that women use to "deal with" their containment on a daily basis. I draw on qualitative data in the forms of surveys and interviews to answer these questions.

## Data and Methods

This study utilizes a mixed-method approach that draws from both questionnaires and semi-structured interviews with incarcerated and formerly incarcerated women.

Interview data are drawn from a larger ethnographic research project, conducted from 2002 to 2005, on prison conditions and radical women's prison activism. For this project, I conducted fifteen interviews of activists in a grassroots prison organization that sought to support incarcerated women and to contest abusive prison conditions. These activists visited and worked with a small group of women in prison to determine what types of support the women needed most. Because I wanted to understand how both activists and prisoners conceptualized the work of the group, incarcerated women were selected to participate in the study if they maintained connections with the activists in the organization at the time I was conducting my fieldwork. I conducted interviews with a total of fifteen prisoners, two of whom identified as white and the rest of whom identified as First Nation, African-American, or Latina; one woman also identified as middle class while the remaining women identified as poor or working class.

Questions on the interview guide that provide data for this chapter include, "Can you tell me a little bit about your social background and life?", "What are your daily struggles in prison?", "What do you think are the issues most important to women prisoners today?", "What do you think has to change in prison, if anything?", and "Is there anything you would like to talk about?" Interviews lasted between forty-five minutes and one hour and were conducted in two separate women's prisons in a western state. I was able to communicate with nine prisoners multiple times, both in person and through letters.

Based on the responses that I previously gathered from interviews—which raised more questions for me about the struggles that women in prison face and the ways that they resist the abuse of prison life—a small sample of twenty questionnaires was sent to formerly incarcerated women, none of whom had been previously interviewed by me, in early 2009. These women resided in the state where the previous study was conducted and where I had contacts with both formerly and currently incarcerated women. Twelve questionnaires were returned. Three of these women were African American, four were Latina, and five were white. Interestingly, eleven of the respondents identified as middle class while one identified as working class. This could be due to middle class women's greater comfort with responding to surveys.

Questions on the survey built on data I had gathered in the first interviews, and asked women to comment on their experiences with imprisonment. Questions included, "What were your experiences with prison?", "How were the conditions, including healthcare and working conditions?", "Did you make close friends?", "Did you feel silenced in any way and how did you voice yourself?", and "What do you want society to know about you or prison life?" The question about friendship was used because interviewed women highlighted the importance of friends in providing emotional support during their incarceration.

I used the program ATLAS/ti to code and analyze interview data and questionnaire responses, looking for trends across the data that I collected. I have changed the names of all respondents to respect their privacy and confidentiality (Lofland and Lofland, 1995), and do not use any identifying information as to where prisoners are incarcerated.

# Findings

## *Experiences with Prison*

### Feelings of Separation, Loneliness, Lack of Control, and Silencing

Incarcerated and formerly incarcerated women identify feelings of separation, loneliness, lack of control, and silencing as crucial experiences that frame and define their time in prison. Women consistently report that prison life is or was extremely lonely. One woman who was formerly incarcerated, Zoe, explains:

> While incarcerated I experienced a depth of separation I had never known before. The minute I was incarcerated my world became divided—I was 'in' and everyone/everything else in the world which existed was 'out.' The isolation I felt by being separated from everyone I love was tormenting.

The loneliness that women feel while incarcerated does not simply stem from being in a place where women initially do not know anyone, but from their separation from family, friends, children, and other loved ones. Once the prison doors close, a dichotomy is created where women inside exist as separate and cut off from the rest of the "outside world" around them. What little interaction women have with the larger society is tightly controlled and restricted: visits are monitored by prison staff and physical affection is not permitted or is severely restricted. The isolation women report is excruciatingly painful. An incarcerated woman named Barbara explains:

> The isolation is the worst part. I rarely see my family or children due to the distance. I am completely cut off from the rest of society in a way where those on the outside have no idea what happens to me on a daily basis. I hurt on a daily basis because I cannot see my children or be a part of their lives.

Prison creates hurdles for people on the outside and makes visiting very difficult for families and friends. Because many prisons are located in rural towns far from prisoners' homes, a trip to a prison frequently means that one's family and friends must have sufficient resources, such as cars, money, and time off from work. For prisoners like Barbara, who come from poor families, such resources are hard to come by. As a result, many women do not often receive visitors and report feelings of isolation and separation. This is emotionally tolling as they lose contact with those to whom they are closest.

Separation from children is especially painful. Upon entering prison women are unable to be an active part of their children's lives. At least 70 percent of incarcerated women are mothers (Golden, 2005; Morash and Schram, 2002; Guevara Urbina, 2008; Girshick, 1999; Owen, 1998; Enos, 1998), and research shows that the mother/child separation leads to increased anxiety, depression, and stress in female prisoners (Craig, 2009). Although maintaining close family ties during incarceration, "has been shown to result in decreased recidivism rates, improved mental health of inmates and other family members, increased likelihood of family reunification following release, and greater potential for parole success" (Reed and Reed, 2004, p. 265), not all prisons offer programs to bring mothers and children together.[3] Because prisons are lo-

---

3. Bedford Hills Correctional Facility in New York is an example of a prison that has nurseries so that women can be with their infants for up to one year, and other facilities, such as Riker's Island, the Minnesota State Correctional Facility, and the Massachusetts Correctional Institutional at Framingham have various mother/child programs (see Craig, 2009; Morash and Schram, 2002). Moreover, community groups are increasingly working to unite mothers and their children. For example, the "Get on the Bus" program in California has been successful at uniting mothers and their children, and offers trips for chil-

cated very far from many women's homes, and because prisoners are all too often poor and do not have families with resources for regular visits, women are torn away from their children for long periods of time. This separation can sometimes be permanent, as when parental rights are terminated because a woman is deemed "unfit to parent" by virtue of her confinement (see Golden, 2005; Morash and Schram, 2002; Guevara Urbina, 2008; Brown and Bloom, 2008).

Women also report that upon entering prison they quickly learned that they had little control over the day-to-day issues in their lives. Barbara states:

> They tell us what to do at all times of the day. I no longer have control over my life. I have to do what guards tell me.

Because of the rigidity of prison life, with staff determining sleeping and eating schedules, work schedules, and the timing of room inspections, women frequently report that they have little control over their lives. This feeling was reported by the majority (20 out of 27) of respondents. Some women tried to retain the notion that they were, indeed, in control of their lives. Zoe states:

> I did not want to give up control and, at times, the tiresome façade I played that I was in control brought me comfort.

Women like Zoe try to maintain some semblance of control so that prison does not dominate all aspects of their lives. Strategies to maintain control run the gamut from simply telling oneself that you are in control of your surroundings to filing complaints about prison conditions, which will be discussed below, under resistance.

The most frequently cited experience that framed women's understandings of incarceration was that of silencing. Upon entering prison, women not only found that their daily routines were controlled by prison staff, but that their thoughts, ideas, and voices were unimportant. An imprisoned women, Laurel, states:

> We don't have much of a voice in here. Speaking out against the conditions, we'll get punished. The staff do not care what we have to say and see us all as manipulative. We are definitely silenced and this is made obvious when we get in here. If we dare to speak out we can be punished, like being put in AdSeg.

----

dren to go and visit their fathers in prison as well. See http://www.getonthebus.us/. The Girl Scouts Behind Bars Program also brings mothers and children together (Craig, 2009).

Laurel explains that there are severe repercussions to contesting the authority of correctional officers, such as being placed in Administrative Segregation (solitary confinement). The message is do not step out of line or challenge the prison's authority; this makes many women fear speaking out against the injustices they encounter.

In addition to outright retaliation by correctional staff, women who have experienced prison identify other ways that they are silenced. Zoe explains:

> I felt silenced by the lack of power I had as an inmate. The minute I was assigned an inmate number I began to view myself differently. The guards only called us by our last name and this in itself created the illusion we did not exist. I was reprimanded and talked down to … by guards and staff.

Women report feeling dehumanized by the assignment of inmate numbers, making statements such as, "We are only a number in here. They don't see us as human." The assignment of inmate numbers serves to chip away at women's individuality and humanity, as they are seen as just one among many. The use of last names, too, puts a level of distance between guards and prisoners so that guards do not have to connect with the women in a more personal way. These tactics make it easier for guards to ridicule and act in a condescending manner toward incarcerated women, as the women are not seen to be on the same "level" as correctional officers.

## Medical Neglect and Guard Abuse

Silencing additionally occurs through medical neglect and guard abuse. All of the women interviewed and surveyed made at least passing reference to medical neglect and guard abuse, indicating that these are defining features of prison life. A formerly incarcerated woman, Anna, states, "I tried not to get sick because women came in walking and ended up in wheel chairs." The state of medical care is exceptionally bad in many or most women's prisons, with women dying unnecessarily. Zoe explains:

> There were women on the compound who had ailments impossible to treat or care for in a facility which was not a medical center. Women taken out for surgery would come back to the compound and receive improper post-op care, often getting infections. I knew a woman, who had been an attorney on the outside who was given wrong medication. In return she had a stroke, and by the time I left the compound, she looked as if she was close to dying. A woman died in her cube …

Everyone knew it was an unnecessary death and could have been prevented with earlier proper action and medical care. One woman I
lived with for six weeks in the "fish bowl"—a converted TV room,
overcrowded with sixteen women and no ventilation—went out to
have a hysterectomy. When she came back, she could barely walk. She
received no post-op care, and I only saw an officer check on her twice.
Mostly the inmates took care of her.

A formerly incarcerated woman, Kristi, states:

The healthcare is horrendous. I met this woman in the yard who was
a lifer. She was going to have some surgery on her toenail—she had
a really bad ingrown toenail. There was this other woman who was
slated for surgery and she was diabetic, and her foot had become gan-
grenous. They got their charts mixed up, and amputated the foot of
the lady who had the ingrown toenail. They then said, "Oh well," and
cut off all of her mail, outgoing, to keep the outside from knowing.
The woman with diabetes had to have her leg amputated higher because they waited so long, and she eventually died. Healthcare for myself, I got hurt and they never gave me physical therapy. I lost 25
percent of the mobility in my foot.

These stories, which may seem shocking to those of us on the outside of prison,
are par for the course on the inside of prison. Medical neglect has physical
consequences for imprisoned women, and it has other, more obscure consequences in that it essentially silences these women. This silence can be blatant,
as when prison personnel cut off outgoing mail to cover up malpractice and
keep women from speaking out about staff "mistakes." But it is also less obvious in that refusing to treat women's ailments, or treating them inappropriately,
frequently keeps imprisoned women physically weak and unable—even
afraid—to speak out about their conditions.

Abuse is another method of silencing that women, both incarcerated and
formerly incarcerated, highlight as defining much of their imprisonment. Although women in the study report that they have been subject or witness to both
physical and sexual harassment, it is the emotional abuse that prisoners identify as the most difficult to negotiate. Laurel states:

The thing is, they can refuse healthcare and get physical with us, but
it is the emotional abuse we go through that hurts the most. They call
us bitches and sluts and repeatedly tell us we are manipulators and

liars. Some of the staff mean well but many just look down on us as the scum of the earth. It gets to you.

Similarly, Zoe states:

Guards and staff belittled and ridiculed the inmates, imposing the position of power they held over us by the simple fact that they were employed by the Board of Prisons.

As Guevara Urbina (2008, p. 155) argues, verbal abuse is "one of the most powerful psychological mechanisms to humiliate, intimate, and control, and this conduct in female prisons seems to be more of a norm than the exception." The rampant emotional abuse that many women endure while in prison leads them to report feeling, "ashamed, doomed for hell, low self worth" (Luz), "powerless, angry, sad and a bad criminal" (Paz), "degraded" (Anna) and "like scum, and bitter with no self worth" (Marta). Although human rights organizations have understandably spent much time exposing the physical and sexual abuses that occur behind prison walls, such emotional abuse is just as damaging, if not more, because it is long lasting: emotional abuse has implications for one's self-esteem, self-confidence, and overall sense of self. The majority of the women in the study report that they believed they were unworthy, horrible people because of the statements that authority figures made about them. This makes it difficult for imprisoned women to accept themselves for their strength and resiliency. It also silences women: because they internalize the perceptions that staff have of them, voicing dissent around prison conditions becomes even more difficult as they believe that their treatment is deserved.

Incarcerated and formerly incarcerated women also tend to blame themselves for their incarceration. They report that they "made bad choices" (Paz) which led to their imprisonment. Although this "choice" framework moves us away from a structural interpretation of incarceration—and mirrors what society and correctional officers communicate to women in prison—it perhaps ironically allows imprisoned women a sense of agency, which may combat some of the powerlessness that they report. Women reported with pride that they had made changes in their lives despite the harsh reality of prison life, including obtaining an education while in prison, attending sober living programs, and changing their ways of thinking. More than merely supporting the idea that people are incarcerated due to poor life choices, the statements women make about individual responsibility also allow them some semblance of control over their lives: they feel that they are able to dictate the trajectory of their lives in a total institution where power, for the most part, comes from the top down.

## *Resistance and Voice*

Despite the silencing effects of prison, incarcerated women do find ways to resist and establish voices for themselves. Generally, women report that they choose their battles wisely because, as Marcus-Mendoza and Wright (2004) underscore, correctional systems punish resistance and expect conformity. Yet resistance has come, for example, in the form of class-action lawsuits, with women prisoners coming together to fight against healthcare conditions and sexual abuse. More often, however, women resist the process of silencing through formal channels within the prison system, such as filing grievances, and more informal channels, such as forging strong bonds of friendship with other prisoners, holding self-help group meetings, and engaging in acts of creativity that they can call their own even as the system labels them one of many.

### Formal Methods of Resistance: Complaints

Several of the women in the study report that they have filed grievances against the prison system for its treatment of women. Paz states:

> I had to be in lockup like three times. I wrote a complaint about a deputy once and I never saw her again after that day.

Erika also explains:

> I filed a complaint about the way I was treated by the staff, and my room got torn up right after that. They get back at us for complaining, but I felt good that I did something.

Both Paz and Erika contested the way they were treated by prison staff. Paz was successful in that she no longer had to deal with the behavior she was enduring; however, both Paz and Erika suffered repercussions. Although waging complaints against the prison system sometimes leads to retaliation by staff and administration, the grievance process is still conceptualized by some women, like Erika, as a way to assert and empower themselves.

### Informal Methods of Resistance: Friendships

While a minority of the women surveyed reported that they filed formal complaints against the prison system, the majority of respondents indicated that resistance can be conceptualized in broader, sometimes more obscure, ways as well. In this study, many incarcerated and formerly incarcerated women identified the friendships they made with other imprisoned women as critical for maintaining strength and a sense of self in the prison system. Indeed, the friendships that women share in prison are sometimes their saving graces, as Zoe explains:

> Women cared for each other and would take on the role of mother, sister, daughter, and even lover. Women of different race and class lived for the most part successfully side-by-side. I can honestly say the friendships I made in prison felt deep and real. The common thread we shared created a unique bond that could not be mimicked by my friends on the outside. I felt like no one could understand what I was going through as well as another inmate. Some women became my closest confidants and friends. Almost everything I did on the compound included a companion and friend by my side. We scheduled everything together including walking, eating meals, shopping, laundry, working out, walking to and from work, going to church, and crocheting. I am still in contact with some of the women I was incarcerated with and believe I will always have gratitude for what we experienced together.

Zoe's reference to women taking on the role of "mother, sister, daughter, and even lover" speaks to group formations in women's prisons, referred to by earlier research as "play families" (Owen, 1998; see also Heffernan, 1972; Giallombardo, 1966), "pseudo families" (Girshick, 1999; Selling, 1931) or "state families" (Girshick, 1999). Research by Owen (1998, p. 134) shows that personal connections in women's prisons have as their base "emotional, practical, and material connections as well as sexual and familial ties." Found particularly in women's institutions, it is not unusual for incarcerated women to form families, where, for example, an older woman may take on the role of mother and younger women may take on the role of daughters or sisters.[4] As Owen (1998) notes, these distinctions are often fluid and may change according to the context of the situation or the women involved in the family. With the exception of one respondent who felt that the members of prison families were constantly "in each other's business," and six respondents who felt that women in prison, on the whole, "can't be trusted," (see also Girshick, 1999; Greer, 2000; Severance, 2005) five incarcerated and formerly incarcerated women in this study were explicit that these families provide women with a sense of closeness that prisons generally discourage, and potentially, practical

---

4. Owen (1998) also notes that women may take on the role of father, son, or brother, but Girshick (1999) points out that the husband role in women's prisons is rare.

and material resources to be shared amongst their members. Although families were described by respondents to a lesser extent than friendships, the families these women created in prison kept their spirits up and are/were a response to the "loneliness and deprivations" of prison life (Girshick 1999, p. 89). Interestingly, Zoe was the only respondent in my study that mentioned romantic relationships between women in prison; none of the other respondents expressed whether they were romantically involved with incarcerated women.

Zoe also references the bonds she forged with women inside based on their common experiences with imprisonment. Unlike Zoe, four of the women in the study identified that they had only one or "some" close friends, one woman said she did not make any close friends at all, and one woman said she made "many associates but only one good friend," differentiating between close, intimate ties and more superficial relationships (Severance, 2005). Yet the majority of respondents talked about their friendships with women in prison in positive terms. These women expressed that they felt that only other women in prison could really understand what they experienced. Some further explained that friendships allowed them to connect with other women when prison administrators want them divided. Erika states:

> I was able to bond with women when the guards just wanted us to shut up and do what they told us. I could relate with the friends I made, trust in them, in ways that I could not with anyone on staff. I think the guards hated when we had friends, they probably thought it went against their authority. My friends were the ones who helped me to get through prison. They helped me to see who I am and helped me to value myself as a person, and to vocalize these things. I guess I felt powerless over my life when I went to prison, and really alone, but I got stronger through the women I met and felt I was part of a bigger picture. I also became more vocal about things I saw going wrong in the prison because I had friends watching my back.

Girshick (1999) draws on prior research (see Larson and Nelson, 1984) to discuss friendships between incarcerated women as a form of adaptation to prison life. Upon entry into prison, a woman may develop primary relations with other incarcerated women (including in the form of families and romantic relationships), and she may also transform a sense of powerlessness into control, through the friendships that she forges (Girshick, 1999). The friendships that Erika and other respondents entered into while in prison allowed them to not only escape feelings of isolation and loneliness, but to turn their feelings of powerlessness into strength. With the support of close friends, respondents like Erika reported that they felt justified in speaking out against conditions that they saw as unjust. In this way, the support of other women allows many women to find a voice in an institution that otherwise demands their silence. While I recognize that relationships among women in prison are complex and cannot be simplified into always being defined as empowering—indeed, some women in this study, as well as many in Girshick's (1999), Greer's (2000), and Severance's (2005) work, reportedly did not feel that they could trust other women in prison—for the majority of the respondents in this study friendships were extremely important to defying the "divide and conquer" mentality of the prison system.[5]

An interesting question is what happens to these friendships once women leave prison? Of the twelve formerly incarcerated women in the study, five indicated in their surveys that they keep in touch with their friends in prison. One responded that she does not keep in touch with women inside, and the rest did not mention whether they continue to maintain contact with incarcerated women. That only five women indicated that they remain friends with imprisoned women could be a function of many women wanting to put prison behind them upon parole, difficulty in maintaining personal connections when life on the outside can be challenging in terms of starting anew, or a separation between women's lives inside of prison verses their lives outside of prison. In any event, the fact remains that friendships have the capacity to help imprisoned women cope with and resist the conditions of confinement.

## Self-Help Groups and Organizing Within Prison

Both incarcerated and formerly incarcerated women also identified self-help groups as spaces where the potentialities for empowerment are realized. In these groups, friendships are forged and some women are able to find voice. Luz states:

> I made three very good friends and voiced myself by sharing in self-help groups.

---

5. Severance (2005, 354) points out that this distrust could result from prior experience with abuse in relationships as well as automatic negative perceptions of other inmates: "After all, the one thing these women know about the others is that they are all convicted felons and inmates are not immune to the influence of stereotypes and prejudices concerning convicts." Women in Severance's (2005) study also identified gossip, jealousy, and theft as reasons not to trust other prisoners.

Shelley expands on this:

> The groups I went to served as a place where I could bond with other women and get away, at least for an hour or so, from the strict rules. I could actually say what was on my mind, and I came to learn that other women went through similar things that I did. Groups were the one place where I felt sane. I felt like others understood me and I felt possibilities for me and the other women. In prison we were never taught there can be possibilities for us, they just cut us down day in and day out. Sharing in groups helped me to see that I may be worth something, and I learned the value of speaking up.

Prisons are places of containment, characterized by hyper-rationality. As Shelley alludes to, every minute and every aspect of prisoners' lives is measured, regulated, and controlled (Lawston, 2008). Incarceration itself includes confinement in a small space, strictly scheduled waking, sleeping, dining, and recreation hours, and control and measurement of prison cells and what is permitted in those cells (Lawston, 2008). In addition, prisoners are subjected to daily verbal degradation and humiliation—also mentioned by Shelley—and also, physical, sexual, and medical violence. All of this determines prisoners' complete subjection to their keepers, and on a larger scale, the state.

Yet within this oppressive social structure, the potential for empowerment, voice, and organizing remains. As Shelley explains, self-help groups serve as one area where women in prison are able to come together, share their stories, draw connections between their lives and the lives of the other women in the group, and importantly, *speak up*. In these spaces there is the potential for women to learn that their insights are valuable and their voice, important.

One example of an empowering self-help group is featured in the recent and compelling film *Sin By Silence*. *Sin By Silence* chronicles Convicted Women Against Abuse (CWAA), which was founded in 1989 by Brenda Clubine. This group is organized and led entirely by incarcerated women and serves as a space for discussions of their experiences with violence, as well as their legal cases. The efforts of this group have led to several women's releases, including Brenda Clubine's. The remaining members continue, as stated on the film's website, "to refuse to accept their status as powerless women prisoners. They choose to create new means to have their voices heard" (Sin By Silence, 2009).

## Creativity as Resistance

Creativity is another way to cope with, and exhibit personal expression in, the prison environment. Respondents reported that they took up writing, knitting, drawing, or other acts of creation as a way to manage the feelings that arose from being incarcerated. Jessica states, "I learned how to be creative making beautiful baskets just to release some of the energy it took to cope with being there." Zoe explains this more fully:

> I felt silenced by the lack of power I had as an inmate. I voiced myself by meditating and using my creativity as an outlet. I studied spiritual books and worked their programs. Because I could not speak out to the guards and staff, I chose instead to process what I experienced through my writing and art. In an odd way I felt as if my imprisonment helped me to find a creative voice. It was between me and God, and I did not want to go through the experience only as a victim to my circumstances and the Board of Prison.

Engaging in creative acts is not only a way for women to get their minds off the monotony of prison life, but a way for them to find their own, unique voices. Their creativity becomes a representation of themselves, one that the system cannot take away from them. Many women report that they shift their attention away from the pain they experience in prison, especially that which is forced upon them by staff, to creative projects and the development of their internal selves. For women like Zoe, this process is sometimes a spiritual one, where they become less engaged with how they are perceived by staff and more concerned with serving and connecting to something larger than themselves.[6]

Creative expression in prison provide women with a greater sense of control over their lives, when waking and sleeping schedules, visiting schedules, dining schedules, searches of living quarters and of their person, and even physical, sexual and emotional abuse and poor healthcare, are determined for them. While such expression may be a way for women to process their lives both before and during prison, it is also a way to escape the abuse and hu-

---

6. Related to creative expressions in prison are more formal programs that are offered in a few facilities across the nation. Art therapy has been used in some prisons so that women may express feelings associated with the violence they have endured over the course of their lives. Merriam (1998) argues that art therapy allows women in prison to express emotions— through their artwork—that they are not ordinarily allowed to process and express in a controlled environment. Although such programs are shown to have positive effects for incarcerated women—especially those who have suffered abuse—few facilities offer them (see also Marcus-Mendoza (2004) and Marcus-Mendoza and Wright (2004) on effective feminist therapies in prison settings).

miliation they endure behind prison walls—a way to resist the separation, loneliness, lack of control, and silencing of the prison system. Like friendships and self-help groups, creative expressions help women to see the value and power of their unique, individual voices.

# Conclusion

Incarcerated and formerly incarcerated women identify feelings of separation, loneliness, lack of control, and silencing as experiences that define their imprisonment. Silencing is especially salient for these women, as prisons are designed so that those within them must be compliant with the rules, regulations, policies and practices of those in power—no matter if they are unjust or unethical. Silencing is achieved in a variety of ways, such as retaliation or threats of retaliation, violence, emotional abuse, and medical neglect.

Yet as this chapter shows, despite the prison system's best efforts incarcerated women still find ways to resist these conditions and establish voice for themselves. There are a variety of means of resistance, such as through formal complaints and lawsuits, but more often than not women resist the silencing effects of prison in more informal ways. For some women these ways include forging strong bonds of friendship with other prisoners, organization of and participation in self-help groups, and/or engaging in acts of creativity. Although some women reported that they do not trust other women in prison and do not or did not have close friends in prison, most of the women in this study report that friendships are especially important for establishing support systems; some of these friendships last long after women are released from prison. In many ways, although women report that separation, lack of control, loneliness, and silencing define their incarceration, friendships, organizing within prison, and creativity as means of resistance also define their incarceration and help them to survive a system that continues to subordinate rather than uplift.

Because I surveyed both incarcerated and formerly incarcerated women for this study, I compared results to determine if there were any differences in responses between the two groups. Does what is experienced in prison look different in hindsight?

Interestingly, there were no observable differences in incarcerated and formerly incarcerated women's reflections on imprisonment. The most obvious difference is the immediate focus of the women. Incarcerated women focused more on conditions of confinement and how they cope with, or resist, those conditions. Formerly incarcerated women's reflections on imprisonment mirrored those of confined women, but women who were now in the "free world" focused more on their continued recovery outside of prison, the steps they had taken toward reunification with family, and the processes they were taking to go back to school. Incarcerated women also looked to the future, but their immediate environment provided formidable challenges that they had to address. This is not to say that formerly incarcerated women were not also faced with challenges upon and after their release (see O'Brien, 2001), but that the challenges the two groups faced, differed.

Additionally, several of the formerly incarcerated women expressed feeling fortunate that they were out of prison, explaining that they would now "learn to live life and enjoy the beauty it has to offer"(Luz). Several of these women explained that they planned to use their experiences in prison to educate society on incarceration; two of the respondents were in school to become drug and alcohol counselors, and one was going to school for a job in the field of mental health (Marta). These women suggested that their experiences, both before but especially during prison, served as powerful influences for how they were now living their lives. While prison and parole experiences—and access to resources, housing, and counseling—undoubtedly influence one's ease with re-entry into society in myriad ways (O'Brien, 2001), what these women suggest is that they have actively worked to reflect upon and use their experiences—as well as their voices—in ways that may benefit others and perhaps even effect powerful social change.

# References

Amnesty International. (1999). Not part of my sentence: Violations in the human rights of women in custody. Retrieved from www.amnestyusa.org/women/womeninprison.html.

Block, D., Wislanka, U., Pierson, C., and Fadem, P. (2008). The fire inside. *National Women's Studies Association Journal, 20*(8), 48–70.

Bloom, B., Chesney Lind, M, & Owen, B. (1994). Women in California prisons: Hidden victims of the War on Drugs. San Francisco, CA: Center on Juvenile and Criminal Justice.

Boudin. K. (1998). *Lessons from a mother's program in prison: A psychosocial approach* supports women and their children. In J. Harden and M. Hill (Eds.), *Breaking the rules: Women in prison and feminist therapy* (pp. 103–126). New York: The Harrington Park Press.

Brown, M. and Bloom, B. (2008). Colonialism and carceral motherhood: Native Hawaiian families under corrections and child welfare control. *Feminist Criminology, 4*(2), 151–169.

Browne, A., Miller, B., & Maguin, E. (1999). Prevalence and severity of lifetime physical and sexual victimization among incarcerated women. *International Journal of* Law and Psychiatry, *22*(3–4), 301–322.

Cook, S., Smith, S., Tusher, C.P., & Raiford, J. (2005). Self-reports of traumatic events in a random sample of incarcerated women. *Women & Criminal Justice, 16*(1/2), 107–126.

Covington, S. (1998). *Women in prison: Approaches in the treatment of our most invisible population.* In J. Harden and M. Hill (Eds.), *Breaking the rules: Women in prison and feminist therapy* (pp. 141–156). New York: The Harrington Park Press.

Craig, S. (2009). A historical review of mother and child programs for incarcerated women. *The Prison Journal, 89*(1), 35–53.

Diaz Cotto, J. (2006). *Chicana lives and criminal justice: Voices from el barrio.* Texas: University of Texas Press.

Dirks, D. (2004). Sexual revictimization and retraumatization of women in prison. *Women's Studies Quarterly, 32*(3/4), 102–115.

Dougherty, J. (2008). *Power-belief theory: Female criminality and the dynamics of oppression.*

In R. Zaplin (Ed.), *Female offenders: Critical perspectives and effective interventions,* (pp. 165–196). Massachusetts: Jones and Bartlett Publishers.

Enos, S. (1998). *Managing motherhood in prison: The impact of race and ethnicity on child placements.* In J. Harden and M. Hill (Eds.), *Breaking the rules: Women in prison and feminist therapy,* (pp. 57–74). New York: The Harrington Park Press.

Freedman, E. (1981). *Their sister's keepers: Women's prison reform in America, 1830–1930.* Ann Arbor: University of Michigan Press.

Giallombardo, R. (1966). *Society of women: A study of a women's prison.* New York: John Wiley & Sons.

Girshick, L. (1999). *No safe haven: Stories of women in prison.* Boston: Northeastern University Press.

Golden, R. (2005). *War on the family: Mothers in prison and the families they leave behind.* New York: Routledge.

Gottschalk, M. (2006). *The prison and the gallows: The politics of mass incarceration in America.* New York: Cambridge University Press.

Greenfeld, L. & Snell, T. (1999). Women offenders. Retrieved from Bureau of Justice Statistics, http://virlib.ncjrs.org/statistics.asp#w.

Greer, K. (2000). The changing nature of interpersonal relationships in a women's prison. *The Prison Journal, 80,* 442–468.

Guevara Urbina, Martin. (2008). *A comprehensive study of female offenders: Life before, during, and after incarceration.* Illinois: Charles C. Thomas, Publisher, LTD.

Harden, J. and Hill, M., eds. (1998). *Breaking the rules: Women in prison and feminist therapy.* New York: The Harrington Park Press.

Heffernan, E. (1972). *Making it in prison: The square, the cool, and the life.* New York: John Wiley & Sons.

Heney, J., & Kristiansen, C.M. (1998). *An analysis of the impact of prison of women survivors* of childhood sexual abuse. In J. Harden and M. Hill (Eds.), *Breaking the rules: Women in prison and feminist therapy*, (pp. 29– 44). New York: The Harrington Park Press.

Human Rights Watch. (1996). All too familiar: Sexual abuse of women in U.S. state prisons." Retrieved from http://hrw.org/reports/1996/Us1.htm#_1_36.

James, J. (2005). *The new abolitionists: (Neo) slave narratives and contemporary prison writings.* Albany: State University of New York Press.

Johnson, P.C. (2003). *Inner lives: Voices of African American women in prison.* New York and London: New York University Press.

Lam, T. (2008, February 1). Jury awards women $15.4 million for sexual abuse in prison. *Detroit Free Press.* Retrieved from http://www.sfwar.org/pdf/ PIC_USAT_02_08.pdf.

Lamb, W. (2004). *Couldn't keep it to myself: Wally Lamb and the women at York Correctional Institution.* Harper Perrenial.

Larson, J. and Nelson, J. (1984). Women, friendship, and adaptation to prison. *Journal of Criminal Justice, 12,* 601–615.

Lawston, J.M. (2008). Women, the criminal justice system, and incarceration: Processes of power, silence, and resistance. *National Women's Studies Association Journal, 20*(2), 1–18.

Lawston, J.M. and Schlesinger, T. Forthcoming. Experiences of interpersonal violence and criminal justice control: A mixed method analysis.

Lofland, J.,& Lofland, L. (1995). *Analyzing social settings: A guide to qualitative observation and analysis.* Belmont, CA: Wadsworth.

Mack, A. (2007). Editor's introduction. *Social Research, 74*(2), xi–xiii.

Marcus-Mendoza, S.T. and Wright, E. (2004). Decontextualizing female criminality: Treating abused women in prison in the United States. *Feminism & Psychology,* 14, 250–255.

Marcus-Mendoza, S. (2004). Feminist therapy behind bars. *Women's Studies Quarterly, 32*(3/4), 49–60.

Marcus-Mendoza, S.T., Klein-Saffran, J., & Lutze, F. (1998). *A feminist examination of boot* camp prison programs for women. In J. Harden and M.

Hill (Eds.), *Breaking the rules: Women in prison and feminist therapy*, (pp. 173–186). New York: The Harrington Park Press.

Mauer, M., Potler, C., & Wolf, R. (1999). Gender and justice: Women, drugs and sentencing policy. Washington, DC: The Sentencing Project.

Merriam, B. (1998). To find a voice: Art therapy in a woman's prison. *Women & Therapy*, 21(1), 157–171.

Moe, A. (2006). Women, drugs and crime. *Criminal Justice Studies* 19(4): 337–352.

Morash, M. and Schram, P. (2002). *The prison experience: Special issues of women in prison.* Illinois: Waveland Press.

Morgan, D. (1998). *Restricted love.* In J. Harden and M. Hill (Eds.), *Breaking the rules: Women in prison and feminist therapy* (pp. 75–84). New York: The Harrington Park Press.

Mumola, C. (2000). Incarcerated parents and their children. Washington, DC: U.S. Department of Justice, Bureau of Justice Statistics.

O'Brien, P. (2001). *Making it in the 'free world:' Women in transition from prison.* Albany: State University of New York Press.

Owen, B. (1998). *In the mix: Struggle and survival in a women's prison.* Albany: State University of New York Press.

Pew Center on the States. (2008). Pew center finds more than one in 100 adults are behind bars." Retrieved from http://www.pewcenteronthestates.org/news_room_detail.aspx?id=35912.

Pollock, J. (2002). *Women, prison, and crime.* Wadsworth: Thomas Learning.

Pollock. J. (2004). *Prisons and prison life: Costs and consequences.* California: Roxbury.

Reed, D. and Reed, E. (2004). *Mothers in prison and their children.* In B. Price and N. Sokoloff (Ed.), *The criminal justice system and women: Offenders, prisoners, victims and workers* (pp. 261–273). New York: McGraw Hill.

Richie, B. (1996). *Compelled to crime: The gender entrapment of battered black women.* New York: Routledge.

Sin By Silence. (2009). www.sinbysilence.com.

Selling, L. S. (1931). The pseudo-family. *American Journal of Sociology* 37, 247–253.

Severance, T. (2005). 'You know who you can go to:' Cooperation and exchange between incarcerated women. *The Prison Journal*, 85(3), 343–367.

Singer, M., Bussey, J., Song, L., & Lunghofer, L. (1995). The psychosocial issues of women serving time in jail. *Social Work, 40*(1), 103–113.

Sudbury, J. (2005). *Global lockdown: Race, gender, and the prison industrial complex.* New York: Routledge.

Talvi, S. (2007). *Women behind bars: The crisis of women in the U.S. prison system*. California: Seal Press.

Tuesday, V.J. (1998). *Girls in jail*. In J. Harden and M. Hill (Eds.), *Breaking the rules: Women in prison and feminist therapy* (pp. 127–139). New York: The Harrington Park Press.

U.S. Department of Justice, Bureau of Justice Statistics. (1999). Women offenders. Washington, DC: US Government Printing Office.

Walker, E., Unutzer, J., Rutter, C., Gelfand, A., Saunders, K., VonKorff, M., Koss, M., & W. Katon. (1999). Costs of heath care use by women HMO members with a history of childhood abuse and neglect. *Archive of General Psychiatry, 56*, 609–613.

Western, B. (2007). Mass imprisonment and economic inequality. *Social Research, 74*(2), 509–532.

Zaplin, R.T. (2008). *Female offenders: A systems perspective*. In R.T. Zaplin (Ed.), *Female offenders: Critical perspectives and effective interventions*, (pp. 77–98). Massachusetts: Jones and Bartlett Publishers.

# Inequality among Female Offenders: Racial Disparities in Substance Abuse and Medical Treatment among Mothers in Prison

*Zina T. McGee, Ph.D., Kaneesha Williams, B.S., Nicollette Strickland, B.A., Tamara Dobson-Brown, B.A., and Mykeya Foreman, B.S.*

## Statement of Problem

*I was unconscious here once for 42 minutes before they called the ambulance. They need better mental health programs, especially for PTSD and bi-polar disorders. You need to be able to get to see a counselor when you need to see one. The case managers want to help but their cases are far too large. I get my meds at 8 am.... for my teeth. I get Motrin and Penicillin because I have had a sore tooth for the past 2 and a half months.... There is only one dentist ... and there is a big waiting list because they can only take so many at a time and many of us have dental issues ...*

(Incarcerated Women's Initiative Vermont Research Partnership Complete Report, 2007)

Research consistently shows a discernible increase in the number of women incarcerated in the United States, many of whom are detained for non-violent, first-time offenses (Schmalleger and Smykla, 2011). Studies have also suggested that among those women incarcerated for low-level offenses, their increased rates of drug addiction are indicative of their need to escape economic hardship and childhood pain, yet they are less likely to receive drug treatment while incarcerated. Further, the majority of women in prison have been victims of domestic violence at some point in their lives, and they are more likely to have been raised in poor and working class families, an issue that is rarely addressed in discussions of counseling female inmates suffering from traumatic victimization (Fernandes, 2009). Moreover, the medical treatment of women who are incarcerated remains far worse than that of men, and female prisoners are more likely to suffer from chronic health problems since the criminal justice system does not adequately address their unique needs. As a result, many female inmates suffer from higher rates of asthma, gynecological disease, seizure disorders, and dietary problems.

The issue becomes increasingly complex when the inmate is a mother or she is pregnant. In fact, an estimated 6.7 % of black women, 5.9% of Hispanic women, and 5.2% of white women are likely to be pregnant at the time of incarceration (Schmalleger and Smykla, 2011). Further, pregnant women who are in jails or prisons are often provided no prenatal care or adequate nutrition, and many do not have access to special facilities or any information given to them about their options, such as termination or adoption. As a result, scholars have recommended that women's penal institutions need to provide adequate counseling for pregnant inmates, extensive prenatal care, and delivery at community hospitals (Fernandes, 2009). The aforementioned issues point toward the multitude of problems that many incarcerated women face, as research continues to suggest that women offenders with histories of substance abuse, in particular, present complex clinical profiles with a range of medical, psychological, and social problems (Nighawan et al., 2010). However, fewer programs have assessed the specific needs of these women and have focused more on the observations of clinicians.

Research has also shown that certain familial background characteristics (i.e., living situation while growing up, family history of incarceration, and parental abuse of drugs and alcohol) relate to the female inmate's own circumstances including abuse prior to incarceration, history of drug and/or alcohol abuse and physical illness, although treatment options to handle these conditions remain limited for many of these women.

Specific race differences regarding familial background characteristics (i.e., living situation while growing up, family history of incarceration, and parental abuse of drugs and alcohol) and/or the female inmate's own patterns of abuse prior to incarceration, history of drug and/or alcohol abuse and physical illness are also investigated as studies show that patterns of treatment including drug/alcohol, mental health counseling, drug treatment, medical attention, group counseling, parenting classes, and reunification counseling differ significantly across the offender's race and social class (McGee and Gilbert, 2010). In this paper, we give attention to the barriers to medical and substance-dependence treatment among incarcerated women and the extent to which access to these services differ by the aforementioned sociodemographic characteristics. Earlier studies have shown that women's criminal victimization and criminal offending, including drug use, are related, and the nature of this relationship has been explored through examinations of race and social class differences among women in prison (McGee and Gilbert, 2010). The present study investigates the nature of this relationship in a sample of female inmates in four states, addressing the following question, "What is the relationship between race and social class as risk factors and treatment for medical disorders and substance abuse/addiction?" The current paper emphasizes medical disorders, drug usage and drug treatment among a sample of incarcerated women in the states of Virginia, Maryland, District of Columbia, and New York.

## Female Offenders: Needs versus Available Services

A review of the literature suggests that research has continued to indicate disparities in substance abuse and medical treatment among incarcerated mothers. In a study of drug dependency among female inmates, for example, Bradley and Follingstad (2003) evaluated the effectiveness of group therapy for incarcerated women with histories of childhood sexual and/or physical abuse. Results revealed that 43% to 75% of the incarcerated women experienced physical or sexual assault and reported symptoms including depression, PTSD, borderline personality disorder, and substance abuse. Their findings suggested that among incarcerated women, skills training should effectively address self-respect, trust in others, and identifying symptoms of depression, anxiety, and PTSD (Bradley and Follingstad, 2003). McGee and Gilbert (2010), in a related study of female detainees, found that half of them engaged in both drug and alcohol abuse at the time of their offense, and although they were likely to display significant substance abuse problems, they were less likely to receive substance abuse treatment while incarcerated. Instead, minimal treatment was offered to these women suffering from a range of other problems, addressing the need for increased group therapy, family counseling, reunification programs, and mental health treatment. Regarding the special population of substance-abusing pregnant female inmates, Hotelling (2008) posits that these women have health-care needs that are minimally met by the prison systems, and many of the mothers have high-risk pregnancies due to the economic and social problems that led them to be incarcerated (i.e., poverty, lack of education, inadequate health care, and drugs) (Association of Women's Health, 2011). Further, Hotelling (2008) has suggested that issues of multicultural counseling awareness, sensitivity, and training are rarely focused on in discussions of what happens to many women who will ultimately be released from jails and prisons, only to recidivate because of the lack of proper aftercare. Yet, studies continues to show that when handling female offenders within a correctional setting, less emphasis is placed on dealing with issues of incest, childhood sexual abuse, pregnancy, neglect despite the fact that many of these women are also mothers with children under the age of 18 (Crossman, 2012; Hotelling, 2008).

Concerning the mental health treatment of female offenders, Muraskin's (2012) research suggests that certain characteristics that are overlooked when developing programs consistently demonstrate the need for gender-specific programs. For example, when considering mental health issues, her results from a study of female detainees shows that 33 percent of female offenders were diagnosed with post-traumatic stress disorder, 12.2 percent were diagnosed with a serious mental illness, and 72 percent presented a dual diagnosis (mental health and substance abuse). However, despite these statistics, many of the female inmates reported inadequate mental health treatment. Here she argues that women bring a variety of unique health and relationship issues to the prison experience, but without understanding the many characteristics of female offenders, treatment programs cannot be appropriately tailored to address their needs (Muraskin, 2012). This poses a particular problem for women offenders since many of them are more likely to have been sexually abused as children with mental health issues that were not properly diagnosed and treated prior to incarceration (McGee and Gilbert, 2010).

Regarding additional specific medical conditions among women in prison, Nijhawan et al. (2010) examined the preventive healthcare needs of incarcerated women in the following areas: cervical cancer and breast cancer screening, sexually transmitted infection (STI) screening, hepatitis screening and vaccination, and smoking cessation. They conducted a cross-sectional survey with a random sample of incarcerated women and found that Hispanic and black females reported being less likely than white females to have been tested for hepatitis C and screened for breast and cervical cancer. Moreover, the survey participants' common social characteristics, such as high rates of mental illness, substance use, and housing instability, combined with low levels of education and health insurance, defined a group of women with a multitude of healthcare needs but limited access to routine medical care in their communities (Nijhawan et al., 2010). The authors concluded that incarceration provides an opportunity to educate, screen, and treat female inmates for illnesses by which they are disproportionately affected.

Finally, Covington (1998) describes different approaches regarding the treatment of the "invisible woman," many of whom suffer from the aforementioned conditions. In an effort to increase the awareness of women's lives in the criminal justice system, she examined four areas of concern that incarcerated women report as being both most challenging and the major precursor to relapse: self, relationships, sexuality, and spirituality. In a review of her research, she found that virtually every survey respondent reported that there was too little funding for treatment services, that there were not enough drug treatment facilities or appropriate placements for drug dependent clients, and there was a lack of qualified personnel to staff treatment programs (Covington 1998). Similarly, Bloom and Covington (2008) found that among a sample of incarcerated women in California, there was less likelihood to have committed a violent offense and more likelihood to have been convicted of a crime involving alcohol, other drugs or property. Most of the female prisoners in the sample were poor, undereducated, and unskilled single mothers, and a disproportionate number of them were women of color. Two-thirds of the incarcerated women had children under the age of 18, and health care, particularly pre-natal care, education, job training and treatment for alcohol/other drug abuse were all absent from the women's prison system according to the respondents. The lack of proper substance abuse treatment programs is evidenced in the fact that in recent years, shrinking tax dollars for community based programs have led judges to believe that the best chance that pregnant, addicted women have for treatment is through sentencing and incarceration. Many women enter the prison system with a poor self-image and a history of trauma and abuse, problems which are further exacerbated by the limited resources afforded them while detained.

In summary, the focus of the criminal justice system is not on the middle- to upper-income white women addicted to prescribed medications, but on the disproportionate number of lower-income women of color, African American women in particular, who abuse illegal substances (McGee and Gilbert, 2010). Research consistently shows that women are still denied comprehensive services including transition programs, alternatives to violence training, aftercare, counseling, mental health treatment, life skills training, parenting skills training, and vocational preparation, and even less emphasis is placed on specialized programs that incorporate women's victimization as part of their treatment for drug abuse and criminal behavior. Strategies for successful intervention often do not include a holistic approach, and fewer programs address the impact of domestic violence on substance abuse, a problem which is more pronounced for African American women (Bloom and Covington, 2008). Situations for these women are worsened by their poor educations, limited resources, and their location in high crime neighborhoods. While many of their crimes are non-violent, they are more likely to face charges of child abuse and neglect, much of which is due to the impact of race and gender oppression on addiction, often not addressed in counseling approaches (McGee and Gilbert, 2010). This is particularly problematic since it has been suggested that the children of incarcerated women may be the next generation of prisoners without access to successful intervention programs and the necessary financial resources to escape poverty and violence.

## Theoretical/Conceptual Framework

Feminist theory is a major contemporary sociological theory which analyzes the status of women and men in society with the purpose of using that knowledge to better women's lives (Crossman, 2012). Feminist theorists continue to question the differences between women, including how race, class, ethnicity, and age intersect with gender. While the approach gives a voice to women, there are four main focuses of feminist theory that attempt to explain the societal differences between men and women: gender differences, gender inequality, gender oppression, and structural oppression. The gender difference perspective examines how women's location in, and experience of, social situations differ from men's. Feminist theorists believe that the different roles assigned to women and men within institutions better explain gender difference. Gender inequality theories recognize that women's location in, and experience of, social situations are not only different from but also unequal to men's (Crossman, 2012). Theories of gender oppression extend theories of gender difference and gender inequality by arguing that not only are women different from or unequal to men, but that they are actively oppressed, subordinated, and even abused by men (Crossman, 2012). Finally, the structural oppression theories posit that women's oppression and inequality are a result of capitalism, patriarchy, and racism (Crossman, 2012). Crossman (2012) states that intersectionality theorists seek to explain oppression and inequality across a variety of variables, including class, gender, race, ethnicity, and age. They also argue that not all women experience oppression in the same way. White women and black women face different forms of discrimination.

With regard to the applicability of this perspective to the current study, the substance abuse and medical treatment of incarcerated women is drastically worse than the treatment of incarcerated men. Furthermore, female prisoners are more likely to suffer from chronic health and mental health problems because the prison medical system is devised to serve males without addressing the unique needs of women. As a result, many female inmates suffer from higher rates of anxiety, depression, PTSD, asthma, gynecological disease, seizure disorders, and dietary problems. Pregnant women may not be afforded prenatal care, while women abusing drugs may not receive adequate treatment from the holistic perspective to examine the family dynamics relating to abuse and victimization. Many of today's administrators and correctional officers still treat women as if they were men (Schmalleger and Smykla, 2011), and prisons do not feel as though they are required to fulfill their specific needs. Hence, there is a dire need for more gender specific programs in light of these disparities for the critical evaluation of existing programs to further determine what is effective, what contributes best to the reduction of recidivism, and what promotes the greatest mental and physical health outcomes among the diverse population of women in prison and the children that they leave behind.

# Methodology

In this research study, we focus on several factors that are of concern when investigating female offenders. Issues central to the current study are the experiences of women in jail and prison particularly with regard to substance abuse and medical treatment. Our intent is to explore the linkage between race, social class and disparate medical and substance abuse treatment among a sample of female inmates. Special attention is paid to the treatment for drug and alcohol problems, and the extent to which such treatment differs across dimensions of race and social class. The study uses two primary sources of information: survey data collected from 200 female inmates and in-depth interviews conducted with 20 women who were either incarcerated at the time of the interview or had been released from the correctional setting. The goal is to address the following research question: "What is the relationship between race and social class as risk factors and treatment for medical disorders and substance abuse/addiction?"

Surveys were conducted with 200 women incarcerated in jails in Virginia, Maryland, District of Columbia, and New York. Twenty interviews were also conducted with some of the women currently housed in the jails and a few who had been released from the correctional institution. We recruited women to the study by requesting volunteers within the female housing unit and obtaining information on other women who would be willing to address their experiences after incarceration. We specifically recruited women with children, and the study reports on a convenience sample since random sampling was not available due to considerable transition and court dates. We obtained informed consent, and research assistants conducted the interviews and distributed the surveys to the women in a private setting within the jails. We also interviewed females released from prison in community centers that provided services to ex-offenders. There was no compensation provided for data collection within the jails; however, women in the community centers who were former jail inmates received $20 for each interview.

Questionnaire items examined familial background characteristics (i.e., living situation while growing up, family history of incarceration, and parental abuse of drugs and alcohol), the inmate's own situations including abuse prior to incarceration, history of drug and/or alcohol abuse, physical illness, patterns of treatment including drug/alcohol treatment, mental health counseling, medical attention, group counseling, parenting classes, and reunification counseling. Items also addressed the mechanisms that female inmates used to cope with their incarceration, particularly in instances where extended separation from children was involved. To further understand the experiences of women in jail and the manner in which they coped with being away from their children, we used a series of open-ended questions in the interviews addressing how the female inmates felt about being away from home, the impact that incarceration had on their lives, the degree to which they received support in jail to assist with rehabilitation, the factors that contributed to their ability to cope while in jail, their goals in life prior to incarceration, and the dynamics of dealing with criminal justice personnel. The questions were later modified for a follow-up interview on released offenders to explore how they adjusted to life after incarceration. For this study, women receiving drug abuse and mental health treatment were compared with women who did not.

## Analysis and Findings

Descriptive statistics were obtained and results show that at the time of their arrest, the plurality of women were between the ages of 35-44 (42%), were divorced (36%), had completed high school (38%), and were employed full time (34%). The majority of the women were black (55%), and a vast majority of the women had children under the age of 18 (71%). They were more likely to have been charged with drug possession (46%), followed by larceny theft (34%), fraud (22%), other offenses relating to drugs (20%), and other property offenses (10%). None of the women reported involvement in violent offenses such as murder, negligent manslaughter, and assault. The findings are consistent with previous studies which suggest that many of the women processed through the criminal justice system are non-violent, first-time offenders (Bradley and Follingstad, 2003; Fernandes, 2009; McGee and Gilbert, 2010). Regarding substance abuse and treatment, results also revealed that most women had a history of prior drug or alcohol abuse (75%), were under the influence of drugs or alcohol at the time of their arrest (52%), and had committed an offense to get money for drugs (60%).

Fewer women reported a history of mental illness or psychiatric condition (28%), although it should be noted that the question did not ask if they had been previously diagnosed with any type of mental disorder or mental illness. Eighteen percent of the women reported being under the influence of psychiatric medication at the time of their arrest. Regarding specific types of drugs, the majority of women reported having used marijuana (80%) and/or cocaine (65%) compared to other drugs such as heroin, stimulants, depressants, hallucinogens, antidepressants, and other drugs such as crack. These figures are supported by research suggesting that women offenders with histories of substance abuse present multifaceted profiles with a range of medical, emotional, and societal problems (Nighawan et al., 2010). However, a smaller amount of programs have evaluated the explicit needs of these women and have focused more on the interpretations of medical personnel. In that regard, results from the current study showed that the majority of women had not received drug or alcohol treatment at some point in their lives (62%), and fewer had received mental health counseling (41% had). Additionally, these women were less likely to report that they had received drug or alcohol treatment (35%) and mental health counseling while in jail (10%). Less than one-fourth of the women received a gynecological examination while incarcerated (23%), while a small percentage reported that they were pregnant at the time that they entered the correctional facility (5%). Few of them reported having received prenatal care while incarcerated (5%). As expected, these findings have treatment policy implications. Too few women are given access to services such as drug treatment, mental health counseling, family reunification, parenting classes and group counseling. Many of these women will ultimately be released without stable housing or legal sources of income. Discussions of the treatment of released jail detainees continue to utilize a pathological framework while denying the multidimensional needs of women who have been victimized by physical abuse and drug addictions. Bloom and Covington (2008), for example, argue that the greatest risk for female inmates is their loss of parental rights, which results primarily from maternal substance abuse and the lack of reunification services for women offenders. The likelihood of mother/child reunification declines with prior maternal incarceration, and as women are arrested, convicted and incarcerated multiple times, the rates at which they will be permanently separated from their children are quickly rising, further suggesting the need to explore additional treatment options for these women beyond the traditional substance abuse programs. The needs of these women are multidimensional, and research findings continue to show that effective treatment programs should be designed to address all aspects of their incarceration and subsequent release.

## *Race, Medical History and Treatment: Quantitative Findings*

Results also show specific racial differences among the women in jail, including information on their family background, history of abuse, relationships with their children, drug addiction, mental health status, physical health, the extent of treatment for drugs and mental illness, participation in specific programs, and patterns of coping with incarceration. Chi-Square Tests for Independence ($\chi^2$) were conducted for this portion of the analysis, and we report all relationships that were significant at the .05 level.

Results indicated that white women were more likely than their black counterparts to report a prior history of drug or alcohol abuse (100%), report a prior history of mental illness or psychiatric condition (40%), indicate that they were under the influence of drugs or alcohol at the time of their arrest (82%), indicate that they were under the influence of psychiatric medication at the time of their arrest (40%), and report that they committed an offense to get money to buy drugs (89%). Compared to black women, they were also more likely to indicate that at some point in their lives they had used marijuana (100%), cocaine (100%), heroin (42%), stimulants (51%), depressants (69%), hallucinogens (51%), and antidepressants (58%). However, with regard to the use of crack (which was categorized as a separate drug from cocaine), black women were more likely to report usage (18%). This finding is consistent with Bloom and Covington's (2008) argument that crack cocaine has had a major impact on African American women, particularly those who maintain their own households and are currently receiving AFDC. Here they suggest that the unique experiences of African American women are often dismissed, and they propose a feminist model to examine the full context of their lives since successful intervention requires a holistic approach. Further, they note that the oppressive intersection of race, class, and gender must be examined within the context of domestic violence and addiction among females, women of color in particular. This is an issue that must be addressed by counselors in an effort to provide effective treatment.

As stated earlier, few of the female inmates reported participation in a variety of programs other than those addressing substance abuse. Additional findings suggest specific racial differences with regard to women's participation in these programs (using Chi-Square Tests for Independence -$\chi^2$). For example, white women were more likely than their black counterparts to report participation in mental health counseling (58%), to report being diagnosed with a physical illness (40%) and treated by a doctor (40%), to report receiving a gynecological examination while incarcerated (40%), to report participation in individual/group counseling prior to incarceration (40%) and while incarcerated (11%), to have received prescription medications in jail (40%), to have been treated for a diagnosed mental condition prior to incarceration (58%) and while incarcerated (40%), and to have received family counseling (51%). However, results also show that black women were more likely to report participation in drug/alcohol treatment in jail (55%). Fewer reported participation in mental health counseling (18%), although the percentage of participation remained higher than that of white women.

Additionally, white women reported greater reliance on the following to cope with detainment: family (100%), friends (100%), and a pastor (60%). Black women were more likely to report reliance on their children (50%) in their efforts to cope with their situation. Concepts of familial bonds and kinship care among women of color are supported by our findings, although it must also be noted that the cumulative effects of poverty, racism, and sexism experienced by many black mothers will ultimately become the experiences of their children, thus creating a new generation of youth at risk.

Findings of racial differences regarding the types of treatment and services offered to female inmates further support McGee and Gilbert's (2010) assertion that minority women continue to face collateral damage within the penal system as they are forced to bear the burden of punitive policies and extreme sentencing, only to find themselves facing another plight as they are denied effective treatment for the problems that they may experience beyond drug addictions. Their consistent lack of participation in programs such as family/ individual counseling and mental health treatment provides further evidence of the discriminatory practices that will prevent them from achieving outcomes relating to economic independence, family reunification and reduced criminal involvement.

**Table 11.1. Zero Order Correlations of Education and Race toward Access to Medical and Drug/Alcohol Treatment in Prison among Female Inmates**

|  | *Highest Level of Education* | *Race/Ethnic Origin* | *Participate in Medical and Drug/Alcohol Treatment Program in Jail* |
|---|---|---|---|
| *Highest Level of Education* | 1.00 |  |  |
| *Race/Ethnic Origin* | -.072 | 1.00 |  |
| *Participate in Medical and Drug/Alcohol Treatment Program in Jail* | .096 | -.453* | 1.00 |

*Significant at the 0.01 level (2-tailed).

For additional analyses, variables measuring medical treatment (i.e., treated by a doctor, seen by a physician, received medication in jail) and drug/alcohol treatment (i.e., received services while in jail) were combined to create an indicator measuring access to medical and substance-dependence services. Thus, categories were collapsed into just two categories measuring the presence/absence of treatment. Relationships between race, social class, and access to treatment were investigated using Pearson product-moment correlation coefficient. Preliminary analyses were performed to ensure no violation of the assumptions of normality, linearity and homoscedasticity. There was a moderate, negative correlation between the two variables ($r = -.453$, $p < .01$), with minority women being less likely to report access to medical and drug/alcohol treatment while in prison. However, there was no significant correlation between education as a measure of social class and access to medical and drug/alcohol treatment program as seen in Table 11.1.

Results from the Chi-Square test in Table 11.2 indicated that there was a significant relationship between race and access to medical and drug/alcohol treatment in prison among the female inmates. Black women were the least likely to participate (73.7%) in comparison to other groups (Chi Square=66.309, $p = <.01$). Regarding class differences, education had no effect on access to treatment among incarcerated women. While the statistics are consistent with previous research, studies have cautioned against over-generalizing when analyzing data with specific characteristics similar to those in this sample. Researchers have also pointed toward discrepancies in self-report data.

Table 11.2. Chi Square Analysis of Relationships between Race and Access to Medical and Drug/Alcohol Treatment among Female Inmates

|  | *White* | *Black* | *Other* |
|---|---|---|---|
| *Treatment* | 62.8% | 26.3% | 34.8% |
| *No Treatment* | 37.2% | 73.7% | 65.2% |

*Significant at the 0.01 level (2-tailed).

Table 11.3. Multiple Regression Analysis of Relationship between Race, Social Class, and Access to Medical and Drug/Alcohol Treatment Programs in Jail

| *Independent Variables* | *b* | *Standard Error* | *Beta* | *t* |
|---|---|---|---|---|
| *Race/Ethnicity Origin* | -.430* | .061 | -.448 | -7.061 |
| *Highest Level of Education* | .039 | .039 | .064 | 1.006 |

*Significant at .01 level (2-tailed).

Finally, results from the regression analysis in Table 11.3 indicate that 20.9% of the variation in medical and drug/alcohol treatment participation was explained by race and education (as a measure of social class). The overall model suggests that when taken together, both variables have an effect (F=26.073, p<.01). The partial model shows that race is the best and only predictor of access to treatment when controlling for education (b=-.430, p<.01), suggesting that the race of the female inmate predicts her access to medical and drug/alcohol treatment regardless of social class.

## *Race, Medical History and Treatment: Qualitative Findings*

A variety of themes surfaced from the interview responses. Among them were concerns about their children and visitation, having limited support and treatment for mental health and substance abuse, being undereducated with few resources, and facing lengthy sentences for non-violent crimes. In addition to the concerns of the mother-child separation, a critical component to the unique experiences of incarcerated women is the pervasive issue of lack of treatment for mental health problems and drug abuse. With conditions that have often been misdiagnosed or untreated, some of the women indicated that substance abuse was the primary factor that caused them to return to jail or prison several times. They also discussed feeling uneducated and unaware about their addictions. During additional interviews with women who had been released from prison, Vanessa, a 54-year-old black woman who served time for shoplifting and drug charges, said in a raspy voice,

> Prison taught me nothing ... it was a waste of my time, it did not treat the problem, I am now clean for 10 years because of Narcotics Anonymous (NA). My help came from learning how to deal with my disease, I was not educated on the disease ... it made me numb ... it made me feel good. But through NA I have learned how to deal with my problems and face them ... prison taught me nothing!

Vanessa, who has been out of the system for 11 years, also said,

> I wanted the feeling everybody else had, I used drugs to numb feelings from my abusive husband. Heroin, coke, I did it all, I had to have it! I even tried to commit suicide, the drugs weren't taking anymore, everything I did, stealing, prostitution, it was for drugs. I was worthless, penniless ... the drugs tear you down, they make you worn out, but now ... I'm worth more than all the gold in the world.

As Vanessa spoke it became even more evident that the hopelessness that once controlled her mind and her life resulted from excessive drug abuse precipitated by domestic violence. This is supported by empirical studies, and understanding the nexus between domestic violence incidents and substance abuse is a critical factor in treating and healing the female offender. As with Vanessa's circumstance, other women interviewed in jail expressed the same concerns with inadequate treatment and limited knowledge of their addictions. Fariah, a 37-year-old black mother, discussed in an angry tone her feelings toward the lack of resources within prisons and jails compared to the resources provided to male inmates. She said,

> They have courses for men here, they are cared for here, there is nothing for women ... no parenting skills, no reunification programs,

nothing. The other local jail has more programs for women but most of us are on the waiting list to get there where we could get better help.

Karen, a 45-year-old biracial woman dealing with a shoplifting addiction, said that she found herself misdiagnosed, misunderstood and frustrated with limited support and assistance. Only recently had her shoplifting problem been linked to severe clinical depression after several years of being arrested and detained in jails. She said,

> I am good away from home, it's a safe haven for me here, I have never abused drugs or alcohol, I was placed on anti-depressants but that is not what I need, I need help with my shoplifting problem, they say I'm a kleptomaniac, they never looked at me to see what was wrong until I asked them, so I'm safe here.

Another theme that emerged was the lack of programs for rehabilitation. For many of the women, jail was not just considered to be a place to confine those who have committed crimes, but also a place that offers rehabilitation from problems they faced prior to incarceration and while incarcerated. While there are programs within the prison to help women recover from drugs and alcohol use, all prisons are not the same and do not provide the same programs to every female. A participant named Saroyal, a 39-year-old African American mother of 4 says,

> I was in a reflection program in jail, it is associated with the CSB. It is a drug program. It is a program that after so many days you have been released from jail they will help you with certain things, but not for the long term. Once I got out I had nothing left to help me with my addiction in the street. The only people who really benefited from this program were the people who were mentally unstable while in jail. For the rest of us, they just gave us Prozac, Abilify or Trazadone, and then they gave us clothes.

Her words express that while there are programs provided to women are incarcerated, many of them are not specific to the unique needs of those greatly affected by histories of drug abuse, addiction, and victimization. The programs Saroyal spoke of are not long-term and have not had a tremendous impact on her life. She was able to get back on her feet but only for a moment as she indicates, and at this point does not know what will happen to her. She feels as though she should head back to prison because it is a place of shelter and food since she is not being rehabilitated outside of prison.

Shakeria, a 23-year-old mother of two expresses some of the same sentiments as Saroyal when she says,

> My goal in life was to finish college and settle down and then have some children. When I met my boyfriend he informed me that he did not want children. He was a drug dealer and I went along with his plans. Not only did we sell drugs … we used drugs. We both got arrested for selling drugs and possessing controlled substances. We were arrested at the same time. The only thing I think about now is when my boyfriend will be released from jail. I don't expect to ever be clean again and there is no one to really help me with that anyway. I didn't get much of that in jail. I don't know what I am going to do.

As Shakeria spoke, it became even more obvious that what controlled her thoughts continued to exist as a consequence from her extreme drug misuse with little or no rehabilitation. As with her situation, other women interviewed in prison articulated the same anxieties with insufficient treatment and inadequate information of their addictions. Crystal, a 40-year-old black mother, for example, also discussed the lack of resources inside penitentiaries. She said,

> They have resources for persons interested in obtaining their GED. The jails are not concerned with whether or not or how the prisoners will interact with their loved ones when they are discharged. There are no lessons on the reunification process or how to stay off drugs. They don't even help us with our physical problems. I suffer all the time with chest pains and migraines, but get no help, just aspirin.

As with Crystal's circumstance, other women interviewed upon release from jail expressed the same concerns with inadequate treatment and limited knowledge of their addictions. Angela, a 30-year-old black mother, addressed her feelings toward the absence of resources. She said,

> There was nothing for me … no counseling for my sexual abuse, no drug treatment programs, nothing. Nothing for my physical pain for my illnesses. The jail had some programs but they treated us all the same no matter what our problems were. We didn't see doctors much, and no one helped me with my drug problem. I won't be able to be any better than I am because now there aren't even other programs for me now that I am out. Just drug court. It helps some but some of the classes they send us to don't even relate to me and my problems.

The themes that materialized from the dialogues with these women support the idea that a woman's experience in prison may be affected by the numerous dimensions of her life such as prior mistreatment, domestic violence, separation from their children, and additional fears exclusive to women in our culture. In spite of the limited investigations on the connection linking reduced contact with children while imprisoned and repeated criminal activities, researchers persistently state that the subject of mother–child interactions is significant to the comprehension of women's criminal behavior after imprisonment (Fernandes, 2009). Several of the female offenders described feelings of hopelessness, humiliation, and guiltiness, yet stated they received no therapy to aid them with their psychological health condition. Many of them also pointed out that they only received substance abuse treatment in prison, and hardly any assistance had been supplied to them that dealt with group therapy, reuniting families, psychological health treatment, and counseling after being discharged. Where there is a scarce amount of rehabilitation and treatment, women will never be able to understand the normal structures of child-rearing because of the haze of addiction (McGee and Gilbert, 2010). The results of this investigation show the necessity for intervention plans that must be made available to women in prisons if they are to reunite with the family unit and flourish in their attempts to become resocialized within society.

## Summary and Conclusion

The release of an incarcerated mother can be a joyous occasion, but for many mothers, it can also be characterized by extreme disappointment. Upon release, many mothers discover that their children have grown and changed in their absence. Additionally, many realize that their children have become adjusted to new settings and caretakers. Unfortunately, many mothers find their children difficult to handle. Research suggests that this occurs because some children are fearful of repeated separations from their mothers (Bloom and Covington, 2008). Additionally, many children who have been separated for a long period of time are more likely to view their mothers as weak authority figures and are unable to understand or sympathize with their situations, leading them to act inappropriately. Research has also indicated that children of incarcerated mothers have an array of developmental problems, further suggesting the need for increasing programs which identify the multiple risks and issues of children of incarcerated women. Factors such as age during time of maternal incarceration and duration of incarceration are critical to understanding the development of children of incarcerated mothers (Covington, 1998).

Effective programs in prison can combat physical and psychological problems of women in the prison system. Presently, correctional institutions provide legally mandated levels of medical resources and services that only target physical health concerns and not mental health concerns. The programs that are most effective include a combination of substance abuse programs, work training, parenting classes, child visitation programs, work release programs, and education and health care programs (McGee and Gilbert, 2010). Women inmates also need a strong network of supportive peers and programs that deal with experiences of childhood sexual abuse, domestic violence, and negative relationships with men. To effectively reduce recidivism and promote healthy life choices and environments among women in the prison systems upon release, it is imperative to address past histories of victimization while dealing with current behaviors involving drug and alcohol abuse (Covington, 1998). Regarding limitations, the interviews for this study lasted only an average of two hours and were conducted on a select group of women drawn from the full sample of female inmates. The study would have benefited from a larger sample of interviewees questioned for an extended period of time. This would have allowed for a more detailed analysis of 200 mothers' narratives. Moreover, the information obtained from the women regarding their lives in jail, including medical and substance abuse treatment programs, cannot be confirmed within the restrictions of the study. Supplementary means of triangulation to substantiate the information provided by the mothers would have strengthened the project. Additionally, there is no reference group, so the extent of selection bias cannot be determined.

Correctional rehabilitative programs must become tailored to the subjective experience of the female offender. The characteristics of promising programs for women in prison must include substance abuse awareness, empowerment with basic life skills, parenting skills, vocational and educational training, as well as relationship empowerment. Other components of effective treatment are well trained staff, individualized and structured programs, sufficient resources, victimization services, and program participation. Because substance abuse is so prevalent among female offenders, programs for those on probation should also provide adequate childcare, which has been a significant hindrance to many women trying to meet probation requirements.

When addressing substance abuse, it is equally important to note the racial and economic differences that accompany usage (Bloom and Covington, 2008). Most minority and lower-income women are not addicted to legal substances, but are instead battling addictions to hard drugs such as crack cocaine.

The findings of this project support the contention that although there are programs that aim to treat the female offender and her addictions, there are fewer that incorporate family reunification, developing parenting skills, and counseling and treatment for mothers and their children. If the criminal justice system will not provide additional alternatives to incarceration, there must be an increase in funding for gender-specific treatment programs and greater emphasis on family-based correctional programs in order to successfully treat the female offender. The findings of this research study have clearly indicated a need for parenting programs, substance abuse treatment, mental health counseling for post-traumatic experiences, vocational/educational training, basic life skills training, and perhaps most importantly, programs for reuniting the mother and child and maintaining contact while she is incarcerated. Only then can we lay the foundation for treating and rehabilitating women in the "concrete womb," many of whom are forced to parent their children behind bars.

# References


Association of Women's Health, O. a. (2011). Shackling Incarcerated Pregnant Women. *Journal of Obstetric, Gynecologic, & Neonatal Nursing*, 817–818.

Bloom, B. E., & Covington, S. S. (2008). Addressing the Mental Health Needs of Women Offenders. *Women's Mental Health Issues Across the Criminal Justice System*.

Bradley, R. G., & Follingstad, D. (2003, August). Group Therapy for Incarcerated Women Who Experienced Interpersonal Violence: A Pilot Study. *Journal of Traumatic Stress, 16,/4*, 337–340.

Covington, S. S. (1998). Women in Prison: Approaches in the Treatment of Our Most Invisible Population. *Women and Therapy Journal, 21*, 141–155.

*Children of Incarcerated Parents Fact Sheet*. (2011). Retrieved November 10, 2011, from FCNetwork.org: http://www.fcnetwork.org/AECFChildren%20of%20Incarcerated%20Parents%20Factsheet.pdf.

*Criminological Theory*. (2005, November 22). Retrieved September 28, 2012, from http://www.criminology.fsu.edu: http://www.criminology.fsu.edu/crimtheory/conflict.htm.

Crossman, A. (2012). *Feminist Theory: An Overview*. Retrieved October 9, 2012, from sociology.about.com: http://sociology.about.com/od/Sociological-Theory/a/Feminist-Theory.htm.

Fernandes, G. K. (2009, November 2). *Pregnant Prisoners: Enduring Labor Behind Bars*. Retrieved November 14, 2011, from MomLogic.com: http://www.momlogic.com/2009/11/pregnant_prisoners_enduring_labor_behind_bars.php.

Hotelling, B. A. (2008). Perinatal Needs of Pregnant, Incarcerated Women. *The Journal of Perinatal Education*, 37–44.

McGee, Z. T., & Gilbert, A. N. (2010). Treatment programs for incarcerated women and mother-child communication levels. *Criminal Justice Studies: A Critical Journal of Crime, Law and Society, 23*(4), 337–345.

Muraskin, R. (2012). *Women and Justice: It's a Crime.* Upper Saddle River: Pearson Education.

Nijhawan, A. E., Salloway, R., Nunn, A. S., Poshkus, M., & Clarke, J. G. (2010, January 19). Preventive Healthcare for Underserved Women: Results of a Prison Survey. *Journal of Women's Health*, 17–22.

Schmalleger, & J. O. Smykla, *Corrections in the 21st Century* (pp. 351–356). (2011). Chapter 10: The Inmate World. New York: McGraw-Hill.

*The first federal prison for women opens.* (2011). Retrieved Novemeber 15, 2011, from The History Channel website: http://www.history.com/this-day-in-history/the-first-federal-prison-for-women-opens.

University of Vermont/ Vermont Research, P. (2007, June). *Incarcerated Women's Initiative Vermont Research Partnership Complete Report.* Retrieved September 17, 2012, from www.uvm.edu: http://www.uvm.edu/~vrp/IWICompleteReport_June_07.pdf.

# Second-Chance Grandparenting: How a New and Renewed Identity Impacts the Desistance Process

*Erin M. Kerrison, Ph.D., and Ronet Bachman, Ph.D.*

## Introduction

Among the recent plethora of research examining criminal desistance, studies have begun to show that popular theories of desistance, including Sampson and Laub's age-graded informal social control theory (Laub & Sampson, 2003; Sampson & Laub, 1993), appear insufficient when predicting desistance using contemporary samples of offenders leaving today's prisons, particularly those who are drug-involved. The sample of men upon which much of early theorizing was based featured a cohort of white males who came of age in the 1950s when well-paying industrial jobs were available and who, as a result, appear to have been amenable to changing their criminal behavior via routes such as gainful employment and good marriages. Recent theorizing about desistance has added to this structural background the psychological manifestations that appear to affect the success of the desistance process for active offenders today. For example, Maruna and colleagues (Farrall & Maruna, 2004; Maruna & Roy, 2007; Maruna, 2001, 2004) assert that desistance involves individuals reinterpreting their past criminal selves with prosocial views of themselves to reconcile their current identities as "good" people. This work was expanded through research by Giordano and her colleagues (Giordano, Cernkovich, & Rudolph, 2002; Giordano, Schroeder, & Cernkovich, 2007) who collected data from a prospective cohort of adolescent offenders transitioning to early adulthood. They contended that cognitive changes within individuals must first occur before they will be open to pro-social opportunities such as employment and good partnerships. This includes offenders recrafting emotional dimensions of their identities as well as "emotional mellowing" (Giordano et al., 2007, p. 1611), which serves to replace an angry or depressive self with one that is both more pro-social and emotionally stable.

Paternoster and Bushway (Bushway & Paternoster, 2011, 2013; Paternoster & Bushway, 2009) offer one of the most recent theoretical formulations explaining desistance, called the identity theory of desistance (ITD). Offenders, Paternoster and Bushway (2009) contend, will retain an "offender" working identity as long as they perceive it will net more benefits than costs. The process of changing an offender identity occurs "when perceived failures and dissatisfactions within different domains of life become connected and when current failures become linked with anticipated future failures" (2009, p.1105). When offenders come to the realization that their criminal offending is either currently more costly than beneficial or is projected to be more costly in the future, they make initial moves to change their identity (and ultimately their life) to one that is law-abiding.

This newly emerging prosocial identity triggers a change in the person's preferences for things like quick and easy money (via theft or drug dealing), and motivates a move to make one's social network more prosocial as well. It is this internal change in identity and the recognition of the kind of person that one wants to be that both motivates behavior consistent with a prosocial identity (change in preferences, desire for legitimate work, and conventional friends) and sends a signal to others (like potential prosocial intimates and employers) that the person is making positive changes in their life. This desistance theory, unlike the theory of informal social control or cognitive transformations, hypothesizes that identity change is necessary for desistance to occur, that identity change must come before prosocial opportunities can arrive and be successfully used, and that desistance can occur even in the absence of conventional turning points.

A great deal of research relying on contemporary samples of offenders has noted the importance of identity change for the desistance process (Aresti, Eatough, & Brooks-Gordon, 2010; Bachman, Kerrison, O'Connell, & Paternoster, 2013; Healy, 2013, 2014; King, 2013; Opsal, 2012; Stevens, 2012). For example, in one of the largest prospective studies to date to examine desistance in contemporary mixed race and gender sample of drug-involved cohort of offenders called the *Roads Diverge Study*, Bachman, Kerrison, O'Connell, & Paternoster (2013) found that the vast majority of offenders who had successfully desisted from both crime and drug use had first transformed their "offender identity" into a "nonoffender working identity." This cognitive process was typically motivated by realizing that if change did not occur, they would likely become what they feared, such as dying an addict or dying in prison. To sustain their new "nonoffender" identity, respondents used various tools including changing their "people, places, and things" by seeking out noncriminal associates and staying away from previous locations that triggered their drug use and/or criminal behavior. While partnership, parenting, and employment did not appear to be turning points for the majority of our respondents, when they were ready to get clean, rekindling relationships with extended family and finding living-wage employment served to solidify new prosocial identities.

One of the relationships that helped solidify a "nonoffender working identity" for many of the women in the *Roads Diverge Study* was the role of the grandparent. After a brief review of the contextual nature of parenting and grandparenting and the methods upon which our analyses are based, we describe the importance of grandparenting in prosocial identity transformation for female offenders in this sample.

# Parenting and Grandparenting after Prison

Approximately 700,000 individuals were released from state and federal prisons (Carson & Golinelli, 2013) and more than half of returning offenders are parents to minor children (Glaze & Maruschak, 2008). Moreover, many of those individuals are grandparents who are charged with primary guardianship of children upon their release (Christian & Kennedy, 2011; Ferraro & Moe, 2003; Schollenberger, 2009). Even for those individuals who are released but do not serve as primary caregivers to their children or grandchildren, the majority do return home to their families (Visher, 2007) and occupy some sort of caregiver role, however cursory (Lattimore & Visher, 2009; Visher & Courtney, 2007). Although the criminological life-course perspective of age-graded social control (Laub & Sampson, 2003; Sampson & Laub, 1993) would suggest that transitions to prosocial roles such as marriage and parenting may serve key positive turning points in the lives of individuals, which may lead them to desist from offending, the literature has proven equivocal about the effects of parental roles on desistance.

For example, some quantitative research has suggested the becoming a mother increases the likelihood of women exiting a criminal career (Kreager, Matsueda, & Erosheva, 2010), while others have found no effects for parenting (Giordano, Seffrin, Manning, & Longmore, 2011). The qualitative literature is similarly equivocal. For example, after interviewing a sample of poor urban women, Edin and Kefalas (2005) concluded that motherhood decreased the likelihood of offending by restructuring daily routines and reducing criminal opportunities. However, after interviewing women on parole, Brown and Bloom (2009) found that mothers reentering the community after prison confront the same problems that mediated their incarceration including poverty, lack of education, unstable housing, and underemployment. As such, although motherhood has the potential of providing a conventional identity, these women often continued to be peripheral members of their households and the stresses associated with reentry appeared only to be exacerbated by their roles as mothers.

It is critical to remark that families marked by concentrated disadvantage, intergenerational patterns of offending, and early onset of parenthood, produce grandparents who are relatively young compared to grandparents whose families do not exhibit a legacy of offending (Christian & Thomas, 2009; Farrington, Jolliffe, & Loeber, 2001; Foster, 2010; Western & Wildeman, 2009). Grandparenting in this context may represent a unique caregiving role, and allows for the fostering and (re)establishment of a certain type of social support network (Cox, 2002; Kemp, 2003) and an opportunity to reunite with their families and gain access to a means of holistic reintegration (Bazemore & Erbe, 2004; Breese, Ra'el, & Grant, 2000; Brown & Bloom, 2009; Duwe & Clark, 2011; Henly, Danzinger, & Offer, 2005; Martinez & Christian, 2008; Schollenberger, 2009). For many grandparent offenders, returning home to their children and grandchildren (re)introduces them to a role and purpose that many of them had otherwise missed or neglected entirely.

While extant literature has been equivocal about the effects of motherhood and desistance, there have been virtually no attempts to examine the salience of grandparenting in this process. In this chapter, we present evidence that the role of "grandmother" often offers drug-involved female offenders a chance for redemption, reclamation of social capital, and an avenue through which offenders can potentially reinvent themselves (Giordano et al., 2002) and an opportunity to secure their prosocial identity (Paternoster & Bushway, 2009).

# Methods

## *Sample*

The data for this study come from a longitudinal analysis of serious drug-involved offenders who were released from the state of Delaware correctional system between the years 1990 and 1996. The original study was designed to examine the effectiveness of a drug therapeutic community (TC), and the sample consisted of 1,250 male and female offenders who were randomly assigned to either a control or a treatment condition (Inciardi, Martin, & Butzin, 2004). Subjects in the study were first interviewed while still incarcerated, approximately nine months prior to release (referred to throughout this paper as the baseline incarceration), and were re-interviewed after release at 6, 18, 42, and 60 months after release. In this paper, we included only white and African-American subjects for this analysis, which resulted in 1,044 subjects, of whom 79% were male and 73% African-American.[1]

Arrest histories for each offender that covered the years 1990 to 2008 were obtained from the Delaware Statistical Analysis Center, which records all arrests and imprisonments in the state of Delaware. These data were augmented by arrest data from the National Crime Information Center (NCIC) in order to capture arrests that occurred outside the state of Delaware. With these data we amassed a count of the number of arrests for each person per year. Incarceration data were collected from each offender since 1990 and included the entrance and exit data from prison for each sentence. This information was used to compute the number of days free per year as a measure of exposure time. Our analysis strategy began with the estimation of a group-based trajectory model (GBTM) for our arrest history data (Nagin, 2005; for details about the estimation procedure, see Bachman et al., 2013). A graph of the offending trajectories for the five-group (all quadratic) model is shown in Figure 1. As can be seen, three of the groups, the Low-Level Desisters (26% of the total), the Mid-Level Desisters (21% of the total), and the High-Level Desisters (15% of the total) had primarily desisted from offending by the end of 2008.[2] Since being released from their baseline incarceration, approximately sixty percent of these offenders who had spent time in a state penitentiary and who were substance abusers had stopped or nearly stopped accumulating arrests by 2008. There are two distinct groups of offenders who continued to be arrested. The

---

1. Because of their small number, Hispanic offenders were excluded from our quantitative analysis and qualitative interviews as were the few subjects from other race/ethnicities.

2. The terms Low-, Mid-, and High-Level refers to the general trend of the arrest trajectories over a period of 30 years. For example, while the Low-Level Desisters started at about 1.75 arrests per year after release, by five years after release they trended downward and consistently had the lowest annual arrest numbers over time. The Mid-Level Desisters started lower, but quickly trended upward, and their trajectory of arrests was consistently between that for the Low-Levels and the High-Level Desisters who generally had higher annual arrests than the Mid-Levels. The same is true for the two persisting groups. Compared with the High-Level Persisters, the Low-Level Persisters consistently had fewer arrests each year.

**Figure 12.1. Trajectories of Arrests 1990–2008**

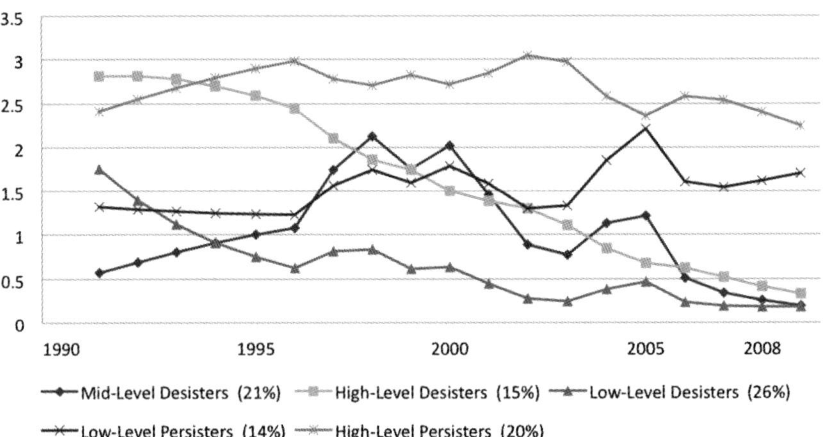


first group, the Low-Level Persisters (16% of the total) started out averaging about one arrest per year and generally remained between one and two arrests per year until 2008. The High-Level Persisters (22% of the total) also had a fairly flat trajectory moving between two and three annual arrests over the 1990–2008 time period. These two groups of persisting offenders comprised thirty-eight percent of the total number of offenders.

To illuminate the mechanisms for change in offending over time, we sampled and conducted intensive interviews with 304 of these former inmates randomly drawn from each of the five offending trajectory groups. The purpose of these qualitative interviews was to allow the offenders to speak directly and for themselves about what changes they felt they had undergone over the years since their baseline incarceration. Our goal was to descriptively examine the role of identity change and the causal sequencing of events throughout the lives of these offenders, as they relate to both criminal offending and substance abuse. This chapter relied on the female respondents only (N=111). The average age of the females at the time of interviews was 44.8, with a range of 30 through 59 and the majority of the sample was African American (72%).

## *Interview Methods*

Respondents selected for in-depth interviews were first contacted by mail requesting that they call a research office phone number at a local university if they were willing to participate in the interview. Follow-up was needed in most cases, and was done first by another letter, then by phone, and finally by personal visits. All interviews were face-to-face, lasted from 1 to 3 hours, and were tape-recorded. Interviewed respondents were compensated $100 for their time and travel expenses.

The interview guide resembled an Event History Calendar (EHC), which has proven to be an extremely useful tool for collecting retrospective data on life events within different domains such as subjects' relationship changes, medical history, and offending (Belli, Stafford, & Alwin, 2009). Another important tool we used in our EHC to facilitate respondents' recall was the placement of arrest and incarceration dates obtained from official data within the calendars, as well as key life events such as birthdays. These cues proved extremely useful for helping respondents recall both their offending histories as well as other life events. However, the interviews were primarily open-ended and resembled conversations rather than an exchange of formal survey questions and answers. The goal was to uncover what Agnew (2006) refers to as "storylines" in understanding criminal offending. A storyline is a "temporally limited, interrelated set of events and conditions that increase the likelihood that individuals will engage in crime" (2006, p. 121). For each criminal and drug relapse event self-reported or obtained from official records, respondents were asked to recreate the event both perceptually and structurally, and interviewers probed for respondents' cognitive decision making processes surrounding those events.

All interviews were transcribed verbatim and imported into NVivo for coding. Codes in our scheme ranged from purely descriptive (e.g., narrative describing first arrest or first incarceration) to more interpretive concepts such as reflections of identity change, or a feared self. The coding process began with a list of initial categories developed from the existing literature on desistance including such key indicators as turning points, indicators of agency and readiness for change, and the psychological indicators of discontent and fear. In addition, all emergent themes were coded, which resulted in over 20 main categories (e.g., Discontent, Turning Points, Incarceration) with over 100 subcategories used in the coding scheme.

This qualitative component of the research not only allowed us to examine the cognitive mechanisms of desistance in the respondent's own words, but also provided self-reported involvement in crime and substance use. We operationally defined crime desistance as those who were not under correctional supervision and who had not engaged in any criminal activity during the past 12 months. Substance-use desistance was defined as those who were not under correctional supervision and who had not used illegal drugs, including illegally use of prescribed medications or using alcohol if alcohol was their drug of choice, during the past 12 months. For ease of presentation, we provide

Table 12.1. Percent Distribution of Self-Report Crime, Drug Use,
and Immediate Desistance by Gender, Race, and Trajectory
Group Membership for Interviewed Females, N=111.

|  | Percent Still Using * | Percent Still Engaging in Crime * | Percent Immediately Desisted After First Incarceration | N |
|---|---|---|---|---|
| White | 55 | 25 | 6 | 31 |
| African-American | 54 | 25 | 1 | 80 |

* Self-reported crime desistance was defined as those who were *not* under correctional supervision and who had *not* engaged in any criminal activity during the past 12 months. Substance-use desistance was defined as those who were not under correctional supervision and who had not used illegal drugs, including illegally using prescribed medications or using alcohol if alcohol was their drug of choice, during the past 12 months.

comparisons between those who desisted and those who were still persisting in drug use and/or crime. Table 12.1 presents descriptive information on desistance for the 111 female interviews in which self-reported desistance could be validly coded in the interviews. As can be seen, there were no significant racial differences in self-reported desistance. About half of both African American and White females reported still using substances and nearly one quarter of both groups were still involved in other types of offending.

# Results

Of the 111 interviews analyzed for this study, whether they had desisted or not, 94 individuals had in some way attributed their patterns of offending and substance use to the acknowledgement of their responsibility to their children. Some desisted outright, while others continued to use drugs but resorted to substances that were innocuous compared to their drug of choice (e.g., transitioning from heroin to the occasional beer). Some women changed their patterns of offending such that they only involved themselves in acts that were minor and carried little risk of arrest, while others still confronted relapse that they attributed to the stress and fear of caring for children. For those desisters whose progress was related to the desire to be better parents, respondents described that coming home and being accepted and trusted by their families provided a platform upon which they could sustain and advance their new prosocial identities.

## *Desistance and Identity Transformation*

Among these women, many grandparent respondents talked explicitly about how their grandparenting role impacted their desistance effort. Most often participants expressed sheer love for these children and how the very existence of their grandchild(ren) afforded them access to a new legacy that they did not want to forfeit. For example, when asked to identify the most important reason for which she had stayed clean for so long, Regina[3] offered the following:

> My pudding pop, my little baby pudding pop. When I was there, I mean I wasn't actually there physically but I was on the phone. My daughter said mom I'm in labor and you are the first one that I called. And my daughter and I really hadn't had our own conversations, it was like brief conversations but our relationship now is so awesome ... But my little pudding pop when she told me that she was pregnant and that would have been my first grandson, oh my God ... I was like, 'I cannot do this.' I wouldn't give him up for the world. I wouldn't give her up for the world. I wouldn't give XX [grandchild's name] up for the world.

Charlene knew she had to make a change in her life when she grew fed up with seeing her grandchildren while behind bars. She could no longer tolerate the shame of having her grandchildren visit her in prison and clearly states that she needed to be the grandmother that they deserved and could respect. She describes,

> *Interviewer*: Anything you think I missed that might help us to understand anything about things in your life that helped you to change?
>
> *Charlene*: One thing, I know that I'm getting older and I look back at my kids and they're getting older and I realize that the amount of grandkids I have, it really hurt me to have my daughters bring my grandkids to a prison to visit me.
>
> *Interviewer*: Wow.
>
> *Charlene*: So that's another factor, I don't want to see another one like that and I don't want to be in no situation like that. So I know in order

---

3. All names are pseudonyms and all geographical locations have been deidentified.

for me to not be in a situation like that I had to change a lot of my behaviors …

Similar to Charlene and Regina, Connie declared that she would do whatever she could to make sure she spent time with her grandchildren, the very people who kept her clean:

> *Interviewer*: What do you think is the toughest part about staying out of trouble? With not having that income and money coming in sometimes you now, you thinking about going back to [criminal behavior]?
>
> *Connie*: You know why not? Because it was the little things I would do with my babies. "Here. Mommy, here." Going somewhere with them, doing something … playing with them, taking them somewhere you know … we find bus tickets [and somehow make outings work] …
>
> *Interviewer*: If you had to list three most important things that helped you stay out of trouble, what would they be? I need three from you.
>
> *Connie*: God, my children, and grandchildren, and my great-grandbabies. Sorry, that's four.

Not only did respondents express how their love and devotion for their grandchildren helped to keep them in line, but they also underscored how good it felt to be back in the fold with their own children and trusted once again or for the very first time. When Janet was asked to describe her decision-making process in greater detail, she revealed,

> *Interviewer*: So what did you do? Tell me about the thought process with "I'm getting on a bus and I'm not going to go back."
>
> *Janet*: Oh, it felt so good though because all I wanted was that relationship with my family again. Because really I didn't think I was going to get it back that time, I thought, OK, I lost them forever, I've done really put a lot of hurt on them and all but my one daughter, my middle daughter … [Now] when I first came home I was with my younger daughter and I stayed with her. I babysat. They paid me to babysit the grandbabies when they worked, but my middle daughter was still iffy-iffy because she didn't want me to come in her life and leave again because she always felt that I abandoned her. No matter what, when I left I abandoned her but after about 4 months of being in there she started coming around and we got that bond back and now I'm living with my son. They just bought a five-bedroom house and four-bath

and that's where I'm living, and they have a little daycare and I babysit all of my little grandbabies and they pay me and that's what I do … Their father didn't really allow me to spend time with them, [but] now that I have that bond and trust back with my family they trust me and allow me to spend time with the grandbabies like before and plus I babysit, ya know? That's my income right now. I feel like myself again, back with them.

Janet's story of redemption not only brought about (re)inclusion with her more hesitant children, but also a steady, legal source of income that could keep her out of criminal involvement.

Consistent with the hypotheses outlined in Paternoster and Bushway's (2009) Identity Theory of Desistance, many of the respondents for whom grandparenting roles positively affected their desistance efforts identify a number of concrete changes in the choices they made, the processes through which they arrived at those decisions, and how those shifts reflected a transformed identity. Many began to see themselves as someone with a family and someone with real obligations to that family. More importantly, they reflect on how the harm they caused, ultimately came back to harm them, too. One respondent shared:

It got to a point where I really couldn't hide it, ya know what I mean? And I got tired of them being hurt by what I was doing, so I had to start thinking about other people other than myself. I had to start thinking about how it's going to affect them if I go back, I got a grandson today, too … He's 1, so it's my oldest daughter's son so I think I gotta, I gotta look at it like the bigger picture. I've been broke, but I refuse to go out and do something crazy. But I'm saying that it's like a mindset that my mindset now is different than it was before, that's how serious you gotta take your recovery. That's how serious you gotta take your freedom and that's what makes a difference in my life today that I'm not selfish like I used to be. And I really didn't know that I was hurting anybody but me ya know what I mean? I'm getting high. That's me, it's my body, I'm not really hurting nobody, I'm not breaking no laws. I work every day. If I wanna go buy a bag I go buy a bag, I ain't hurting nobody … I saw doctors, lawyers, they come over from a hard day of work and they want a drink, I want a bag ya know? But that's what I'm saying! I had to change that sort of thinking … I had to think about my daughters. I had to think about my grandson … I had to think about me … Shit I'm almost 50 now, man. Shit.

Paternoster and Bushway (2009; Bushway and Paternoster 2012, 2013) contend that offenders will retain an "offender" working identity as long as they perceive it will net more benefits than costs. The process of changing an offender identity begins when perceived failures and dissatisfactions within different domains of life become connected. They also assert that this linkage of failures is often coupled with a "feared self." That is, offenders perceive that without making a behavioral change, their future is bleak and will only contain more pain and hardship. Some grandparents expressed a real fear of living and dying alone and knew that they had to get clean and right with their children and grandchildren if they ever hoped of reclaiming their families. Regina explained,

> The night before I went I got this phone call and I found out my daughter was pregnant ... I was going to get ready to get high and I turned on the answer machine after she called and she said "Mom, if you are going to continue to be a crackhead you will never ever see your grandchild. When you die I will not be at your funeral and neither will he." And from that day on, I can't do it, no more. I cannot do this, no more. So I went to detox for five days and I told them before I left there, I said I cannot go home. If I go home I will be high again, put me somewhere until a bed is ready for me and I need to go out of [City Name], I need to get out of [City Name].

Some respondents offered that their desistance effort was directly linked to their fear of putting their grandchildren at risk or losing them entirely. Carol was the primary guardian of her grandchildren and expressed that she had to stop for fear of having her grandchildren taken from her:

> *Interviewer*: Have you become ... Well, you said you're working on becoming the person you wanted to be.
>
> *Carol*: Yes. Yes. Well, when I go back home, I'm gonna stop by, get my little grandbaby and take her from my sister's house and take her back. Because boy does she miss me.
>
> *Interviewer*: What's your pattern of drinking now? You still doing it?
>
> *Carol*: No. I might have a beer because XX [daughter's name] don't play, because she already said, "Momma, you ever, ever, ever do drugs or drink liquor ... you'll never see her again." I ain't trying to blow that. That's my little grandbaby.

*Interviewer*: They're near and dear to your heart, aren't they? I've got two of my own.

*Carol*: I love them.

## Conscientious Persisters

Not all grandparents desisted entirely, but those who self-reportedly still used drugs or committed crimes shared their commitment to minimizing the risk of harm done to their grandchildren and the relationships that they treasured. One respondent was a high-offending persister who used and sold cocaine throughout all of her adult life. She consciously chose to tailor her illicit substance use and sale, however, in order to protect her grandchildren's safety and maintain some measure of positive rapport with her family. This respondent discusses the ultimatum she confronted and how she consequently tailored her habits below:

> *Interviewer*: Your family had been supportive but they said no more?
>
> *Respondent*: Yeah they were like, "Man, if you don't stop, then hey, you're on your own." It was like, "You getting high, you coming in here all crazy," and even though I wasn't bringing the crack and stuff to the house once I was in the house that meant that the crazy stuff went with me. Because I was robbing niggas and all that, if they knew, they were going to kick in my grandkids' door. Woulda been a rap, you know what I mean?
>
> *Interviewer*: Yeah.
>
> *Respondent*: So it was like nah, and I had to respect that, and which I did. I didn't like it but I had to respect it because I put myself in that situation.
>
> *Interviewer*: Right.
>
> *Respondent*: And today I'm telling you, man, every time anyone in my family sees me that's all they do is give praise, like, "Yo, I knew you could do it."
>
> *Interviewer*: That's an awesome feeling.
>
> *Respondent*: Yeah it's a high that substance can never get.

Jackie shared a similar set of circumstances where she did not reach a full point of desistance (nor did she intend to) but she did make strides to reduce the harm that her use patterns created for her family.

*Interviewer*: You said you wanted to change, you knew you had a problem, but you didn't want to change because … ?

*Jackie*: No, I wanted to change but that coke, guess you're gonna tape this, that coke, you know what I'm going to say, like meth, they won't let you put it down. The time you do that, you sit down, then you looking for another one … So all this paperwork you're doing right here [referring to interviewer's field-note taking], it's all gonna be the same questions, it's all for drugs.

*Interviewer*: Alright then.

*Jackie*: Yes.

*Interviewer*: Now you did say at some point you cut down.

*Jackie*: I don't mess with it anymore, but I ain't gonna stop drinking my beer and my liquor, I don't mess with drugs.

*Interviewer*: So that's a change we are talking about.

*Jackie*: … I gotta worry about XX [grandson's name] now, my little grandbaby, that's all.

In sum, a majority of the respondents who were still using were not ready to make a change, and still appeared to accept a "user" identity. The decision to keep using and offending had cost them many things including resources, freedom, and tenuous family ties. Despite these costs, most appear to have accepted this identity, at least for now.

# Conclusions

For many, grandparenting positively affected the desistance process and gave rise to an inverse relationship between grandparenting and reoffending. These narratives suggest that a fear of losing familial ties proved remarkably sobering for respondents unwilling to forfeit yet a second generation of loved ones. However, the assumption of the grandparenting role, purpose, and responsibility came *after* these women found the courage and agency to design and pursue a prosocial "nonoffender" identity. Grandparents made a conscientious decision to see themselves as grandparents first, and then took the necessary steps to diminish their ties to their "offender" identity, if not sever them completely.

Not every grandparent in the study had also desisted from crime at the time of their interview. However, all of them had positive things to say about their grandchildren and their desire to realize a healthy and integrated grandparenting role. Furthermore, beyond regrets of having missed their grandchildren's childhoods, no one had anything negative to say about their grandparenting status. There were parents of minor children in this study who did identify how tensions, burdens, and challenges associated with parenting negatively affected their reentry efforts but many grandparents were willing and ready to go the extra mile that they struggled with as parents raising their own children. Grandparents spoke very differently about their desistance struggles, as there appears to be something particularly worthwhile about working to retrieve or reclaim a status that was once lost or that they had never had a chance achieve. Within that struggle lies an identity transformation dependent upon the realization that the stakes are higher with every second chance. Perhaps, the rewards reaped are infinitely greater, too.

# References


Agnew, R. (2006). Storylines as a Neglected Cause of Crime. *Journal of Research in Crime and Delinquency, 43*(2), 119–147.

Aresti, A., Eatough, V., & Brooks-Gordon, B. (2010). Doing time after time: An interpretative phenomenological analysis of reformed ex-prisoners' experiences of self-change, identity and career opportunities. *Psychology, Crime & Law, 16*(3), 169–190.

Bachman, R., Kerrison, E., O'Connell, D., & Paternoster, R. (2013). *Roads Diverge: Long-Term Patterns of Relapse, Recidivism and Desistance for a Cohort of Drug Involved Offenders (Grant Number 2008-IJ-CX-1107)*. Washington, DC: National Institute of Justice, United States Department of Justice.

Bazemore, G., & Erbe, C. (2004). Reintegration and Restorative Justice: Towards a Theory of Practice and Informal Social Control and Support. In S. Maruna & R. Immarigeon (Eds.), *After Crime and Punishment: Pathways to Offender Reintegration*. Portland, OR: Willan Publishing.

Belli, R. F., Stafford, F. P., & Alwin, D. F. (2009). The Application of Calendar and Time Diary Methods in the Collection of Life Course Data. In R. F. Belli, F. P. Stafford, & D. F. Alwin (Eds.), *Calendar and Time diary: Methods in Life Course Research*. Thousand Oaks, CA: Sage Publishers.

Breese, J. R., Ra'el, K., & Grant, K. (2000). No Place Like Home: A Qualitative Investigation of Social Support and its Effects on Recidivism. *Sociological Practice: A Journal of Clinical and Applied Research, 2*(1), 1–21.

Brown, M., & Bloom, B. (2009). Reentry and Renegotiating Motherhood. *Crime & Delinquency, 55*(2), 313–336.

Bushway, S. D., & Paternoster, R. (2011). Understanding desistance: Theory testing with formal empirical models. In J. MacDonald (Ed.), *Measuring crime and criminality: Advances in criminological theory* (Vol. 17, pp. 299–333). New Brunswick, NJ: Transaction Publishers.

Bushway, S. D., & Paternoster, R. (2013). Desistance from crime: A review and ideas for moving forward. In C. L. Gibson & M. D. Krohn (Eds.), *Handbook of Life-Course Criminology* (pp. 213–231). New York: Springer.

Carson, E. A., & Golinelli, D. (2013). *Prisoners in 2012—Advance Counts* (Vol. NCJ-242467). Washington, DC: Bureau of Justice Statistics, Office of Justice Programs.

Christian, J., & Kennedy, L. W. (2011). Secondary narratives in the aftermath of crime: Defining family members' relationships with prisoners. *Punishment and Society, 13*(4), 379–402.

Christian, J., & Thomas, S. S. (2009). Examining the Intersections of Race, Gender, and Mass Imprisonment. *Journal of Ethnicity in Criminal Justice, 7*(1), 69–84.

Cox, C. B. (2002). Empowering African American Custodial Grandparents. *Social Work, 47*(1), 45–54.

Duwe, G., & Clark, V. (2011). Blessed be the Social Tie that Binds: The Effects of Prison Visitation on Offender Recidivism. *Criminal Justice Policy Review.*

Edin, K., & Kefalas, M. (2005). *Promises I can keep: Why low-income women put motherhood before marriage.* Berkeley: University of California Press.

Farrall, S., & Maruna, S. (2004). Desistance-focused criminal justice policy research. *The Howard Journal of Criminal Justice, 43*(4), 358–367.

Farrington, D. P., Jolliffe, D., & Loeber, R. (2001). The concentration of offenders in families, and family criminality in the prediction of boys' delinquency. *Journal of Adolescence, 24*(5), 579–596.

Ferraro, K. J., & Moe, A. M. (2003). Mothering, Crime, and Incarceration. *Journal of Contemporary Ethnography, 32*(1), 9–40.

Foster, H. (2010). Living arrangements of children of incarcerated parents: The roles of stability, embeddedness, gender, and race/ethnicity. In *Children of incarcerated parents: Theoretical, development, and clinical issues* (pp. 127–157). New York, NY, US: Springer Publishing Co, New York, NY.

Giordano, P. C., Cernkovich, S. A., & Rudolph, J. L. (2002). Gender, Crime, and Desistance: Toward a Theory of Cognitive Transformation. *The American Journal of Sociology, 107*(4), 990–1064.

Giordano, P. C., Schroeder, R. D., & Cernkovich, S. A. (2007). Emotions and crime over the life course: A neo-meadian perspective on criminal continuity and change. *American Journal of Sociology, 112*(6), 1603–1661.

Giordano, P. C., Seffrin, P. M., Manning, W. D., & Longmore, M. A. (2011). Parenthood and crime: The role of wantedness, relationships with partners, and ses. *Journal of Criminal Justice, 39*(5), 405–416.

Glaze, L. E., & Maruschak, L. M. (2008). *Parents in Prison and their Minor Children*. Washington, D.C.: Bureau of Justice Statistics.

Harper, C. C., & McLanahan, S. S. (2004). Father absence and youth incarceration. *Journal of Research on Adolescence, 14*(3), 369–397.

Healy, D. (2013). Changing fate? Agency and the desistance process. *Theoretical Criminology, OnlineFirst*.

Healy, D. (2014). Becoming a desister: Exploring the role of agency, coping and imagination in the construction of a new self. *British Journal of Criminology, OnlineFirst*.

Henly, J. R., Danzinger, S. K., & Offer, S. (2005). The Contribution of Social Support to the Material Well-Being of Low-Income Families. *Journal of Marriage and Family, 67*(1), 122–140.

Inciardi, J. A., Martin, S. S., & Butzin, C. A. (2004). Five-year Outcomes of Therapeutic Community Treatment of Drug-Involved Offenders After Release from Prison. *Crime and Delinquency, 50*(1), 88–107.

Kemp, C. L. (2003). The Social Demographic Contours of Contemporary Grandparenthood: Mapping Patterns in Canada and the United States. *Journal of Comparative Family Studies, 34*(2), 187.

King, S. (2013). Early desistance narratives: A qualitative analysis of probationers' transitions towards desistance. *Punishment & Society, 15*(2), 147–165.

Kreager, D. A., Matsueda, R. L., & Erosheva, E. A. (2010). Motherhood and Criminal Desistance in Disadvantaged Neighborhoods. *Criminology, 48*(1), 221–258.

Lattimore, P. K., & Visher, C. A. (2009). *The Multi-Site Evaluation of SVORI: Summary and Synthesis*. Research Triangle Park, NC: RTI International.

Laub, J. H., & Sampson, R. J. (2003). *Shared Beginnings, Divergent Lives: Delinquent Boys to Age 70*. Cambridge, MA: Harvard University Press.

Martinez, D. J., & Christian, J. (2008). The familial relationships of former prisoners: Examining the link between residence and informal support mechanisms. *Journal of Contemporary Ethnography, 38*(2), 201–224.

Maruna, S. (2001). *Making good: How ex-convicts reform and rebuild their lives*. Washington, DC: American Psychological Association.

Maruna, S. (2004). Desistance from crime and explanatory style: A new direction in the psychology of reform. *Journal of Contemporary Criminal Justice, 20*(2), 184–200.

Maruna, S., & Roy, K. (2007). Amputation or Reconstruction? Notes on the Concept of "Knifing Off" and Desistance From Crime. *Journal of Contemporary Criminal Justice, 23*(1), 104–124.

Nagin, D. S. (2005). *Group-based Modeling of Development.* Cambridge, MA: Harvard University Press.

Opsal, T. (2012). "Livin' on the straights": Identity, desistance, and work among women post-incarceration. *Sociological Inquiry, 82*(3), 378–403.

Paternoster, R., & Bushway, S. (2009). Desistance and the "feared self": toward an identity theory of criminal desistance. *The Journal of Criminal Law and Criminology, 99*(4), 1103–1156.

Sampson, R., & Laub, J. (1993). *Crime in the Making: Pathways and Turning Points through Life.* Cambridge, MA: Harvard University Press.

Shollenberger, T. L. (2009). *When relatives return: Interviews with family members of returning prisoners in Houston, Texas.* Washington, D.C.: The Urban Institute.

Stevens, A. (2012). "I am the person now I always meant to be": Identity reconstruction and narrative reframing in therapeutic community prisons. *Criminology and Criminal Justice, 12*(5), 527–547.

Visher, C. A., & Courtney, S. (2007). *One Year Out: Experiences of Prisoners Returning to Cleveland.* Washington, D.C.: Urban Institute.

Western, B., & Wildeman, C. (2009). The Black Family and Mass Incarceration. *The Annals of the American Academy of Political and Social Science, 621*(1), 221–242.

# Staying Out or Going Back? A Qualitative Study of Women Prisoners, Recidivism and Reintegration

*Susan F. Sharp, Ph.D., and Juanita Ortiz, Ph.D.*

The rate of women's imprisonment grew significantly during the last decades of the twentieth century and first decade of the twenty-first century. Most of those women eventually are released. Some return to prison, while others stay out. Among the latter group, many remain marginalized, struggling to integrate into society. However, some women are able establish more stable lifestyles. Yet little is known about what facilitates successful reintegration. That is the focus of this chapter.

Women prisoners are likely to be poor, non-white, and lacking formal education (Bloom, Owen, Covington & Raeder, 2002; Bloom, Owen & Covington, 2005; Mauer, 2013; Sokoloff, 2005). They are also likely to come from disadvantaged and disorganized communities (Clear, Rose & Ryder, 2001). About half of the women in U.S. prisons are African American or Hispanic (Bloom et al., 2002; Mauer, 2013), and slightly more than half have only a high school diploma or the equivalent.

Because there are fewer African Americans in Oklahoma, the site of this study, the demographics of women prisoners are somewhat different. Slightly under two-thirds are white, while African Americans comprise slightly more than 25 percent of the women and Native Americans account for about 12 percent (Oklahoma Department of Corrections, 2010; 2012). However, like their national counterparts, Oklahoma's women prisoners tend to be undereducated. Nearly 75 percent of those admitted in 2012 had a need for basic education, yet two-thirds of those released did not receive any education while in prison (Oklahoma Department of Corrections, 2012). Additionally, women offenders tend to have unstable work histories, yet they are often single mothers with the responsibility of supporting children. Almost two-thirds were unemployed or underemployed at the time of arrest. When employed, they tended to be in low-paying jobs making little more than minimum wage (Bloom et al., 2002). Furthermore, nearly two-thirds are mothers of minor children (Bloom et al., 2002), and more than 60 percent of those mothers reported living with their minor children prior to incarceration (Glaze & Maruschak, 2008). When released from prison, they confront issues similar to those they faced prior to incarceration (Fortune et al., 2010), often linked to their roles as mothers and the necessity to resume caregiving for their children (Cobbina, 2010; O'Brien, 2001). Issues such as safe affordable housing, paying fines and restitution, and finding work that provides sustainable living are intertwined with the responsibilities they face as mothers.

The current study examines unsuccessful reentry as evidenced by returning to prison versus more successful reintegration. Cobbina (2010) examined women's constructions of reintegration and defined reentry as successful "if they did not return to prison for committing an offense two to three years post release" (p. 215). We focus on *successful reintegration*: being able to reestablish oneself in the community in a safe and sustainable way. We have defined *recidivism* as those who returned to prison within three years of release for a new offense or a technical violation. *Reintegration* reflects the ability to establish oneself in the community. This distinction is important, as not all who remain out of prison also integrate successfully into their communities *when success is defined as being able to develop a safe and economically sustainable life.* It is our contention that those who successfully reintegrate may have unique characteristics, and lessons can be learned and policies developed by examining those who are successful and those who are not. This study addresses those issues by comparing the experiences of two groups of women released from state prisons in Oklahoma: those who returned to prison in less than three years and women who stayed out and had some degree of success rebuilding their lives. Our goal is to uncover characteristics and experiences that may help prevent recidivism and improve the reentry experiences of former women prisoners.

## Women, Reentry and Reintegration

Recent research indicates that nearly half of all state prisoners return to prison within three years (Pew Center on the States, 2011). Women are less likely to recidivate than their male counterparts (Beck & Shipley, 1989; Langan & Levin, 2002), but many do return to prison or at least reoffend. Nationally, almost two-thirds of all women released from prison are arrested for a new crime within three years, with whites being the least likely and blacks the most likely to be rearrested (Durose, Cooper & Snyder, 2014). Almost 60 percent of the females in the Langan and Levin 2002 recidivism dataset were rearrested within three years of their release although only about 30 percent returned to prison, with recidivism highest among those who served time for property or drug offenses (Deschenes, Owen & Crow, 2006). Furthermore, the highest risk of recidivism is in the initial time following release. In one state, 47 percent of former women prisoners were reconvicted or reincarcerated, with most recidivating within the first two years (Huebner, DeJong, & Cobbina 2010). However, recent data from Oklahoma indicate only 16.1 percent of released women prisoners returned to prison in under three years (Oklahoma Department of Corrections, 2012). To understand this, one must take into account the high female incarceration rate in Oklahoma (135 per 100,000), double the national rate of 67 per 100,000 (Guerino, Harrison & Sabol, 2011). Policies that contribute to the high incarceration rate of women include the likelihood of using incarceration rather than probation for low level offenses. Additionally, the rate of drug court failures is almost 50 percent (MGT. 2007). Drug offenses account for nearly half of Oklahoma's women prisoners, with more than half of those admitted each year assessed with a need for substance abuse treatment. Only about one in four of released women received the recommended treatment prior to release (Oklahoma Department of Corrections, 2010; 2012).

Both men and women who are released from prison face a number of problems, but these are often exacerbated among women (Rettinger & Andrews, 2010). In a society that remains patriarchal, women are more likely to be economically marginalized than men and to have extensive histories of abuse. Indeed, Holtfreter, Reisig and Morash (2004) argue that their victimization histories, economic marginalization and high rates of substance abuse make it difficult to avoid a criminal lifestyle. Furthermore, their risks of returning to prison vary according to their pathways into crime and may be difficult to measure using instruments such as the Level of Services Inventory-Revised (LSI-R), which has been found to less effective for predicting recidivism among women with highly gendered pathways into crime (Reisig, Holtfreter & Morash, 2006). Ideally, assessments are used to direct resources and programs to those most in need. If the tools used to measure needs are ineffective, those most in need may not obtain essential programs and services, reflected in unsuccessful release.

There is still limited research on the reentry needs of women prisoners (but see Arditti & Few, 2006; Cobbina, 2009; Cobbina, 2010; Covington, 2003; Deschenes et al., 2006; Fortune et al., 2010; Harm & Phillips, 2001; Huebner et al., 2010; O'Brien, 2001; Rettinger & Andrews, 2010; Richie, 2001). What we do know is that women's pathways into prison differ from those of men, and they have different needs (Brennan et al., 2012; Holtfreter & Morash, 2003; Wright et al., 2007). Furthermore, they often engage in their crimes with males and are less culpable. Programs for women should thus be designed with their specific pathways and needs in mind. However, research into women's reentry experiences documents the common practice of taking programs designed for men and applying them to women (Bloom et al., 2002; Bloom, Owen, & Covington, 2005; Holtfreter & Morash, 2003).

While some reentry needs of women offenders are similar to those of men, women's pathways into crime are reflected in their reentry experiences (Belknap & Holsinger, 2006; Daly, 1992; Owen, 1998). Thus, it is important to consider the distinctive reentry needs of women and to create programs accordingly. Put simply, without effective intervention, released women have the same issues they had prior to incarceration, with the additional burden of a felony conviction. From a feminist perspective, however, it is not solely an issue of reducing the likelihood of returning to prison or being arrested that should be the goal. While many released women are not counted in official recidivism statistics, they remain on the margins of society. Programs to promote successful reentry should therefore focus on improving their lives as well reducing recidivism.

# Problems Faced by Women Prisoners in Reintegration

Women prisoners have more physical and mental health problems than their male counterparts (James & Glaze, 2006). While prisoners of both sexes have high rates of mental illness, Anderson (2003) found that women prisoners were more likely to have recurring and more severe mental health issues as a result of their victimization histories. Yet they often leave prison with mental health issues that are untreated (Richie, 2001). Part of the problem is that services tend to be given based on assessment scores. Lower scores may result in not receiving services (Farr, 2000), or available services may not be appropriate (Bloom et al., 2002; Covington, 2003). Once home, the problem continues. Community mental health services for low-income individuals are often limited or unavailable in some areas, especially non-urban communities. The same is true for physical health problems (Richie, 2001). Chronic disease and poor health are further exacerbated in certain groups. Hispanic women offenders have higher rates of chronic disease than white women offenders (Anderson, Rosay and Saum, 2001). Additionally, incarcerated women with histories of abuse are more likely to engage in problematic risky sexual behavior such as unprotected sex, multiple partners and sex under the influence of drugs and alcohol (Fogel & Belyea, 1999). However, prison medical services are often underfunded, and the under-diagnosis and under-treatment of these issues in prison can lead to unsuccessful reentry efforts (Baer et. al., 2006; Belknap, 2015).

Substance abuse is another problem released women experience (Richie, 2001). At the national level, nearly half of incarcerated women reported daily drug use (Greenfeld & Snell, 1999). One study found that 57.7 percent of their sample of women prisoners in Oklahoma reported daily drug use prior to prison (Sharp, Peck & Hartsfield, 2012). While some women do receive substance abuse treatment in prison, many do not. In Oklahoma, only 28 percent of those needing treatment actually completed a program prior to release (Oklahoma Department of Corrections, 2012). Notably, victimization, mental health issues and substance abuse in this population are interrelated. Failure to treat the underlying trauma leads to unsuccessful substance abuse treatment (Bloom et al., 2002), underscoring the need for trauma-informed treatment (Covington, 2008). Finally, research indicates that the greatest impact on substance abuse occurs not from treatment in prison but from combining in-prison treatment with aftercare upon release (Messina, Burdon & Prendergast, 2006).

Employment is another area that can be problematic, and challenges in securing employment after prison are correlated with higher recidivism (Richie, 2001). Women parolees must struggle not only with lack of education and job skills but also with the stigma of convictions (O'Brien, 2001; Richie, 2001; Seiter & Kadela, 2003). Many states legally restrict convicted felons' work opportunities further (Dietrich, 2002; Harris & Keller, 2005). When these women do find work, it is typically in low-paying, secondary-labor-market positions (Bloom et al., 2002; Western, 2002). Negative experiences finding work can lead to disillusionment about working in the legal job market, especially in the face of larger profits in the illegal economy (Rose et al., 2008). Yet they are burdened by fees that they encounter upon their release from prison, such as restitution, court costs, and parole supervision fees (Arditti & Few, 2006).

Reliable transportation is linked to finding and keeping employment as well as avoiding parole violation for failure to keep required appointments. The newly released woman is faced with many requirements: meeting with her parole officer, work, and attending mandated programs. Not only must she juggle the timing, but she must also find a way to get to each place. Since many no longer have a driver's license, they rely on family, friends or public transportation (Cobbina, 2009; Cobbina, 2010). This can be even more difficult for women who do not live near family or who are not in a major metropolitan area with adequate public transportation, and they may end up driving without a license, which can result in revocation of parole.

Prisons also work against empowerment and self-efficacy. Basic needs such as housing and food are met by the institution (O'Brien, 2001; Owen, 1998). Upon release, the woman is suddenly faced with many responsibilities, including finding a place to live (Richie, 2001). Some will parole to family, but only slightly more than half have that option (Mallik-Kane & Visher, 2008). The remainder must pursue other avenues. Many leave with insufficient funds to rent a place, and even those who have money face barriers due to their criminal histories (Cobbina, 2009). Those with drug convictions are often barred from subsidized housing (Legal Action Center, 2004). Even when there is no legal bar, many landlords will not rent to convicted felons. In some jurisdictions, transitional housing may be available, offering the newly released woman a temporary option, but again, availability is limited (Cobbina, 2009).

Family reunification is a major issue (Richie, 2001). While male prisoners face challenges in reuniting with their families, they are more likely to return to an intimate partner or spouse upon release (Arditti & Few, 2006; King et al., 2007; Leverentz, 2006; Walt et al.). However, many women prisoners are not married and do not have an intimate partner to whom they will return. Presence or absence of an intimate partner during incarceration and upon release from prison is important, as a *stable* partner can often provide social and financial support (Huebner et al. 2010). However, relationships with men may actually *increase* women's likelihood to offend (Cobbina, 2010; King et al., 2007; Leverentz, 2006; Sharp, 2014). Instead, their success is often linked to support from other family members and to their relationships with children (Cobbina, 2009; Giordano et al., 2002; Sharp et al., 1999; Sharp, 2014; Uggen & Kruttschnitt, 1998).

Women face additional problems trying to regain their children (Brown, 2003). Often they must meet stiff state social service requirements such as employment, substance abuse treatment, stable housing, and desistance from crime (Dodge & Pogrebin, 2001). In other cases, worn-out families want the woman to take over her responsibilities as a mother, even though she may be ill prepared to do so (Brown, 2003). Incarcerated mothers are also more than three times more likely than fathers to have been the only parent in the household at the time of incarceration (Mumola, 2000). Thus, incarceration of a mother comes with a higher likelihood that a child will be left without a parent in the home (Bloom, 1995; Mumola, 2000; Sharp & Marcus-Mendoza, 2001).

# The Current Study

In-depth interviews were conducted in 2008 and 2009 with two groups of women using a semi-structured interview instrument. Thirteen women were interviewed in the "staying out group." They were selected using a snowball sampling technique. Women selected had not only remained out of prison but reported feeling stable in their environments, often having well-paying jobs. The mean age was 39.8 years, ranging from 28 to 54. The mean time since incarceration was six years. Six were white, six were black, and one was Native American. The "going back" group was identified by the Department of Corrections, who drew a sample of 50 women between the ages of 18 and 65 who had returned to prison in less than three years. This group was composed of twenty-one women reincarcerated for a second or subsequent time who were interviewed in the prison. Nine had been transferred or released at the time of the interview, reducing the sample pool to 41. The researcher interviewed all who were willing to participate (n=21). The mean age was 38.6 years, ranging from 25 to 55. Eight were white, eight were black, and five were Native American. It is noteworthy that the majority of those reincarcerated had not committed a new offense but instead violated terms of their probation.

The women in both groups chose pseudonyms and were given the option of being recorded. All but one of the women in the "staying out" group allowed recording of the interview. Three women in the "going back" group requested that they not be recorded, so extensive notes were taken. The women were asked about problems they faced leaving prison, the impact of their imprisonment on their personal relationships, and programs they had participated in both inside and outside of prison. In particular, we focused on health issues, employment, housing, and transportation, as well as on relationships with partners, family and children. The women who were back in prison were also asked to describe what they believed led to their reincarceration. We coded the data separately using an open coding strategy and then compared coding. During the process two unanticipated themes emerged that will be discussed. We then went back through the interviews to code these themes.

While the two samples were not drawn in the same manner, in both cases the sample was not representative. We realize that this was not ideal, but it would be impossible to use the same sampling technique with the two groups we wished to study. For the prison group, the Department of Corrections drew a sample of those who had recidivated within three years. There is, however, no defined population of former prisoners, especially those who have completed required post-release supervision. They are a hidden population, making it difficult to know if our sample matched the population. Unlike Cobbina (2009;

2010) who interviewed women on parole, we focused on women who had successfully reintegrated into society, most (n=10) no longer on parole. Because our interest was about success rather than simply a lack of reincarceration, snowball sampling provided the best method of tapping into this population.

# Leaving Prison

The women who returned to prison averaged slightly less than two years out. Vanda (white, age 39) was out the shortest period of time (279 days), while Pooty (Native American, age 29) stayed out the longest—1084 days. Three returned in under one year, eight more in under two years, and the remaining ten in under three years. In contrast, the women who stayed out of prison had been released anywhere from three to twelve years, with an average time of slightly over six years out of prison.

## *Physical Health, Mental Health and Substance Abuse*

Looking at the two groups of women, it was quickly evident that those who went back to prison were more likely to report severe physical health problems than those who stayed out. Seven reported severe physical problems that interfered with their ability to work upon release. Laci (white, age 46) developed cancer during her prior incarceration and was released in a wheel chair, with no insurance and no housing. She told a women's shelter that she was being battered in order to get housing and medical care after she had accumulated $100,000 in medical debt. She was often unable to fill prescriptions and eventually relapsed on drugs, leading to revocation of her parole. Likewise Dirty Lucy (white, age 49) described leaving prison with a bacterial condition in her stomach she claimed was life-threatening. She said that the appropriate treatment would have cost her $4,000 per day. She worked for about ten months before becoming unable to work due to her health. So she began dealing drugs to help pay for her medical care, eventually leading to her arrest for a dirty urinalysis. She stated, "So I had major medical issues … And I was so sick, so I was like, 'Well, I'll do a little bit of morphine here, and it'll make me feel better.' And one thing led to another and I was right back in the place I was before." Another woman, Cody (black, age 37) reported she had been severely injured in an automobile accident. Vivian (white, age 49) also reported health problems that started in her previous incarceration but were left untreated. She said she had difficulty breathing but was unable to get medical care when released. It was upon her return to prison that she finally was diagnosed. "They were trying to say I had asthma. I never had asthma before. And the lady told me that the memo said COPD … I went about two years before I got any help." Vanda was diagnosed with asthma, but she reported she could not afford to see a doctor to get a prescription for an inhaler, so, "[w]hen my asthma started bothering me, I'd have to go to the ER to get a breathing treatment." In another case of breathing difficulty, Tamara (white, age 25) was released with chronic asthma, and she went to a free clinic where she received a prescription for an inhaler. However, at the pharmacy she was told it would cost her $275 to fill the prescription, so she did not get it. Then she became pregnant, and according to her, she often went without eating for days during the pregnancy. When asked by the researcher why she did not get food stamps, she commented, "I thought I was ineligible since I was a convicted felon." Her health declined due to poor nutrition and failure to take prescribed medication. Finally, Shoshone (Native American, age 55) was released with torn ligaments in her shoulder and elbow that limited her ability to work. According to her, the Indian Clinic would not repair her ligaments although she was eligible for routine medical care, stating, "Here, the Indian hospital, they only do ligament tears and things like that for active students in sports and everything. So they don't do it if you're my age and they don't see that you're a very active person." It is noteworthy that five of the eight white women reported serious health issues after release, compared to only one of the eight black women and one of the five Native American women. We considered age as the potential explanation of this, finding that on average, the group of white women were older (40.4 years average) compared to the black women (35.6 years), but whites and Native Americans did not differ in age. The sole Native American who reported physical health problems was 55, suggesting that age did indeed predict differences in the women's experiences. Their stories point to the dearth of adequate care in the corrections system, lack of knowledge of available resources, and difficulty for marginalized women to find adequate care once released.

The women in the staying out group reported either no significant health problems or being able to get treatment when needed. Only one woman, Arlena (black, age 54) reported severe physical health problems, and she was the oldest in the "staying out" group, consistent with our observation regarding age and physical health. She was insured through Medicaid, allowing her to obtain care. Arlena had significant physical health problems, including congestive heart disease. She commented, "They got my SSI started while I was still at Mabel Bassett, so I was able to just go to the same doctors at the Health Sciences. And, then I got Medicaid started so that helps with my prescriptions."

Another woman (Misha, age 31, black) noted, "Well, I don't have any ... And so far I haven't gotten really sick where I have to get prescriptions." Tara (black, age 40) utilized a community clinic, noting that she had not experienced any major health problems prior to getting a job that included insurance, saying, "What I did was, I went to ... Variety Health Clinic for five years until I was able to get insurance at this job now. So ... I just continued to do my yearly pap smear and things right there." Almost all of the women who stayed out reported few health problems, with the exception of Arlena. She was also the only one who reported having to be on regular medication for physical problems.

However, the situation was reversed with mental health problems. Only three of the women who had returned to prison—Bree (black, age 34), Young (black, age 35) and Bad Girl (black, age 47)—acknowledged having mental health issues. Two of them had negative opinions about the mental health treatment field and did not seek services in the community. Young claimed that a prison mental health worker told her that she did not need help, stating, "This was before I got out ... she just patted me on the leg and told me I was just being self-pitying and all this and that. I just kind of looked at her and was like, 'I'm not telling you this so you can feel sorry for me. I'm telling you this because these are things I just have replaying in my mind, and it's keeping me from moving on.' She just more or less acted like she didn't know how to help me."

Bad Girl, who was treated with psychotropic medications while in prison, was released without transitional medication. However, she eventually got mental health support in the community after she was diagnosed with tuberculosis. Several of the other women reported histories of abuse and depression, but they were not provided counseling. Vivian reported, "I only get counseling in drug programs, and usually it's group." Prison can also exacerbate existing problems, as Beth (white, age 38) noted, stating, "There's a lot of violence here. I noticed that I was quick to violence out there, and I had never been ... But I guess you get more prone to violence in here."

Many of the women who returned to prison reported extensive histories of abuse, including Bree, who attributed her problems to her devastating childhood where she was abused and eventually abandoned by her mother. She and her siblings went into the foster care system and were separated. For Young, her sexual abuse by an older cousin when she was ten led to a lack of self-worth: "I just never said anything to my family, because it happened to me once before, me saying anything, and it just felt like ... it was my fault." Most of the women who reported abuse began using substances at a young age, perhaps to self-medicate. For example, Vanda began drinking at age nine, moving on to methamphetamine in her teens, while Laci first injected drugs at age eight, "I've been shooting dope ever since." Dirty Lucy and Tamara reported they started drug use in their mid-teens, while Angel (Native American, age 28) stated she first used drugs at age eleven. However, only Dirty Lucy reported participation in drug treatment during her prior incarceration. Lack of available mental health care in the prisons and subsequently in their communities and self-medication with alcohol or drugs following release led many of these women to reincarceration. Sweet (black, age 35), for example, said she had not been able to get into a treatment program in prison, during either incarceration. She credited lack of availability and high need for the programs, stating, "It's just waiting until you can get into it and they prioritize those people that are in delayed sentencing ... for anybody that's just waiting on the yard, you just be waitin' up to a year, two years to get out to those programs."

Both Bree and Tamara reported that they relapsed immediately upon release. Tamara's boyfriend offered her drugs when he picked her up at the prison, while Bree was around alcohol and drugs. She reported, "Alcohol and crack cocaine. It was right there in my face when I got out ... And that has always been an issue for me ... There was a guy staying with my dad, and he was a drug addict. And I had my little money, my little check, from where I had been in prison so long ... I fell right back into it."

In addition to Bree and Tamara, Young quickly returned to drugs, poignantly noting, "To me, I mean, that's all I knew, and that's what I turned back to. I guess like a therapy. I just did it to numb the pain and to make me forget what was going on around me." The environments to which these women returned hastened their relapse. Living in communities teeming with drugs or having family and partners in the drug world increased the probability of returning to drugs.

Similarly, other women who returned to prison had difficulty staying off drugs. Laci had been using drugs intravenously since she was eight and quickly returned to drug use. Lone Wolf's (Native American, age 34) drug of choice was alcohol. She was often homeless, sleeping under bridges or in parking garages. When asked what she would do when she woke up under a bridge, she noted, "First thing I'd be thinking is that I've got to get me another bottle." Lone Wolf's alcohol abuse created additional problems, including lost jobs, homelessness, and sometimes placing her life in danger. She did not receive treatment during her prior incarceration, and she quickly started drinking again, commenting, "When I quit my job, I just walked to the next place where I'm going to go get drunk."

In contrast, Tara, one of the women who stayed out, reported that she was able to get excellent psychological care while incarcerated and had no drug problem. She credited her success to dealing with her abuse issues. Prior to counseling in prison, she had kept her childhood sexual abuse secret. Her first disclosure was to a prison psychiatrist who helped her understand that the abuse was not her fault:

> I took a lot of counseling and psych—psychological help ... my first time experiencing getting to talk to a psychiatrist. I was able to get out a lot of things that were on my heart and I was blaming myself for a lot of things that, uh, I should have not been blaming myself for and, uh, I had a lot of childhood trauma that I had—didn't realize that I had.

Arlena, Dorothy (white, 28), Gina (black, 46), Kathy (white, 45) and Tara reported being able to obtain needed psychotropic medications through community mental health providers. Tasha (black age 35) and Misha reported that while they were not on psychotropic medication, they received counseling services in the community. This is in contrast to many of the women who had returned to prison who seemed unaware that they might need assistance or were unaware of resources that could assist them. It is significant that those who were able to get help had supportive families and lived in communities that provided more services for those in need. In contrast, several of the women unable to find assistance lived in less urban areas with few sources of help.

Other women who stayed out more successfully also either did not have problems with drugs, like Tara and Jonetta (black, age 39), or were able to get treatment while in prison. Gina received both counseling and drug treatment in prison, as did Kathy, Misha, Twyla (white, age 47) and Barbara (Native American, age 41). Arlena was able to get one of the coveted spots in the trauma-informed "Helping Women Recover" program (Covington, 2008). On release, she was ended up in a homeless mission's long-term drug treatment program, where she participated in substance abuse treatment and relapse prevention planning. This was her second release from prison. She noted that the first time she had received no treatment and quickly relapsed. Her parole was revoked before a treatment bed became available. She felt the trauma-informed treatment better prepared her for successful reintegration. She reported feeling more confident, stating, "I feel confident now that I can stay strong and not use."

Some of the women who stayed out quickly developed support networks outside of prison to enhance their abstinence, including Arlena, Kathy and Tara, who had mentors from prison. Several women also mentioned time spent living in sober living houses and participation in 12-Step groups as important tools for staying clean and sober. Arlena, Dorothy (white, age 28), Gina, Kathy, and Mandy (white, age 39) all reported being involved in either AA, NA or Celebrate Recovery, while Misha, Tara and Twyla reported counseling and church as important support. In addition to helping them stay off drugs, these programs provided an additional source of non-drug-using support.

## Employment, Transportation and Juggling Fees and Appointments

The majority of both groups of women experienced difficulties finding employment. This is unsurprising given that the women prisoners in general have low educational attainment and spotty work histories. Their economic marginalization further leads to low-paying jobs in the secondary labor market. With a felony conviction, their opportunities become even more constrained. Interestingly, the majority of the women who stayed out found jobs through friends or their social support network, which speaks to the importance of having a strong safety net of support in place prior to release, or, even better, a job that pays a living wage lined up for the woman prior to her return to the community.

Those who returned to prison reported even more difficulties than those who were able to stay out, with 15 of the 21 saying that they experienced "serious" difficulties. Two of the remaining six women had jobs set up with family or friends, one had family to support her, and one was disabled. According to Vanda, "As soon as they see that prison or ex-felon, you're out. They're not even gonna look at your application … Especially if you're a woman … Over half of the jobs that I applied to wouldn't even look at it." Beth, who returned to prison after a little over a year, made looking for work her full-time occupation, with no success. She claimed to have looked very hard for work, stating, "And it was six months, of Monday through Friday, focusing, like that was my job, finding a job. And so from 8 in the morning until about 6 in the evening, I was actually beating the pavement … I did the newspaper thing, I got out and walked, I did applications … And it was rejection straight for six months." Bree applied for 29 jobs in 45 days, turned down by all. Her parole officer, not believing her, made her return to each place to get a statement of why she was not hired. The vast majority responded that it was because of her conviction. B-Dog claimed that most jobs required going through temporary employment agencies and that the agencies sent her places that would not hire her due to her criminal record. The jobs that Beverly (black, age 32), Dirty Lucy, and Tamara did find were in the fast-food market and part-time.

The women were also unsure how to handle the question about convictions. Anne (black, age 35) said she wished she had lied about her record. She believed that because she was honest on her application forms that she was not interviewed. However, Missy (black, age 30) did not lie because she believed she would be fired if they found out she had failed to disclose her conviction. She was unable to find work, despite having education and skills, saying, "I have a lot of computer skills, and I went to school for business management. But I can't go and get a job in the business management field, with my background." Several of the women lied on their applications and were initially hired, but when their background checks were returned, they were terminated. Pooty commented, "That crushed my spirit, seriously … It knocked my self-esteem down, when it came to that, because I was excited."

In contrast, several of the women who stayed out were more successful. Tara found work with Goodwill Industries, working at minimum wage at first. While there, she enrolled in college. Eventually, she was able to land a better job through connections she made at Goodwill. She offered the following advice, "When I got my job it was $5.15 an hour … and it didn't matter. I was so happy to get a job. Okay, maybe I don't get that job that is paying $15 an hour. Maybe I can look for a $7.35 an hour." A number of the women who stayed out were able to find work through friends. For example, after being turned down by multiple employers, Mandy went to work for a friend's house-cleaning business. Dorothy, a waitress, got her pre-prison job back. Kathy went to work in a drug-treatment program where she had volunteered, and Twyla, who returned to her husband upon release, started keeping the books for his business. Misha reported more difficulties that were eventually resolved through friends:

> I looked for work for—I used my computer, I got bonded … I got the felon-friendly job list. Some of them don't hire felons … they say felony friendly, but when you say you're a felon, they still do a background check, and then they won't hire you … And the only reason I got the job I have now is because my friend is the manager … And I just happened to walk in there and she asked me if I was still looking for a job. I told her, "Yeah." She called me the next day and told me to come that evening. That I would start the next day.

Gina's situation was unique. Her aunt supported her so that she could go to school. She worked part-time at a motel at night. She enrolled in the petroleum engineering program at a university, and she was placed in internships making a significant amount of money by telling her story to a Human Resources person in the office of a large oil company. That individual decided to give her a chance. However, when she was scheduled to do a final internship in a different location, a background check was run. She was immediately terminated. A friend helped her find a different job working for a state senator.

Several of the women who were successfully staying out also enrolled in higher education programs. Two attended a local community college upon release (Misha and Tara), and five were eventually able to obtain degrees from a large public university (Gina, Jonetta, Tara, Barbara and Kathy). This eventually led to better jobs. However, universities in the state now carefully screen applicants for felony convictions, resulting in an automatic denial of admission that requires an appeal to a board.

Transportation was linked to employment difficulties (see Cobbina 2010). Oklahoma has limited public transportation available in only a few of the largest towns, and those systems are inadequate for going to and from many locations. Furthermore, most women released from prison have little money to pay for public transportation or to pay to friends for giving them rides. This led to difficulties for women who had to walk to work and appointments. It limited the places where they could apply for jobs and often put them at risk of not meeting mandatory appointments, thus having their parole revoked. Missy said that at release, "I had no money, and I had no means of transportation … I couldn't just get on the bus, because I don't have money just to get on the bus." She was able to save enough money to purchase a car that broke down two weeks later. She then used a friend's car to get to work and pick up her children from school, also committing to pick up her friend's children from school. This schedule grew too complicated, and Missy lost her friend, her job, and transportation. If there were children in the home, the problems were magnified, as Missy noted, stating, "I had to think about how was I going to be home on time, for my kids to come home from school. Because I had little kids … So there was no being home by themselves. So I had to think about that … It would have to be in walking distance."

Many parole requirements required access to transportation, as not having a ride was not considered a reasonable excuse for failing to make an appointment. Bree and Vivian reported being paralyzed with fear of missing the bus to their appointments or jobs. They both also commented that relying on public transportation put them in contact with illegal opportunities and individuals engaging in crime. Cody worked late at night but the bus quit running at 6 p.m., so she started going to work early. Tamara walked five miles each way to work. This became problematic because she was pregnant and it was midsummer. At her doctor's urging, she eventually quit the job.

The women who stayed out of prison fared better on average. In many cases, they had support from friends or family that helped them overcome the structural barriers to transportation. Gina's aunt purchased a car for her to use. Several others (Arlena, Barbara, Dorothy, Jonetta, Kathy, Misha, and Nelda) lived in the state's larger cities that had more reliable public transportation.

Tara rode the bus or depended on her family for rides at first. After she had established her own home and kept a job, her grandfather gave her a car. Dorothy was able to save enough money to buy a car while she was in a transitional living program. Cassie (white, age 39) drove a car that belonged to her sister. However, she no longer had a driver's license, and it took her about six months to save enough to get her license reinstated. Misha initially rode the bus, commenting, "When you leave prison … they give you resources. Some people don't use the resources but the ones who really want it, they do." She also had assistance. Initially, her grandparents drove her to places to apply for work. Later, her mother sold her a car cheaply.

Overall, transportation issues for the two groups were different. Those who returned to prison had no assistance and often lived or worked in areas with little or no public transportation. Those who stayed out were more likely to have access to reliable transportation, public or private.

Safe housing is one of the most important needs women released from prison have. The two groups had different experiences in this area as well. Those who returned to prison had far greater difficulty finding housing, especially safe housing. For example, Sweet could not find a place that would rent to her and ended up moving in with her addicted sister, putting her around drugs and leading to relapse. Vivian was also unable to find a place to live. She ended up staying in what she described as a "meth house." The result was that she began using. Bree walked to her father's house when she was released. Her father commented, "It's good to see you but you can't stay here." After that, she bounced around friends' homes and was homeless at times:

> Staying from pillar to post … maybe one night I could stay over at this person's house, and the next night I could probably stay at this person's house … About seven months that I moved from friend to friend … I remember sleeping in a parking garage … Well, I slept in the stairwells, with no blanket or anything. I just had what I had on my back … housing has been very unstable.

Lone Wolf (Native American, age 34) remarked that she would have been able to seek housing assistance from her tribe but not with a felony. She initially went from friend to friend, ending up homeless.

In contrast, the women who stayed out either had supportive friends and family to assist them, or they were able to get into a halfway house. Gina's aunt paid for an apartment for her, while Misha went to her grandparents' home, where she still lives. Kathy paroled to her sister, a teacher. Tara first went to a halfway house and then to her grandfather's home. She saved her paychecks and was able to rent an apartment, apparently due to a failure in the background check:

> When I went and did my, uh, my background check, for my apartment ... And nothing came up on the OSBI ... But, a year into it, on the re-cert, it came back ... So they were saying that, you know, you have a felony. And I was like, yeah, but I had the felonies when I came into the apartments. And they looked back on the application and I had put that I had a felony. I never lied about it or anything. And we got past that but that's why I think they didn't kick me out.

Arlena, who had been to prison before, was well aware that she would need help. She had some initial difficulties before finding safe housing:

> The last time, I tried to stand on my own too soon, you hear what I'm saying? I had been locked up so long I just wanted my own place with nobody telling me what to do. And I couldn't handle it. This time, I went to a sober house but I was the only prisoner there and the only black person. And they treated me bad, so I just took off. And, I was on the streets, crying, no money. I went to a church and sat down on the curb in front. This man came up and ... took me to the mission, and I am still there.

It is apparent that having supportive family or a halfway house available on release helps improve the likelihood of successful reintegration. For family to enhance success, however, it is imperative that they be stable. Being homeless or having criminal or drug-using family increased the likelihood of reincarceration. When there is not a family support network, supportive transitional housing is essential. Without adequate housing, women often find themselves back in criminal or dangerous environments, making it difficult to develop and sustain a noncriminal lifestyle.

## *Family Reunification and Support*

As might be expected, the women who returned to prison and those who stayed out differed in the support they reported from family and others. Those who returned to prison either had no family or friends willing to help or they only had family and friends who were using drugs or engaged in criminal activities. For example, Amanda (white, age 42) was in a relationship with a man when she went to prison, but the relationship quickly died. Not only did that relationship end, but her mother and sisters quit communicating with her. She noted, "They don't believe in me no more ... I wasn't the smart granddaughter, the intelligent niece ... I was just the bad person, the one that didn't have any sense ... And nobody trusted me, and nobody would help me." Beverly had support from her mother while in prison, but that ended upon release because her mother disapproved of the homosexual lifestyle she began in prison. In other cases, family members were engaged in crime, leading to problems for the women. Young was paroled to her grandmother's home where her cousin lived. He was an addict, and she eventually relapsed with him, leading to revocation.

In contrast, those who successfully stayed out reported more support. For example, Gina's aunt bankrolled her getting back on her feet and attending school. As Gina noted, "I didn't have any fear and I had—I was very well resourced." Twyla's husband stood by her during prison, and she returned to their home in a middle-class neighborhood. Kathy had strong support from her sister both during incarceration and post-release, while Misha and Tara both received support from grandparents and lived with them. In both cases, the grandparents lived in stable neighborhoods in homes they owned. Even those who did not report family support reported assistance. Arlena first went to a sober-living house, but she left there. However, due to the intervention of a stranger, she ended up in a mission treatment program. Dorothy went into transitional housing arranged from prison.

Another difficulty for women coming home is relationships with intimate partners. While healthy relationships can enhance success for women prisoners, their options for relationships with men are usually limited and often unhealthy for them. Those who come from poor and criminogenic communities are even less likely to find a supportive partner, instead finding their choices limited to drug-using and criminal men (King et al., 2007; Leverentz, 2006; Walt et al., 2013). Both groups acknowledged the role of relationships with intimate partners. Unsurprisingly, only one woman, Twyla, felt her partner was beneficial to her reintegration. A number of those who returned to prison reported histories of intimate partner violence, layered upon their childhood histories of abuse. These relationships can prevent self-empowerment in the women, increasing their likelihood of recidivism. Tamara returned to an abusive partner. He pressured her to use drugs with him the day she left prison, and she relapsed. She was unable to go to her family for help, commenting, "I was just too fearful to even leave the situation … because he would beat on me and my kids was there and I didn't want them to even see what I was going through." Vivian tried to stay away from her abusive husband when released, but she said her family would not help her so she reunited with him. Since he was a meth cook, it quickly led her back to drugs.

The women who stayed out also saw relationships with intimate partners, especially men, as problematic. Tara noted, "And the ones in for life—drug crimes. They're basically in prison because the boyfriend did something." Both

Tara and Jolene went to prison for crimes they committed with their boyfriend and for which they took the fall. It is noteworthy that the *same man* was involved in both women's cases. Nelda (white, 32) ended up in prison in part because of her relationship with a man who continued to engage in law-violating behavior while she was on probation. She avoided him when released. Gina saw relationships with criminal men as a roadblock for women trying to successfully reenter society, stating, "I mean, that's what a lot of women do, they return … and they want to … our core need when we get out of prison is we want somebody to love us." As evidence, Arlena had personal experience with the need to be loved and its negative consequences. She reported that after her release, she got involved with an old boyfriend who was still selling drugs. This led to a relapse, but she was able to break off the relationship when she caught him with another woman. She reflected on the lack of emotional preparation she had leaving prison and the difficulty that women faced due to loneliness, saying, "The women need to know that the dumbest thing they can do is to go back to one of their old men or find a new one. And they need to have some way to deal with the loneliness. I wasn't prepared for that, and I ended up messing up." Overall, the women who stayed out appeared to be better able to stay away from unhealthy relationships with men than those who returned, perhaps because they also received more support from others on the outside.

Most of the women were also mothers, and their ability to reunite with those children also played into success or failure. Many of the women who returned to prison reported difficulties with reunification with children due to the physical and emotional absence their incarceration had created. As Beverly stated, "You have to re-bond with them, you have to, you know, reestablish your bond with your family." Similarly, Young noted, "My daughter was two years old when I started going to prison … She's 16 now … [My daughter] was like, 'Well, what do you care? You ain't ever been in our lives. You haven't ever been here for me or my brother.'" She went on to say, "I don't know how to be a mom, and it scares me. They don't know how to be around me. I don't know them … I just know that they're mad, they're angry and confused." Likewise, Anne's son asked, "How can you be a mom to me and you've stayed in prison all this time … You can't tell me what to do. You're not my mama." Beth's son, however, would not let her out of his sight when she came home, often sleeping on the floor so he would wake up if she tried to leave or was taken away. Others lost all contact with their children while in prison. Laci commented, "I lost my kids when I came to prison … And I tried to have a relationship with them, but they've grown now. The relationships are gone…. It destroys relationships. It destroys your family. It destroys everything." Vivian's children were in state custody after being moved around among family who did not take care of them. She lost contact with the children. Lone Wolf had little contact with her children who lived with her parents with no telephone.

Several women reported children having a multitude of problems during the incarceration period, including bulimia and running away. Anne, Vivian and Laci reported their children had been molested while they were imprisoned. Most of the women were extremely anxious about their children's well-being. Lone Wolf provided financial support to her parents through crime, stating, "If it took me tricking with a guy to get money, then I'd tell my mom and dad I borrowed the money, instead of telling them the truth." Incarceration was not only hard on the women's children—other family members were also affected, often resulting in estrangement, as Missy expressed: "And my family had to take on all my responsibilities, and it affected hard my family."

Many of the women who stayed out of prison were able to maintain relationships with their children while in prison and rebuild those relationships upon release. In several cases, family continued to care for the children after the woman's release, allowing her time to get back on her feet. Gina noted that getting full responsibility of children too soon could sabotage the chance of successful reintegration. However, she also thought that not being able to get children back could set a woman up for disillusionment and potential relapse, saying, "And devastation can happen with women as far as the—So, for instance, they get out and somehow the state/DHS has their kids and they won't return them or DHS has their kids and they return them too quickly." In Gina's case, the children were with her ex-husband who was in the military. This relieved her, as she knew the children were safe. She has spent a number of years rebuilding those relationships. Still, her guilt about her absence led to some problems: "I felt very guilty about being absent from their life ... And so, you know, there's a lot of guilt associated with ... me doing the things I did to land me in prison. And so ... instead of parenting, I overcompensated with money, and then they learned how to manipulate that."

Misha's grandparents cared for her daughter while she was in prison and put effort into maintaining contact. She moved into their household on release. She has a relationship with her daughter, but she said that she does not try to parent her since she was gone for so much of her life. Tara's sister cared for her children. Once released, she was able to see them daily to rebuild the relationships. After several months of stabilizing, she was able to take over parenting. Kathy's children were raised by her sister, who allowed contact. Although she never regained custody, she has been able to strengthen the relationship. Recently, she became a grandmother. As she put it, "Being a grandmother is sort of like a do-over. With my grandchildren, I have the chance to do it right this time."

## *Final Themes*

Two related but unanticipated themes emerged in the interviews. The women who stayed out consistently described the importance of internal motivation. For Tara that motivation came when she looked at her environment. She reported, "I think that when I first had a sense of direction … my main goal was to get home. And what I was going to do to not come back here … And when I say sense of direction is that you don't have to keep going to jail …" She also noted that success was dependent on a well-developed plan for reintegrating into society, commenting, "They have to leave with a plan. And somebody has to be out there to help them work their plan … And if you do mess up, if you can't accomplish everything in it, if you can accomplish a little of it. Because it builds up our self-esteem." Tasha agreed with Tara, commenting, "I finally came to believe in myself. I knew I could do this." For Gina, part of success meant that she had to stay away from her drug-using friends and family. She commented, "There were some things that I came to, that I concluded in prison that were very important. And that was that, you know, I can't be around drugs and that kind of environment at all." She went on to say that she had no fear of failure when she was released because she had resources and a plan. Additionally, she felt that she needed to succeed to justify her aunt's support and faith in her. Arlena attributed her success to her willingness to change, while Misha talked about the role of internal motivation. She acknowledged that having resources to assist with reintegration was important but that in the end, a woman had to want to not only stay our but to succeed:

> If the person doesn't make … their own choices, then those resources, those support groups, those mentors they've been in contact with, then, then … they're gonna go back … the state can help but the person has to want help, too. They can do only so much for a person before a person has to help themselves.

In contrast, several of the women who returned to prison spoke about not seeing any options or having any hope. They believed that the lack of reentry support doomed them to failure, and that without assistance they could not change their lives. For example, Vanda stated, "You've got to have a future to look forward to, and a lot of women don't because they have nothing. They don't have nobody. If you have nobody, you're going to go back out there alone, by yourself, back to your old ways. Because that's all you know," while Bad Girl summarized the dilemma, saying, "Out of prison, they pretty much force you back out into that atmosphere." Others acknowledged that returning to prison seemed easier than facing the daunting task of reintegration. According to

Pooty, "[It} was scary because, as bad as I wanted out of here, they provided everything for me ..." Dirty Lucy noted, "It was scary going back, because I know that I have a problem, and I know that there's plenty of drugs out there ... I'm not afraid in here." Others also reported feeling ill-prepared and afraid to return to society. Cody commented, "I want my life back, but I'm afraid to go home...," and this was echoed by B-Dog, who stated, "And now, right now, I'm supposed to be getting back out and I'm not even looking forward to it." Some women even expressed being, if not glad, at least relieved to return to prison. The challenges on the outside, the lack of resources and support, and their own feelings of inadequacy combined to make prison seem a better alternative than reentry. Amos (Native American, age 56), commented, "I don't even know if you'll understand this, I was relieved ... tired of struggling. I was just tired, and once I got right with everything and I was provided everything when I got put in jail, I do my time better now." Her thoughts were not unique. Missy struggled to reunite with and care for her children, who were with her family. She was unable to find work, despite her skills. She struggled with transportation, and she eventually returned to prison for committing a robbery to help support herself and her children. She stated that returning to prison was not the worst thing, commenting, "I was kind of, not happy, but relieved, because I was going through a lot out there. Not having a job, not going to school, barely making it with my children."

# Discussion and Conclusions

There were a few limitations in the current study. First and foremost, the two samples were drawn in different ways, bringing the comparability into question. We have addressed this as best as we can. Because we wanted to study women who had some *success* in true reintegration, not simply non-recidivism, matched random sampling was not possible for the "staying out" group. Nor was matched sampling the best option. Additionally, we did not record data about specific offenses in most cases, or their arrest history, although the majority of both groups indicated that they were in prison for drug offenses, even the two who did not use drugs. Clearly, future research should take those issues into account. However, our data do provide insight into not only reentry but also characteristics of women who *successfully* reintegrate. We believe that the focus on *reintegration* rather than just not recidivating is an important contribution.

The experiences of the women in this study suggest that there are differences between those who returned to prison and those who stayed out. The pathways that initially led most of the women into prison still existed when they were released. Our successful group was composed of women who had managed, either through their own efforts or the efforts of others, to overcome many of the challenges. They were able to obtain safe housing, adequate employment, and, in many cases, higher education, even though they had struggled with those things in the past. Reflecting back on their post-prison struggles, they were able to identify how they were able to improve their life circumstances. Admittedly, many were able to parole to supportive and non-criminal families, unlike their peers who returned to prison. They also were more likely to recognize that relationships with intimate partners could play a negative role in reintegration (see Cobbina, 2010; Leverentz, 2006; Walt et al., 2013). Most who stayed out had better physical and mental health, and they had been able to either obtain treatment or else had no problems with alcohol and drugs. This does not mean those who have poorer physical health and mental health or families unable or unwilling to support them are doomed to recidivate. Instead, it provides further evidence of the need to have better treatment, both while in prison and upon release (Baer et. al., 2006; Bloom et al., 2002; Covington, 2003), as well as more options and reentry planning for transitional, supportive housing and supportive networks (Cobbina, 2010).

In addition, the gendered nature of abuse, both in childhood and adulthood, indicates the need for trauma-informed therapy and treatment. As noted by Huebner et al. (2010), victimization and offending are not easily separated, and many women who offend have themselves been victims. Without appropriate intervention and treatment, prison only exacerbates their problems. While both groups of women reported victimization and abuse that led to the choices that put them in prison, many of the successful women had been able to obtain counseling and drug treatment while in prison. Given the reported differences in their families, there may be a selection bias involved in obtaining services while in prison. Interestingly, race did not appear to be a factor, unlike in earlier research (Richie, 2001). However, many of the successful women had more stable and affluent families. Thus, they may have presented themselves as more like the middle-class service providers in prison. While we hope that class was not involved in determining who did or did not receive counseling and drug treatment in prison, the study suggests this possibility. It would be impossible to eradicate what might be unrecognized prejudices against lower-class women. However, if effective treatment was made available to *all* of the women in prison, this problem would disappear. The majority of women who commit crimes are drug offenders, and it is ineffective to incarcerate them for actions resulting from addiction but not offer them any real assistance. Research has consistently indicated that women prisoners have a high probability of being addicted (Bloom et al., 2002). If addiction and the related underlying trauma are not treated, the probability of returning to drug use as a coping mechanism is high. Carefully crafted trauma-informed approaches to substance abuse treatment are thus imperative, and the importance of providing treatment to all who need it is underscored (Bloom et al., 2002; Covington 2003.

Because women prisoners are largely drawn from poor communities that have ill-prepared them for success (Clear et al., 2001), it is a huge task for them to overcome barriers. Employment in particular created problems for the women in this study (see O'Brien, 2001; Seiter & Kadela, 2001). Without a stable income source, they were faced with the inability to secure housing and meet the requirements of parole. We found that success in obtaining employment was often a result of serendipity rather than actions taken by the women. Indeed, like their returning peers, those who stayed out had difficulty getting hired. However, those who improved their situations had been able over time to find better-paying jobs after a while, and more than half went on to obtain at least some college education. Those who returned to prison often became disillusioned and returned to illegal sources of income (see Rose et al., 2008). Thus, preparing women for work as well as having jobs with sufficient pay in place prior to release is vitally important for successfully reintegration and should be available to all reentering women.

Transportation presents a thornier problem. Similar to Cobbina's (2009) research, most of the women in this study no longer had a driver's license and were forced to depend on public transportation or rides from family and friends. The women who stayed out were able to secure transportation, often family giving them a car or selling it to them cheaply. They also were more likely to live in areas with public transportation. For some who returned to prison, inadequate or nonexistent public transportation posed a problem that was insurmountable. While reentry programs can and should provide returning prisoners with vouchers for public transportation, this does not address the issues faced by those living in smaller towns that lack adequate public transportation. More research on this issue is definitely needed.

The two groups of women also differed in their access to safe housing. The successful women were almost unilaterally able to stay with non-criminal family members or in some type of transitional or sober living facility (see Cobbina, 2009). In contrast, inability to secure safe housing was widespread among those who returned to prison, placing them in situations where drug use and crime were likely. It is vital to secure some type of safe housing for all women *prior to* release. They are largely drawn from communities rife with crime and drugs (Clear et al., 2001) where finding safe housing is difficult. Many who returned to prison found themselves homeless or in environments that made relapse into drug-using or criminal behavior likely. Thus increasing the availability of sober living houses and transitional programs for women leaving prison is essential.

Family support also differed between the two groups and was integral to success. Those who returned to prison were more likely to describe either lack of support or support from family and friends who were still involved in the criminal and drug-using lifestyle (see Cobbina, 2009; Uggen & Kruttschnitt, 1998). However, there are other ways to provide needed support. In particular, helping women prisoners develop strong bonds with supportive women on the outside who can serve as mentors is a potentially viable alternative. In at least one of the successful reentry cases, a relationship with a mentor in a faith-based program was an important resource for the prisoner. Therefore, instituting programs to foster relationships between the women inside the prison and supportive women on the outside could assist women in transitioning to the free world.

Relationships with children can also be an important protective factor (Uggen & Kruttschnitt, 1998; Giordano et al., 2002), and we found that the women who stayed out of prison were more likely to be in contact with their children during imprisonment and upon release. This strongly suggests that women's prisons place emphasis on programs that will help maintain and strengthen the bond between mothers and children. Institutional policies frequently impede rather than promote the mother–child relationship (Bloom, 1995). Visitation policies that promote healthy interaction, telephone policies that are not cost-prohibitive, and programs that provide transportation for visitation are sorely needed.

Finally, we suggest that the motivation of women prisoners to succeed is not solely dependent on them. Those who feel hopeless and face overwhelming difficulties in reentry can and should be given the tools to increase the likelihood of success. Motivation is at least in part dependent on whether success is seen as possible. Programs designed to increase self-esteem and self-efficacy can help convert fatalism to hope, hope into motivation. As a society we should revisit current policies that are designed to maximize failure. Unrealistic parole demands, exorbitant fines and fees, and policies that limit choices in housing and employment must be addressed. The problem of successful reentry is a societal problem, in the end. Thus, the solutions must come from society as well as from the women. If we are going to continue imprisoning women for low level drug and property offenses, we need to offer them solutions. Appropriate drug treatment, education and job training, and comprehensive reentry planning and implementation would be a good beginning (Bloom et al, 2002; Cobbina, 2009; O'Brien, 2001).

# References


Anderson, T. L. (2003). Issues in the availability of health care for women prisoners. In S. F. Sharp (Ed.), *The incarcerated woman: Rehabilitative programming in women's prisons* (pp. 49–60). Upper Saddle River, NJ: Pearson Education, Inc.

Anderson, T. L., Rosay, A. B. & Saum, C. (2002). The impact of drug use and crime involvement on health problems among female drug offenders, *The Prison Journal, 82(1)*, 50–68.

Arditti, J. A. & April L. Few, A.L. (2006). Mothers' reentry into family life following incarceration. *Criminal Justice Policy Review, 17(1)*, 103–123.

Baer, D., Bhati, A. Brooks, L., Castro, J., La Vigne, N., Mallik-Kane, K., Naser, R., Osborne, J., Roman, C., Roman, J., Rossman, S., Solomon, A., Visher, C., & Winterfield, L. (2006). *Understanding the challenges of prisoner reentry: Research findings from the urban institute's prisoner reentry portfolio.* Urban Institute Justice Policy Center.

Beck, A. R. & Shipley, B.E. (1989). *Recidivism of prisoners released in 1983.* Bureau of Justice Statistics Special Report No. NCJ 116261. Washington, DC: U.S. Department of Justice.

Belknap, J. (2015). *The invisible woman: Gender, crime and justice* (4th ed.). Belmont, CA: Wadsworth.

Belknap, J. (2010). "Offending women": A double entendre. *Journal of Criminal Law & Criminology, 100*, 1061–1097.

Belknap, J. & Holsinger, K. (2006). The gendered nature of risk factors for delinquency. *Feminist Criminology, 1*, 48–71.

Bloom, B. (1995) . Imprisoned mothers. In K. Gabel & D. Johnston (Eds.). *Children of incarcerated parents* (pp. 271–284). New York: Lexington.

Bloom, B., Owen, B. & Covington, S. (2005). Gender-responsive strategies for women offenders: A summary of research, practice, and guiding principles for women offenders, NIC 020418. Washington, DC: National Institute of Corrections. Retrieved from https://s3.amazonaws.com/static.nicic.gov/Library/020418.pdf.

Bloom, B., Owen, B., Covington, S. & Raeder, M . (2002). *Gender-responsive strategies: Research, practice, and guiding principles for women offenders.* Washington, DC: National Institute of Corrections. Retrieved from http://www.nicic.org/pubs/2003/018017.pdf.

Brennan, T., Breitenbach, M., Dieterich, W., Salisbury, E.J. & van Voorhis, P. (2012). Women's pathways to serious and habitual crime: A person-centered analysis incorporating gender responsive factors. *Criminal Justice & Behavior, 39*, 1481–1508.

Brown, M. (2003). *Motherhood on the margin: Rehabilitation and subjectivity among female parolees in Hawaii.* University of Hawaii, Manoa: Department of Sociology, Unpublished dissertation.

James, D.J. & Glaze, L.E. (2006). *Mental health problems of prison and jail inmates,* NCJ 213600. Washington, DC: U.S. Department of Justice.

Clear, T., Rose, D. & Ryder, J. (2001). Incarceration and the community: The problem of removing and returning offenders. *Crime & Delinquency, 47,* 335–351.

Cobbina, J. (2009). *From prison to home: Women's pathways in and out of crime.* Unpublished dissertation. Retrieved February 7, 2014 from https://www.ncjrs.gov/pdffiles1/nij/grants/226812.pdf.

Cobbina, J. E. (2010). Reintegration success and failure: Factors impacting reintegration among incarcerated and formerly incarcerated women. *Journal of Offender Rehabilitation, 49,* 210–232.

Covington, S. (2008). *Helping women recover.* Somerset, NJ: Jossey-Bass Publishers.

______. (2003). A woman's journey home: Challenges for female offenders. In J. Travis & M. Waul (Eds.), *Prisoners once removed: The impact of incarceration and reentry on children, families, and communities* (pp. 67–103). Washington, DC: The Urban Institute.

Daly, K. (1992). Women's pathways to felony court: Feminist theories of lawbreaking and problems of representation. *Southern California Review of Law and Women's Studies, 2,* 11–52.

Deschenes, E., Owen, B. & Crow, J. (2006). *Recidivism among female prisoners: Secondary analysis of the 1994 BJS recidivism data set* (document no. 216950). Final report submitted to the U.S. Department of Justice. Retrieved from https://www.ncjrs.gov/pdffiles1/nij/grants/216950.pdf.

Dietrich, S. (2002). Criminal records and employment: Ex-offenders thwarted in attempts to earn a living for their families. In A. Hirsch, S. Dietrich, S., R. Langau, P. Schneider, I. Ackelsberg, J. Bernstein-Baker & J. Hohenstein (Eds.). *Every door closed: Barriers facing parents with criminal records.* Philadelphia: Center for Law & Social Policy & Community Legal Services, Inc.

Dodge, M. & Pogrebin, M.R. (2001). Collateral costs of imprisonment for women: Complications of reintegration. *The Prison Journal, 81*(1), 42–54.

Durose, M. R., Cooper, A.D. & Snyder H.N. (2014). *Recidivism of prisoners released in 30 states in 2005: Patterns from 2005 to 2010,* NCJ 244205. Washington, DC: Office of Justice Programs/Bureau of Justice Statistics.

Farr, K. A. (2000). Classification for female inmates: Moving forward. *Crime & Delinquency, 46,* 3–17.

Fogel, C. I. & Belyea, M. (1999). The lives of incarcerated women: Violence, substance abuse, and at risk for HIV. *Journal of the Association of Nurses in AIDS Care, 10*(6), 66–74.

Fortune, D., Thompson, J., Pedlar, A. & Yuen, F. (2010). Social justice and women leaving prison: Beyond punishment and exclusion. *Criminal Justice Matters, 13,* 19–33.

Giordano, P. C., Cernkovich., A. A., & Rudolph, J.D. (2002). Gender, crime, and desistance: Toward a theory of cognitive transformation. *American Journal of Sociology, 107(4),* 990–1064.

Glaze, L.E. & Maruschak, L.M. (2008). Parents in prison and their minor children, NCJ 222984, Bureau of Justice Statistics Special Report. Washington, DC: National Institute of Justice. Retrieved July 24, 2014 from http://www.bjs.gov/content/pub/pdf/pptmc.pdf.

Greenfeld, L.A. & Snell. T. J. (1999). *Women offenders* (NCJ 175688). Washington, DC: US Department of Justice/Office of Justice Programs.

Guerino, P., Harrison, P. M. & Sabol, W.J. (2011). Prisoners in 2010 NCJ 236096. Washington, DC: Office of Justice Programs/Bureau of Justice Statistics.

Harm, N.J. & Phillips, S.D. (2001). You can't go home again: Women and criminal recidivism. *Journal of Offender Rehabilitation, 32,* 3–21.

Harris, P. M. & Keller, K. S. (2005). Ex-offenders need not apply: the criminal background check in hiring decisions. *Journal of Contemporary Criminal Justice, 21*(1), 6–30.

Holtfreter, K., & Morash, M. (2003). The needs of women offenders: Implications for correctional programming. *Women and Criminal Justice, 14,* 137–160.

Holtfreter, K., Reisig, M. & Morash, M. (2004). Poverty, state capital and recidivism among women offenders. *Criminology & Public Policy, 3,* 185–208.

Huebner, B., DeJong, C. & Cobbina, J. (2010). Women coming home: Long-term patterns of recidivism. *Justice Quarterly, 27*(2), 225–254.

King, R. D., Massoglia, M., & MacMillan, R. (2007). The context of marriage and crime: Gender, the propensity to marry, and offending in early adulthood. *Criminology, 45,* 33–65.

Langan, P. A & Levin, D. J. (2002). *Recidivism of prisoners released in 1994* (BJS No. 193427). Washington, DC: U.S. Department of Justice.

Legal Action Center. (2004). *After prison: Roadblocks to reentry: A report on state legal barriers facing people with criminal records.* New York: The Legal Action Center.

Leverentz, A. M. (2006). The love of a good man? Romantic relationships as a source of support or hindrance for female ex-offenders. *Journal of Research in Crime & Delinquency, 43*(4), 459–488.

Mallik-Kane, K. & Visher, K. (2008). *Health and prisoner reentry: How physical, mental, and substance abuse conditions shape the process of reintegration.* Washington, DC: The Urban Institute.

Mauer, M. (2013). The changing racial dynamics of women's incarceration. Washington, DC: The Sentencing Project. Retrieved July 20, 2014 from http://sentencingproject.org/doc/publications/rd_Changing%20Racial%20Dynamics%202013.pdf.

Messina, N., Burdon, W. & Prendergast, M. (2006). Prison-based treatment for drug-dependent women offenders: Treatment versus no treatment. *Journal of Psychoactive Drugs, 38: sup3,* 333–343, DOI: 10.1080/02791072.2006.10400597.

MGT of America, Inc. (2007). Performance Audit of the Oklahoma Department of Corrections for the Legislative Service Bureau of the Oklahoma Legislature: Final Report. Retrieved October 26, 2010, from http:// www.okhouse.gov/Documents/OKRVSDFinalReport080103.pdf.

Mumola, C. (2000). *Incarcerated parents and their children* (BJS Special Report No. NCJ 182335). Washington, DC: U.S. Department of Justice.

O'Brien, P. (2001). *Making it in the "free world": Women in transition from prison.* Albany, NY: SUNY Press.

Oklahoma Department of Corrections/Division of Female Offender Operations (ODOC). (2012). *Fiscal year 2011 annual report.* Oklahoma City, OK: Oklahoma Department of Corrections. Retrieved from http:// www.ok.gov/doc/documents/FY%202011%20Annual%20Report%20Final.pdf.

Owen, B. (1998). *"In the mix": Struggle and survival in a women's prison.* Albany, NY: State University of New York Press.

Pew Center on the States. (2011). *State of Recidivism: The revolving door of America's prisons.* Washington, DC: Pew Charitable Trusts.

Reisig, M., Holtfreter, K. & Morash M. (2006). Assessing recidivism risk across female pathways to crime. *Justice Quarterly, 23,* 384–405.

Rettinger, L. J. & Andrews, D.A. (2010). General risk and need, gender specificity, and the recidivism of female offenders. *Criminal Justice & Behavior, 37,* 29–46.

Richie, B.E. (2001). Challenges incarcerated women face as they return to their communities: Findings from life history interviews. *Crime & Delinquency, 47,* 368–389.

Rose, D.R., Michaelsen, V., Wiest, D.R., & Fabian, A.(2008). Women, reentry, and everyday life: Time to work? The Women's Prison Association. Retrieved from http://66.29.139.159/pdf/Women%20Reentry%20and%20Everyday%20Life%20%20Final%20Report.pdf.

Seiter, R. P & Kadela, K.R. (2003). Prisoner reentry: What works, what doesn't, and what's promising. *Crime & Delinquency, 49*(3), 360–388.

Sharp, S.F. (2014). *Mean lives, mean laws: Oklahoma's women prisoners.* New Brunswick, NJ, Rutgers University Press.

Sharp, S.F. & Marcus-Mendoza, S.T. (2001). It's a family affair: Incarcerated women and their families. *Women & Criminal Justice*, 12: 21–49.

Sharp, S. F., Marcus-Mendoza, S.T., Bentley, R. G., Simpson, D.B. & Love, S. R. (1999). Gender differences in the impact of incarceration on the children and families of drug offenders. In *Interrogating Social Justice: Politics, Culture, and Identity*, eds. M. Corsianos and K. A. Train. Toronto: Canadian Scholars' Press.

Sharp, S.F., Peck, B. M. & Harstfield, J. (2012). Childhood adversity and substance use of women prisoners: A general strain theory approach. *Journal of Criminal Justice, 40*, 202–211.

Sokoloff, N. (2005) Women prisoners at the dawn of the 21st century. *Women & Criminal Justice, 16*, 127–137.

Uggen, C. & Kruttschnitt, C. (1998). Crime in the breaking: Gender differences in desistance. *Law & Society Review, 32*, 339–366.

Walt, L.C., Hunter, B., Salina, D. & Jason, L. 2013. Romance, recovery and community reentry for criminal-justice involved women: Conceptualizing and measuring intimate relationship factors and power. *Journal of Gender Studies*, DOI: 10.1080/09589236.2013.795113.

Western, B. (2002). The impact of incarceration on wage mobility and inequality. *American Sociological Review, 67*(4), 526–546.

Wright, E. M., Salisbury, E. J., & Van Voorhis, P. (2007). Predicting the prison misconducts of women offenders: The importance of gender-responsive needs. *Journal of Contemporary Criminal Justice, 23*, 310–340.

# Conclusion

# Total System Failure

*Susan Marcus-Mendoza*

Although this title may seem overdramatic, I believe it is a fitting description of women's experience with systems they encounter before and after entering the criminal justice system. Chapter after chapter in this book add to the increasing body of scholarship about how this happens. That does not mean that nothing positive happens along the way, or that there are not individuals who are genuinely interested in helping the women, and who work hard to do so, or that women are not responsible for the choices that they make. However, the structure that should support girls and women is so full of holes and poorly constructed that it collapses under the weight of the vast number of those who enter it—total system failure.

I refer to the death of my kitten in the same manner, and it occurred to me when reading these chapters that total system failure is descriptive of what happens to girls and women in the criminal justice system as well. After the death of my two elderly cats, I adopted a kitten through a rescue organization. The organization is comprised of dedicated volunteers who rescued and fostered cats and dogs, made sure that they receive medical care, and find them new homes. I adopted my kitten, Lily, at 3 months of age, and I noticed a slight limp when I got her home. As it did not go away, I took her to the veterinarian, who gave her some anti-inflammatories, and the kitten seemed fine a few days later. However, the condition reoccurred, and over the next few weeks, more symptoms emerged. There were many trips to the veterinarian, but eventually, it became clear that Lily was dying. By the end, she was partially blind, incontinent, 3 of her legs were not working well, other organ failures were sure to follow, and yet she continued to snuggle and purr. The veterinarian said that she was the sickest cat who didn't seem to know that there was anything wrong with her. The death of this kitten at 6 months just seemed so wrong to me, and when asked how the kitten died, I usually reply, "Total system failure." Despite the good work and intentions of the doctors and volunteers, no one really understood what was happening to Lily. They assumed that she had been injured before she was caught, and failed to look beyond that idea. Therefore, any chance that Lily had to receive help that might have kept her from her fate (if indeed it could have been cured, which is still unclear) was missed, despite all the compassionate and skilled people who cared for her and were devastated by her demise. In the course of her short life, she had been in a foster home, a store where I had adopted her, and had seen one veterinarian under their care, and a different one under my care. Not until I started making calls and asking questions of others who had her before me did I learn that everyone had noticed problems, but no one really investigated the origins as they assumed it was an injury, and the separate entities had not communicated with each other about her condition after she left their care. In that sense, both the system of volunteers, owners, and veterinarians, and Lily's body, experienced total system failure.

This idea is a theme throughout the book. In chapter after chapter, it is clear that there were multiple points of intervention along the path of the female offenders highlighted in this book, and yet they end up in an unstable system that fails them. As a society, girls and women encounter many institutions, including family, social services, schools, religious organizations, medical and mental health providers, and in the case of girls and women in these chapters, prisons, jails, and parole and probation. With so many structures available to care for them, it seems surprising that many girls and women are not adequately cared for, or supported, and yet the jails, prisons, juvenile detention centers, and halfway houses would not be filled beyond capacity if that were not the state of affairs. Again, I must reiterate that there are many knowledgeable and hardworking individuals who produce scholarship, develop programs, and work in organizations, who are dedicated to helping these women and girls, and yet somehow, the system fails. Why?

Many concepts and themes presented in this book help to explain aspects of how the system fails, and taken together, it is not surprising that the network or structure they comprise is unsound. The concept of strain theory is one piece of the puzzle. Van Gundy-Yoder's chapter demonstrates the unique way in which strain theory applies to women's criminality. She examines how gender roles and expectations of women create untenable conditions. Although the cases of Yates and Montgomery had many differences, they had in common the gender-role expectations often ascribed to women who are mothers. These expectations create conditions that require more than some women can handle, and the women who cannot or will not meet them are "disappointments," or "deviants"—which is one piece of the unstable structure. In the case of Yates, as described in the chapter by Van Gundy-Yoder, despite growing evidence that Yates was increasingly struggling, no one intervened to stop the tragedy.

The systems that might have helped her, including family, medical providers, and her church, did not work together to prevent the tragic events that occurred in this case. In fact, they seemed to ignore all the signs, encouraged her to stop treatment, and continued to expect her to have more children. Montgomery's case differed in that she was more self-centered, and her priority seemed to be her own happiness, and yet her inability to have more children, and her desire to continue her role as mother and wife, led to her crimes. In this way, strain was a factor in her case as well. Although strain theory is not mentioned in every chapter, these patterns can be seen throughout the book. Adherence to gender roles, and disapproval and punishment of those who do not adhere, creates strain and is one explanation why those who might help are ineffective.

Smith and Klepfer show the logical consequences of chronic system failure. In their study, many battered women who become offenders still do not access the systems that are designed to help them. This is not surprising if such organizations have failed them in the past. Distrust of the system is a frequent complaint by women who have been battered. The authors use Maslow's hierarchy of needs to explain how battering is a threat to their fundamental needs for safety, esteem, belongingness, and love, and this threat is often escalated by the failure of the judicial system to protect them. Once in the system, the focus is on their status as an offender, and their needs as victims are often not considered. Within the criminal justice system, even when resources are available, they are limited or scarce. Thus, this is another way that the system set up to help women can fail them.

Another common and important theme in the book, one which contributes to system failure, is multiple marginalities, as discussed in Sharp's article on Wanda Jean Allen. This examination highlights the complexity of women and girls, who are not just female, black or white, or rich or poor. Female offenders, as do all people, exist in a unique culture consisting of their experiences, and of such factors as their socioeconomic status, level of education, sexual orientation, physical and mental health, geographic location and others. This construct of multiple marginalities exists in different forms across disciplines, but in all cases, requires that we recognize the contexts in which people live their lives, and how their interactions which those entities shape who we are. Sharp's case study is a splendid example of how Jean's status as marginalized in a number of ways led to her demise, the ultimate system failure. The systems through which she passed failed to understand the complexity of Jean as a multifaceted person, and therefore did not help her or even understand her needs in many cases. Durfee's chapter about arresting teenage girls for dating violence takes a broader look at this issue. She finds that African American teenage girls are more likely be victimized and arrested for dating violence. In this case, the combination of being female and being black leads to more arrests. Durfee suggests that the systems with which they interact, especially schools and the criminal justice system, fail to recognize that women of color disproportionally use defensive violence, and then punishes them for it, which is a form of social control unequally applied to African American teenage girls. Again, with no understanding of the context of their actions, the system turns them from victims into perpetrators, and they fail to get the help that they need.

These themes continue as authors examine women's experience with several different types of offenses. Dragon, Oberman and Meyer researched mothers who have killed, and the familiar theme of histories of violence is prominent here. As in the previous chapters, we see women who were victims of abuse and violence, during their childhood and as adults, become offenders. Women in Dragon, Oberman and Meyer's study describe relationships that contributed to their victimization and their crimes. They conclude that blaming and punishing women is not the answer, and that professionals and community members must create a network to address issues such as domestic violence. Even where programs exist, they do not reach all women due to lack of resources. Caputo's chapter on dancing, stripping and escorts is an illustration of just how women enter such jobs, which provides entry into the world of drugs and violence. In this chapter, we see how marginalized women become further marginalized due to the world they come to inhabit. Both their entry into such a life, and the subsequent progression of their lives, can be seen in the context of system failure.

The chapters by Jenkot and Markovic emphasize the issues of gender roles and motivation. In Jenkot's chapter on selling and trading methamphetamine, it is notable that most of the women do not identify themselves as "drug-dealers," a title they find repugnant and reserve for the mostly male group of violent dealers. In fact, women in this study had a variety of motivations, including economic gain, but many saw themselves as helping others, whereas that is definitely not the role of drug dealers. Their role as women in domestic life mandates caring and providing, which is how many see their participation in the drug market. Markovic's chapter on female suicide bombers also looks issues of motivation and entry into terrorism. This chapter provided a comprehensive review of the history of women in terrorist and military groups. According to this chapter, women participate in such activities for a variety of reasons, many similar to that of men—the avenger, religious or nationalist fanatic, or exploited. Among the exploited are those who may have suffered losses and believe they have little to live for (loss of the caring role perhaps), and those who were told to do so by their husbands (obedience to their husbands). In both chapters, their roles as obedient women, homemakers, and caretakers were in the mix of issues that led to their crimes, and in some cases, to their deaths.

The last group of chapters looks specifically at the interaction with the criminal justice system, although all chapters look at this issue to some extent. Fox examines wrongful convictions and unjust sentencing practice. Central to his study is the practice of punishing women who are offensive to the judicial system because they have behaved in ways that are contrary to proscribed gender roles, an offense additional to the one for which they are charged. Fox reminds us that "good women" do not associate with criminals and do not let their children be harmed or killed. This idea of good mothers who protect their children at all costs represents a social expectation that has been passed down from generation to generation by fairy tales, in which the good mother has been killed off either before the story begins or early in the story, because otherwise, the children would never be in peril. Fox shows that the judicial systems' biases against "bad" or "fallen" women lead to wrongful convictions and unjust sentencing practices.

Lawston's chapter on women's experiences with incarceration does a wonderful job of allowing us to not only hear women's voices, but also observe their strengths. The women in her study want to be heard and understood. As Lawston's participants speak, we hear about the conditions they faced in prison, characterized by loneliness, separation, lack of control, and silencing. In prison, they faced sexual, physical, and verbal abuse, and felt dehumanized. However, Lawston also allows us to hear how the women find creative ways to resist, using such strategies as self-help groups and creative expression, which gives them a more indirect, and therefore safer and more acceptable, route to explore their feelings, find their voice, and make it heard, if only by those who are also oppressed. The women in Lawston's study certainly are being failed by the correctional system, but find ways to care for themselves and others.

System failure happens at all phases of interaction with the criminal justice system. The chapter by McGee, Williams, Strickland, Dobson-Brown, and Foreman addresses recidivism by women with substance abuse problems. In their study, as in others, the findings indicate that the resources they need to be successful after prison are lacking, which is part of the reason they reoffend. McGee et al. reveal that the women in their study often did not receive programming that would help them succeed after release, including programs for parenting, family reunification, and family counseling. They conclude that such programming, in addition to treatment for such issues as substance abuse, mental illness, and posttraumatic stress, and education for life skills and job skills, are important to reducing recidivism.

In the last chapter, Sharp and Ortiz examine what happens when women are released that makes them successful leads to reoffending. They allow us to hear from women who succeed after prison, women who succeeded in spite of flawed systems. In the "staying out" group, women overcame challenges that they had struggled with prior to incarceration. They were able to obtain safe housing, jobs, were more likely to have received treatment in prison for substance abuse, had fewer mental and physical health issues, had supportive family, and had been in regular contact with children while incarcerated and upon release. Sharp and Ortiz point out that women who feel hopeless and helpless need treatment in prison to increase their sense of self-esteem and self-efficacy. They say that where the society fails women at this point is by not preparing them to be successful, and by creating such seemingly insurmountable barriers to success as excessive fines and fees, unrealistic parole demands, and policies that create carriers to housing and employment. This is a system failure indeed.

The scholarship in this book represents a broad spectrum of research in terms of theory, type of offenses, and experiences in the system, so that readers will see the depths and breadth of the women's experiences with the criminal justice system. However, it is also a book about women's experience with being women, their place in society, and how many aspects of society are failing them by staying in their own "silos," working from their own frame of reference instead of taking into account the multiple contexts (and in many cases multiple marginalities) of women's lives, and not working together effectively to create a structure that supports girls and women. As I stated earlier, there are many extremely dedicated and knowledgeable people working on prevention, treatment and education for women. The failure is at the community, state and national levels, as well as the organizational level. As demonstrated in this book, there is ample knowledge to inform the transformation of this network of system into a sturdy system. Clearly, women bear some responsibility for their situations. However, there is not enough purposeful working together to create a solid structure to support them, and to help them see other choices than the ones that many of them make, that lead to their entry into the criminal justice system. That process, of building a solid structure, must include the girls and women. You have heard the voices of many women in this book telling you what happened, what didn't happen, and why they are or were "in the system." They are telling you how the system failed them, and what they needed to succeed, and given what we heard in this book, they seem very willing to participate in such a process. To me, the most hopeful aspect of this text is the persistence of many of the women. Like Lily, these women persist despite tremendous odds and much prejudice, showing great strength. They keep fighting for a better life, for a place in the community, and for their identity as mothers, partners, friends, family members. Many clearly want to be productive members of society. Those voices must be the loudest in such a transformational process if we are to build a system with fewer holes that can support all women and girls, a system that will not fail.

# Discussion Questions

## Chapter 1

1. In what ways does strain theory help to explain female criminality?
2. In what ways is strain theory limited in explaining criminal behavior?
3. How do women respond to strain differently from men? How does this impact female offending?
4. Does strain theory give us insight into the connection between female victimization and female criminality? Explain.
5. What can strain theory offer to explain the cases of Yates and Montgomery? What are the limitations of strain theory in these cases?

## Chapter 2

1. How has the response to IPV changed since the 1970s and 1980s?
2. What are some of the barriers that prevent victims of IPV from seeking help?
3. How is the police response problematic in helping victims of IPV? How are the courts ineffective?
4. How does Maslow's hierarchy of needs help to explain how IPV victims respond?
5. What can we learn from the victims themselves?

## Chapter 3

1. What is meant by "multiple marginality" and how does this affect female offending?
2. In what ways are female offenders "doubly deviant"?
3. How does mental retardation marginalize offenders and how is this illustrated in the case of Wanda Jean Allen?

4.  How does sexual orientation intersect with other forms of marginality in the criminal justice system response to female offenders?
5.  Of the variables discussed in the pattern of multiple marginalities, do you see one as most significant? What other factors might contribute to female offending?

## Chapter 4

1.  What is the rationale for implementing IPV mandatory arrest policies in cases of dating violence?
2.  What are some problems with mandatory arrest in adolescent violence?
3.  What research questions did this chapter explore? How does this analysis go beyond looking at gender? What is meant by "intersectional perspective"?
4.  What were the findings of the study and how can these inform mandatory arrest policies?
5.  Discuss the implications of school anti-violence policies for girls of color. What can we learn from these about mandatory arrest laws?

## Chapter 5

1.  How does the phenomenon of mothers who kill challenge classical assumptions of biological determinism that females are nurturers by nature?
2.  How does the criminal justice system response towards mothers who kill their children differ from the response to fathers who commit this crime?
3.  In what ways do gender expectations contribute to filicide? How are these related to societal definitions of romantic love?
4.  What is the difference between active and passive filicide? In the cycle of intimate violence, what factors might be significant in active or passive maternal filicide? How are these different for each?
5.  As a society, what are some of the challenges we face in responding to maternal filicide? What recommendations would you propose?

## Chapter 6

1.  What motivates women to choose the adult entertainment industry as an occupation? Why do they stay in it?
2.  How is the "industry" attractive to female drug users?
3.  Describe the sample of women from the Caputo study. What do you see?
4.  Are the findings from Caputo's study consistent with your answer to #1?

5.  What have you learned about sex work from Caputo's interviews? How do
    these findings challenge your assumptions about sex work?

## Chapter 7

1.  How does lifestyle explain women's involvement in drugs? Describe the
    lifestyle continuum.
2.  What are "gendered pathways" and how do these provide insight into
    women who deal drugs?
3.  What four categories of pathways affect women's choices and how are these
    pathways interconnected?
4.  Discuss the "gendered distribution of methamphetamine" in terms of
    women's identity and dealing.
5.  Discuss gendered distribution in the context of the norm of reciprocity, sex,
    and power.

## Chapter 8

1.  How has the role of women in terrorist activities evolved over time? When
    do we see the emergence of female suicide bombers?
2.  Why do women choose to participate in suicide bombings? What are their
    personal motivations?
3.  What are the typologies of suicide bombers and how do these explain fe-
    male terrorism?
4.  What motivates terrorist groups to use women as female kamikazes?
5.  How do historical trends shed light on female suicide bombers? How can
    this knowledge be used in the war on terrorism?

## Chapter 9

1.  Discuss some of the ways in which women are unjustly convicted. Do you
    see any common threads in these stories?
2.  How are mothers of murdered children a unique case? Which of these sto-
    ries do you think is most telling?
3.  What are some of the reasons women are wrongfully convicted? Which of
    these did you see most often in the cases you read?
4.  Why is the case of Avis Lee significant?
5.  What recommendations would you make in the cases you read? Is there one
    case that spoke to you more than others? Why?

## Chapter 10

1. Describe the women in our prisons. What is their story?
2. In what ways does sexual victimization continue for women who are incarcerated?
3. What other forms of abuse do female inmates experience?
4. What questions inform the research in this study? What common themes were uncovered in these interviews?
5. How was resistance manifest both informally and formally by the women in this study? Which of these do you think had lasting consequences?

## Chapter 11

1. In what ways do female inmates lack adequate medical treatment? How does this reflect their lives before incarceration?
2. What kinds of mental health treatment are neglected? What unique challenges does this pose for female inmates?
3. What theoretical approach frames the study? How does this shape the research questions?
4. Describe the methodology used in the study. What is the research question it seeks to address?
5. What do the quantitative findings tells us about race, class, and medical history? What do the qualitative findings tell us about race, class, and medical treatment services for female inmates?

## Chapter 12

1. What is the "identity theory of desistance" and how does it explain offenders' motivation to change?
2. For female offenders, how does grandparenting impact changes in identity?
3. Describe the sample and methodology used in the study. What was the goal of the interviews?
4. What were the findings of the study about the effects of grandparenting on desistance?
5. Was there an impact of grandparenting on substance abuse?

## Chapter 13

1. What is meant by "successful reintegration" and how is this different from recidivism?
2. What are some of the risks of recidivism faced by female prisoners? What are some of the reentry issues unique to women?
3. Describe the samples used in the study. What did the findings show about women who returned to prison?
4. What did the study find about women who successfully reintegrated? What was a key factor in their success?
5. Did you see any commonalities between women who went back and women who stayed out?

## Conclusion: Total System Failure

1. If you were a warden of a women's prison:
   A) what programming would you provide to ensure that the women had the greatest chance of success upon release?
   B) on which topics would you need to provide containing education for the staff, to ensure that they were prepared to work with the women, and to understand the many contexts of the women's lives?
   C) what aftercare connections to the community would you want your staff to make for each inmate to ensure their success?
2. In what ways do the problems of women in prison reflect the problems of all girls and women in society? Why do some women and girls facing issues such as substance abuse and violence commit crimes?
3. If the problems of women and girls who enter the criminal justice system are the responsibility of society as a whole, what can individuals who are not part of the criminal justice system do to bring about change?

# About the Editors and Contributors

**Alana Van Gundy-Yoder, Ph.D.,** is an Associate Professor at Miami University. Her teaching and research interests center around corrections and criminal behavior, criminological theory, gender and crime, and the National Inside-Out Prison Exchange Program. Her published works concentrate on human rights violations, social justice, feminist criminology, and women's experiences in prison. Her research and service strengthens and supports local communities, domestic and international penal institutes, and public policy legislation.

**Alisa Smith, J.D., Ph.D.,** earned her law degree and Ph.D. from The Florida State University, and she is a professor, of law and justice at The University of Tampa. Dr. Smith's research interests include empirically evaluating the law and courts with recent publications that examined Supreme Court decisions on 'consensual encounters' with the police and the processing of misdemeanor court cases in Florida. Her co-author,

**G. Jeffrey Klepfer, Ph.D.,** earned his doctorate in clinical psychology and is associate professor of psychology at The University of Tampa. His 30-year career in higher education encompasses both administration and teaching. He has served in a variety of roles, including vice president of student affairs and dean of the college of liberal arts and sciences. His teaching has focused on studies in theories of personality, the history of ideas in psychology and the psychology of religion.

**Alesha Durfee, Ph.D.,** is an Associate Professor and Graduate Director in Women and Gender Studies at Arizona State University. She has a Ph.D. in Sociology and a Graduate Certificate in Women Studies from the University of Washington. Her research and teaching focus on social policy and domestic violence using quantitative and qualitative methods; her work has been published in journals such as *Gender & Society, Crime & Delinquency, Violence Against Women,* and *Feminist Criminology.* Her current research includes legal mobilization and the use of protection orders by domestic violence survivors, the effects of mandatory arrest policies, the social construction of domestic violence victimization, and how gender influences the interpretation of survivors' narratives of violence by the justice system. She has also volunteered as a victim advocate for law enforcement and served as Board President for the Purple Ribbon Council, a grassroots organization working to prevent domestic violence.

**Wendy Dragon, Ph.D.,** is an Assistant Professor at Wright State University School of Professional Psychology. She has clinical experience in the assessment of psychological issues that inform criminal decision-making, as well as interventions with individuals with personality disorders and severe mental illness with or without a forensic focus. In addition, she has published peer-reviewed articles in the field of personality assessment.

**Michelle Oberman, J.D.,** teaches at Santa Clara University School of Law in California and is an internationally renowned expert on legal and ethical issues surrounding adolescence, pregnancy, and motherhood. She works at the intersection of health law and criminal law, focusing on domestic (U.S.) and international issues, and has authored two books and numerous articles on filicide. Her book, *When Mothers Kill* (2008), co-authored with Cheryl Meyer, won the Outstanding Book Award from the Academy of Criminal Justice Sciences. She has written numerous articles employing a combination of ethnographic interviews and legal analysis, with the goal of deepening our understanding of the law and its limits in addressing problems arising at the intersection of sexuality, reproduction and the law. She is writing a book, due out in 2016, that explores the purpose and the impact of abortion laws in three distinct geopolitical settings: El Salvador, Oklahoma and California.

**Cheryl L. Meyer, J.D., Ph.D.,** has blended together a unique combination of degrees including a Master's degree in Clinical Psychology, a Ph.D. in Social Psychology and a law degree. Her research has an interdisciplinary focus incorporating legal, feminist, psychological and sociological perspectives. Dr. Meyer is the author of *The Wandering Uterus: Politics and Reproductive Rights of Women* and the co-author of two books on maternal filicide, *Mothers Who Kill Their Children* and *When Mothers Kill.* She is a faculty member at Wright State University in Dayton, Ohio.

**Gail A. Caputo, Ph.D.,** is a Professor of Criminal Justice and Director of the Women and Gender Studies Program at Rutgers-Camden. Her research employs a rich intellectual tradition of ethnography to study social issues relevant to criminology and public policy, particularly women in conflict with the law. Her latest book, *A Halfway House for Women: Oppression and Resistance*

(June, 2014, Northeastern University Press), is an ethnography of reentry at halfway house that promises to help women returning from incarceration to rebuild their lives and relationships. Findings take the reader into the lived experience of reentry in the real, reveal patriarchal oppression in a system of social control designed for the care of women, demonstrates the influence of women's agency among other important contributions.

**Robert Jenkot, Ph.D.,** is an Associate Professor and Chair of the Sociology Department at Coastal Carolina University. He earned his doctorate in sociology at Southern Illinois University-Carbondale. His research leans heavily on the intersection of race, class, and gender as they interact with criminal and deviant behavior, especially with regard to illicit drugs. He is also keenly interested in the way that criminals and deviants overcome the moral and ethical boundaries learned through socialization in order to take part in nonconforming behavior.

**Vesna Markovic, Ph.D.,** is an Assistant Professor and Assistant Dean in the Department of Criminal Justice at Henry C. Lee College of Criminal Justice and Forensic Science at the University of New Haven. She has published extensively on transnational criminal organizations, terrorism and organized crime. She holds a Ph.D. from Sam Houston State University. Dr. Markovic is a senior lecturer for NATO COE-DAT in Ankara, Turkey.

**Michael H. Fox, Ph.D.,** is an Associate Professor at Hyogo University in Japan. A fascination with wrongful convictions lead to the creation of the Japan Innocence and Death Penalty Information Center (jiadep.org). After observing the glaring similarities in the wrongful convictions of women across borders he launched the Worldwide Women's Criminal Justice Network (wcjn.org). With fascination clearly an obsession, and appalled at the use of junk science in the courtroom, he uploaded a third website, the Network for Innocent Arson Defendants (niad.info). He seeks advice on how to maintain focus and remain sane.

**Jodie Michelle Lawston, Ph.D.,** is an Associate Professor and Chair of Women's Studies at California State University-San Marcos. She holds a B.A. in Psychology and Women's Studies from the State University of New York at Stony Brook, an M.A. and Ph.D. in Sociology from the University of California, San Diego.

**Zina T. McGee, Ph.D.,** is an Endowed University Professor of Sociology at Hampton University. She received the Ph.D. in Sociology from Tulane University. Her areas of specialization include juvenile delinquency, victimization among youth, violence against women, and maternal incarceration. She recently received the State Council for Higher Education in Virginia Outstanding Faculty Award, and is one of the recipients of the Top 26 Female Professors in Virginia Award. She is also the recipient of a faculty research grant examining female delinquency, victimization and maternal incarceration, and received the President's Ambassadors Award for Excellence. She is also co-investigator of the National Institute of Mental Health Minority Men's Health Initiative grant sub-project addressing youth violence prevention. Her co-authors are students at Hampton University.

**Kaneesha Williams** received a B.S. Degree in Criminology/Criminal Justice from Hampton University and is currently pursuing a Master's Degree in Forensic Science.

**Nicollette Strickland** received a B.A. Degree in Sociology from Hampton University.

**Tamara Dobson-Brown** received a B.A. Degree in Sociology from Hampton University and is currently pursuing a Master's Degree in Sociology.

**Mykeya Foreman** received a B.S. Degree in Criminology/Criminal Justice from Hampton University.

**Erin Kerrison, Ph.D.,** is a Vice Provost's Postdoctoral Fellow in the Department of Criminology at the University of Pennsylvania. Her mixed-method research agenda explores the relationship between punishment, law, and life course health outcomes.

**Ronet Bachman, Ph.D.,** is a Professor in the Department of Sociology and Criminal Justice at the University of Delaware. She is coauthor of several books on research methods and statistics as well as books on violence and victimization. Her most recent grant was from the National Institute of Justice to study the long-term desistance trajectories of drug-involved offenders who were originally released from prison in the 1990s and re-interviewed from 2009–2011.

**Juanita Ortiz, Ph.D.,** is the Dean of the Social Sciences Division at Rose State College. She received her doctorate in Sociology from the University of Oklahoma, and her research focuses on incarcerated women and recidivism. She was previously a faculty member in the Criminal Justice Department at the University of Illinois-Springfield. Her work on female offender recidivism includes a chapter in Susan F. Sharp's *Mean Lives, Mean Laws: Oklahoma's Women Prisoners* (Rutgers University Press, 2014).

**Susan F. Sharp, Ph.D.,** is the David Ross Boyd Professor of Sociology at the University of Oklahoma and has been named a Presidential Professor. Her areas of interest encompass gender and the criminal justice system, gender and deviance, and the effects of criminal justice policies on families. Recent research includes *Mean Lives, Mean Laws: Oklahoma's Women Prisoners* (Rutgers University Press, 2014), *Hidden Victims* (Rutgers University Press 2005), her edited book, *The Incarcerated Woman* (Prentice-Hall, 2002) as well as work published in a variety of journals.

**Susan Marcus-Mendoza, Ph.D.,** is a Professor of Human Relations, and Women's and Gender Studies at the University of Oklahoma, and a licensed psychologist. She has served as chair of the Department of Human Relations for 13 years. Dr. Marcus-Mendoza has a Ph.D. in clinical psychology from Texas A&M University, and completed a pre-doctoral internship at Baylor College of Medicine. She has been licensed as a psychologist since 1992. Dr. Marcus-Mendoza's research area is female criminality. She has published articles in such journals as *Women & Therapy, Women & Criminal Justice, Women's Studies Quarterly,* and *Feminism & Psychology.*

**Elycia S. Daniel-Roberson** is the Executive Master of Administration of Justice Program Director and Adjunct Professor in the Barbara Jordan-Mickey Leland School of Public Affairs at Texas Southern University. She has publications in the *International Journal of Crime, Criminal Justice and Law, Journal of Texas Probation* and was Managing Editor of the *Encyclopedia of Race and Crime* (2009, Sage Publications). She was also funded by the National Institute of Justice to present crime mapping research. Daniel-Roberson has been teaching in higher education for over 15 years.

**Kathleen A. Cameron, Ph.D.,** received her doctorate in Justice Studies from Arizona State University and is an Associate Professor of Justice Studies at Pittsburg State University in southeast Kansas. She has led the design and development of the interdisciplinary Justice Studies curriculum since 1997. Her areas of specialization include social justice and pedagogy, criminal offending, and legal philosophy. She is currently researching meditation practices in correctional facilities.

# Index